shopping center management

principles and practices

by Horace Carpenter, Jr.
CSM-ASPD

D1616666

INTERNATIONAL COUNCIL OF
SHOPPING CENTERS
New York

Copyright © 1978 International Council of Shopping Centers

First Edition and First Printing 1974

All rights reserved. No part of this work may be reproduced or used in any form or by any means—graphic, electronic, or mechanical, including photocopying, recording, taping, or information-storage and retrieval systems—without written permission of the publisher.

LIBRARY OF CONGRESS CARD CATALOG NUMBER 77-91683
INTERNATIONAL STANDARD BOOK NUMBER 0-913598-05-4

PRINTED IN THE UNITED STATES OF AMERICA

International Council of Shopping Centers
665 Fifth Avenue, New York, N.Y. 10022

Contents

a special acknowledgment

The author is indebted to S. O. Kaylin for his valuable suggestions during the planning of this book, for his careful and critical reading of the manuscript, and for his generous contributions of data and insights on shopping center management, which were derived from his long career as a reporter on and participant in the industry's growth.

—H. C., Jr.

foreword

the shopping center as a functional entity has existed in some form since mankind first developed an organized society. The present-day shopping center as a real estate form is largely a product of the last 30 years. Its forms are endlessly diverse, but all have one thing in common—the need for continuing management.

There exists a substantial body of literature on the siting, planning, designing, leasing, financing, constructing, and valuing of shopping centers. Those matters—the more creative phase of the industry —will receive only incidental mention here. This book, therefore, will focus on what takes place after the development process has been completed and the center is in being.

During the past 25 years, a growing number of individuals have been engaged full-time in the management and operation of shopping centers. Since its formation in 1956, the International Council of Shopping Centers has been the agency through which these men and women have pooled and exchanged their knowledge. It is from that by now quite large reservoir that the book's contents have been distilled, with the scope and presentation based on two concepts of the shopping center manager's role.

People, Property, and Money

The manager is principally involved with three interrelated elements—people, property, and money. The people, some of whom he

1

will see daily and many others whom he will probably never see, have widely diverse, and sometimes contradictory, interests; and it is his role to reconcile those interests to the greatest possible advantage of all parties. The property starts to deteriorate both physically and functionally the day after the center opens, and it is his responsibility to retard both kinds of obsolescence. Threading through all of his dealings is money, with its infinite variations of availability, cost, and time-value.

Successful Manager Is a Generalist

The successful manager is a generalist—he knows what needs to be done, and how to get it done in the most efficient manner, without necessarily having the technical ability to do it himself. Specifically:

■ He understands the procedures by which a shopping center is created without having actually functioned as a developer.

■ Although neither an accountant nor a lawyer, he knows what financial controls and legal guidance are necessary to ensure that his operating records and contracts are sufficient for their purposes.

■ In attending to maintenance, he need have only enough knowledge of the manner in which the principal components of real property function to know how, when, and where to direct the attention of experts.

■ Similarly, in matters of real estate economics, financing, insurance, taxation, security, retail store operation, promotion, personnel management, and community relations, he can be expected only to have a working knowledge sufficient to understand their place in the overall scheme of things and see that they receive proper attention.

A broad choice of published material is available on all of the specialized aspects mentioned, some of which will be referred to at appropriate points but not incorporated into the text. The purpose of this book is to identify and bring together in one place all of the principal phases of the manager's responsibility in a manner that relates the individual parts to the whole.

A word of caution to the reader. The contents have been organized into eleven topical chapters and a twelfth of miscellany. An at-

2

tempt has been made to present in each of the chapters the material peculiar to one portion of the total management function. However, each of the chapters does not constitute a definitive presentation of that particular topic. Rather, the chapters must be taken in the context of the entire book where material pertinent to several topics may be concentrated in one chapter to avoid repetition.

The author hopes that what follows will be helpful to the student considering a career in the shopping center industry, to the novice now in the business who seeks advancement, to those in related fields wishing an overview of the subject, and perhaps even to some of those experienced professionals whose valuable contributions have made this book possible.

Included at the conclusion of each chapter are a series of questions and discussion suggestions that can be helpful guides in developing educational programs structured around this book. The reader also will find the recommended reading lists of value in gaining further insight into each subject.

CHAPTER **1**

Physical and Financial Composition of Shopping Centers

as of the end of 1976 there were more than 17,000 identifiable shopping centers in the United States, over 1,100 in Canada, and a growing number in many other countries around the world. In addition, 700 or 800 new centers are built each year and many others are enlarged. Shopping centers cannot be easily stereotyped for several reasons. They range in size from a half-dozen small shops providing parking for thirty or forty cars to those with as many as 200 stores, including several department stores, and parking space for thousands of automobiles. They can be strictly utilitarian in appearance or the epitome of architectural splendor. Some are situated at the outer edge of suburban areas, others are parts of urban redevelopment in city downtowns, and many are somewhere in between. In age, they include some centers that have been in operation more than forty years; others opened for business only yesterday morning.

Faced with such diversity, it is not easy to provide a complete, yet concise, definition of the term "shopping center." Indeed, if your dictionary was published prior to the late 1960s, it probably is silent on the subject. Two standard works, published in 1969 and 1970, respectively, contain the following definitions, given here in their entirety.

One says, "A group of stores and shops forming a central retail market within a given rural or suburban area."

The other puts it in fewer words: "A collection of stores and restaurants grouped around a common parking lot."

In this book we are going to be concerned with a more precise definition, one reading something like this:

4

A shopping center is a group of retail stores and related business facilities, the whole planned, developed, operated, and managed as a unit, with commensurate on-site parking, and generally related in size and type of shops to the trade area intended to be served.

Historical Perspective

Since very early times, men who had goods or services for sale or exchange have grouped together because collectively they could attract more customers and benefit all concerned, both buyers and sellers. The place chosen was commonly one that was easily accessible to a large number of people. In the American city, this historically resulted in the establishment of a central business district at the focal point of public transportation. Larger cities also developed outlying secondary retail concentrations at lesser transportation hubs.

The advent of mass-produced automobiles set the stage for a change in the established pattern during the 1920s—a change that continued slowly through the 1930s and then began to accelerate after the close of World War II. A detailed chronology would not serve the purposes of this book, but a few landmark events may help provide a perspective on the evolution of the shopping center industry.

Sears, Roebuck & Co. was the first retailer to recognize the significance of the automobile revolution. Early in the 1920s, in its transitional period from mail-order to over-the-counter retailer, Sears began to establish large, free-standing stores with on-site parking, far from the centers of the big cities and, because of the land requirement, usually on the extreme edges of existing retail areas.

Among real estate developers, J. C. Nichols of Kansas City, Missouri, is generally recognized as the shopping center pioneer. His Country Club Plaza, built in the mid-1920s, was constructed as the business district for a large-scale residential development. It had selective tenancy, unified architecture, shared off-street parking, overall management control, and other characteristics of the modern shopping center. In fact, Country Club Plaza was so well known and widely studied that for two decades "plaza" was the generic term for what later became commonly known as "centers" and, more recently, as "malls."

During the second half of the 1930s, small strip centers, usually referred to as "plazas," began to appear on the outskirts of most large cities. These were commonly anchored by a supermarket, which itself was a new form of retail organization, and a drug store, supplemented by a few other convenience-type retail or service shops and designed to serve the needs of a fairly small neighborhood. The typical pattern was a straight line of stores—hence the term "strip"—backed up to a service alley and set back from the street far enough to permit a double line of parking, perpendicular to the stores, in front. Even when neighborhood centers began to assume other shapes—such as "L's" and "U's"—the term "strip" was often applied to them, leading to a certain amount of semantic confusion.

There was very little commercial construction during World War II, but the immediate postwar period saw a sharp resurgence in the building of strip centers of steadily increasing size, and much more ambitious projects were being planned. This proliferation was greatly influenced by the fact that the nation's department stores began to realize that if they wished to expand, or even survive, they must follow their customers to the suburbs. It was this factor that shifted some of the industry's emphasis from satisfying the retail shopping needs of neighborhoods to catering to the much more complex requirements of entire trade areas, measured in miles rather than blocks. That, of course, meant developing very large centers.

The year 1950 saw the opening of the first two shopping centers anchored by full-line branches of downtown department stores. Northgate in Seattle, Washington, was the original mall-type center; it consisted essentially of two strip centers face to face, with a pedestrian walkway between them. Northgate also pioneered with a central heating plant and an underground service tunnel. Shoppers World in Framingham, Massachusetts, was also of mall design, but the length was shortened by placing the stores on two levels, with the upper levels connected by pedestrian bridges. The mall type of layout was immediately adopted widely and, with variations, has been used ever since. The two-level concept, however, did not take hold at the time. A number of years later, high land costs, shrinking land availability, and the need to limit parking-lot sprawl brought about a rebirth of the two-level idea.

Northland Center in Detroit, Michigan, opened in 1954, was the first to use the cluster layout in which the single department store anchor was placed in the center of the site, with the satellite stores ringed around it and the building group, in turn, surrounded by parking spaces. Northland was also the first to have central air-conditioning as well as heating, and was the first to strive for esthetic appeal

6

through the lavish installation of amenities such as landscaping and sculpture.

In 1956, the opening of Southdale Center in Minneapolis, Minnesota, marked another major advance. It was the first fully enclosed, heated, and air-conditioned mall; the first two-level design since the Shoppers World of 1950; and probably the first center to be anchored by branches of two strongly competitive department stores. That last characteristic was of considerable significance.

In the ten-year period from the late 1940s to the late 1950s, the major department stores were not willing to establish branches in shopping centers other than on an exclusive basis, and this had two important effects on the industry that are still apparent. First, it automatically limited the size of the so-called regional centers because of the generally accepted rule-of-thumb that the total floor area of the satellite stores should not exceed that of the department store anchor. Second, it tended to result in an uneconomic proliferation of centers in some suburban areas because of the desire of several competing department stores to be represented.

By the end of the 1950s, the department store thinking had largely reversed and they sought one another's company. The result was a sharp increase in the size of regional centers. The single-anchor developments of the 1950s, however, are still in operation and many of them, as they age, are a challenging management problem.

The standard unit of measurement used by the shopping center industry is the square foot of gross leasable area (GLA). GLA is the total floor area designed for tenant occupancy and exclusive use, including basements, mezzanines, and upper floors, and it is measured from the center line of joint partitions and from outside wall faces. In short, GLA is that area on which tenants pay rent; it is the area that produces income.

Size of the Industry

The most recent statistical data on the various dimensions of the shopping center industry are contained in the third Biennial Census published in the January 1977 issue of *Shopping Center World*, a monthly trade magazine. The methodology of gathering and classifying the information was originally developed by S. O. Kaylin. The mass of detailed information represents the most authoritative statistics available.

As of the end of 1976 there were 17,523 shopping centers in the

United States, which contain a total of 2,338,210,000 square feet of GLA and account for estimated annual sales of $217,454,000,000. The study includes those developments containing a minimum of 10,000 square feet and complying with the definition of a shopping center cited earlier. The sales figure represents 36.3 percent of all retail sales in the United States, including such things as automobiles, gasoline and building materials which had been excluded from previous studies.

A distribution by size in the United States takes the following form:

GLA (square feet)	Number of centers	Percent of total number	Total GLA (000's omitted)	Est. 1976 sales (000's omitted)
10,000– 100,000	11,716	66.9%	666,009 sq. ft.	$ 69,637,000
101,000– 200,000	3,404	19.4	502,540	45,198,000
201,000– 400,000	1,379	7.9	397,303	34,689,000
401,000– 800,000	661	3.8	381,795	33,124,000
801,000–1,000,000	192	1.1	174,784	15,414,000
More than 1,000,000	171	0.9	215,779	19,392,000
	17,523	100	2,338,210	$217,454,000

At the time of this writing similar statistical material for Canada is not available. However, reasonably comparable results are obtained by a "best-guess" upward adjustment of the figures contained in the *Shopping Center World* census as of the end of 1974. Applying an arbitrary 15 percent increase to the physical numbers and an increase of 40 percent to the dollar amounts results in the following 1976 pattern for Canada:

GLA (square feet)	Number of centers	Percent of total number	Total GLA (000's omitted)	Est. 1976 sales (000's omitted)
10,000– 100,000	846	70.8%	49,358 sq. ft.	$ 4,293,000
101,000– 200,000	175	14.6	23,736	1,893,000
201,000– 400,000	120	10.0	34,082	3,052,000
401,000– 800,000	47	3.9	27,074	2,425,000
801,000–1,000,000	3	.2	2,139	192,000
More than 1,000,000	6	.5	7,435	666,000
	1,197	100	143,824	$12,521,000

There are no accurate statistics on shopping centers in the rest of the world, but it is interesting to note that the membership of the International Council of Shopping Centers includes representatives from a total of 37 countries. There is a particularly heavy concentration of shopping centers in Western Europe, Australia and South Africa, and all indications point to growth of the industry elsewhere in the world.

Centers Classified by Function

Within the industry, centers are generally classified by functional type. These categories are usually related to size but are not controlled by it. The three functional types are:

1. *Neighborhood center:* designed to provide convenience shopping for the day-to-day needs of the immediate neighborhood. Usually anchored by a supermarket supported by stores offering drugs, sundries, snacks, and personal services, the majority of neighborhood centers range from 25,000 to 75,000 square feet of GLA.

2. *Community center:* in addition to convenience goods and personal services, they typically offer a selection of apparel and home furnishings. In addition to one or more supermarkets, community centers are commonly anchored by a junior department store and/or a large variety store. The typical range is from 100,000 to 250,000 square feet of GLA.

3. *Regional center:* always anchored by one or more full-line department stores and including enough other stores to provide a broad selection of general merchandise in both soft and hard lines, plus food and personal services. Regional centers are designed to meet all of the shopping needs of a large residential area and usually range upward from about 400,000 square feet of GLA.

Recent years have seen an increase in the development of what are called "specialty" and "theme" centers, with some centers being a combination of the two varieties. The specialty center is composed mainly of facilities that appeal to a relatively narrow segment of the total market. The center may offer products such as apparel, usually high priced; furniture and home improvement; food and entertainment; handicrafts and hobbies; or contain stores specializing in price appeal, commonly referred to as discounters. The theme center is

9

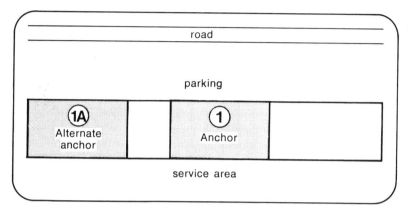

Figure 1—Strip

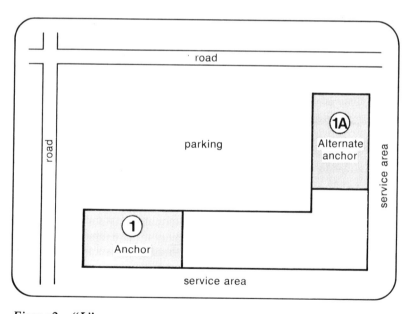

Figure 2—"L"

10

usually characterized by a distinctive architectural and interior design treatment usually related to a historical structure or event associated with the site.

By their nature, specialty centers tend to be limited in size to less than 250,000 square feet of GLA, but in terms of function they are of a regional nature because they must attract business from a wide area to survive. Given that requirement, such a shopping center has special marketing problems, and establishing a theme identity is an approach sometimes taken for that purpose.

Centers Classified by Pattern

In the course of the evolutionary process of the past 30-odd years, certain patterns of building arrangement have developed. Subject to the variations caused by site conditions, most of today's centers fit into one of the patterns described below and illustrated in *Figures 1–8.*

Strip. A straight line of stores with parking in front and a service lane in the rear. The anchor store, commonly a supermarket in small strip centers, is placed either at one end or in the center of the strip. A strip center is usually a small neighborhood center and the terms have come to be used interchangeably; although a strip may also be a large center. *(Figure 1)*

"L." A strip center with a line of stores placed at a right angle to it, forming an "L," with parking in front of the stores and service lanes behind them. Anchors are usually placed at the ends, but it is possible to place an anchor in the crook formed by the two lines of stores. The "L" shape is adaptable to corner locations and is used widely for both neighborhood and community-type centers. *(Figure 2)*

"U." A strip center with two lines of stores placed at right angles to the strip, forming a "U," with parking in front of the stores and service lanes behind them. "U"-shaped centers usually have more store space than strips or "L"s and consequently tend to be community-type rather than neighborhood-type centers. Because of their size, they may have as many as three anchors, one at each end and one in the middle, with the major anchor generally located in the middle. *(Figure 3)*

Cluster. An early form of regional center design. Stores are arranged in a rectangular area, with parking on as many as four sides of the center and with service provided through a tunnel or shielded service bays or a combination of both. Early cluster centers were

11

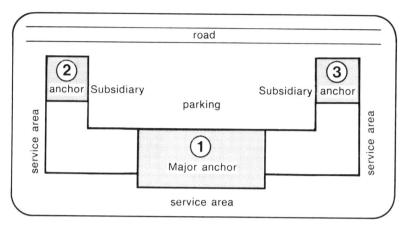

Figure 3—"U"

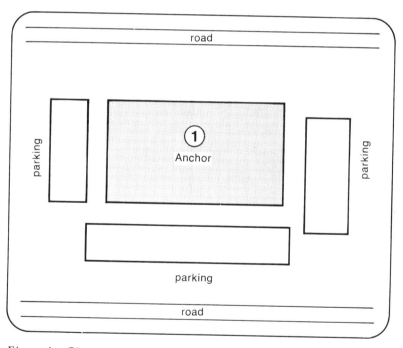

Figure 4—Cluster

12

built as open centers, although some have since been enclosed. The design results in a series of malls. A single-anchor cluster would probably have its anchor store extending from the periphery to the center of the cluster. *(Figure 4)*

"*T.*" A center designed to accommodate three anchor stores, the "T" type has parking on all sides, with service provided through a tunnel or shielded service bays or a combination of both. "T" centers may be open or enclosed. Note that one anchor is not visible from the front entrances of the other two. Some authorities consider this a

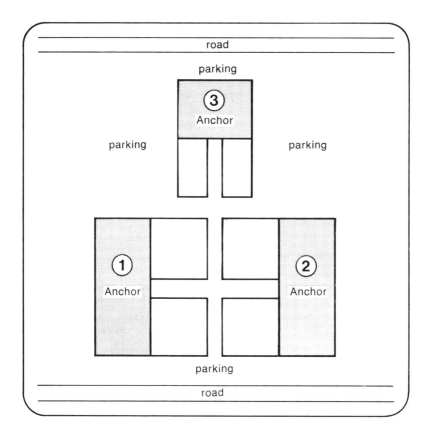

Figure 5—"T"

13

disadvantage in that shoppers may not be drawn to all parts of the center. Other authorities, however, consider this an advantage in that each anchor store provides an attraction helpful to the satellite stores in its vicinity. The "T" may be a two-level center. *(Figure 5)*

Triangle. Similar in many respects to the "T" but with the added factor of providing visibility of all anchor stores from the front of each. A triangular design is likely to be somewhat wasteful of land, but it may be the optimum design for those sites that are not rectangular. Designed to accommodate three anchors, the triangular center may have two levels, with parking around its perimeter.

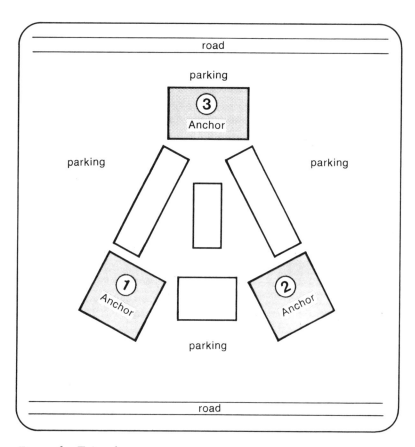

Figure 6—Triangle

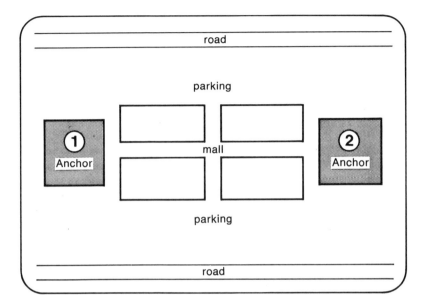

Figure 7—Dumbbell

Dumbbell. Essentially a double strip of stores placed face-to-face along a mall, with anchor stores placed at both ends of the mall, and with parking on all sides. The dumbbell is designed so that the anchors draw traffic along the mall in an effort to achieve maximum interchange of shoppers. *(Figure 7)*

Double Dumbbell. Essentially a dumbbell-type center. One dumbbell runs longitudinally and a second dumbbell runs latitudinally, forming malls that cross in a central court. This design accommodates four anchor stores and provides parking on four sides of the center and in the intervening U-shaped areas. Service to stores is available through a tunnel or service bays. *(Figure 8)*

Large centers may be double dumbbells minus one leg. They may be multilevel—generally two levels but not excluding three levels. Some large centers have basement levels.

The service tunnel is found in many large centers built during the 1950s, but is less prevalent in those of more recent construction.

Large centers built in years past had open malls. Those being built today are almost invariably closed-mall centers.

Since the purpose of this book is to serve as a guide and refer-

15

ence work to the management of shopping centers, the preceding material is intended to assist readers in identifying centers within the perspective of the past. It is not within the purview of this book to be a guide to the future development of shopping centers, a field in which much excellent literature is already available.

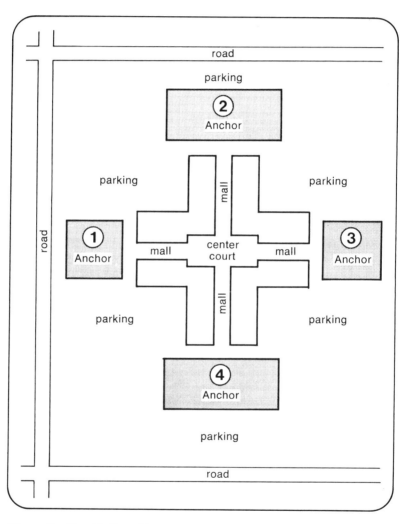

Figure 8—Double Dumbbell

Creating a Typical Shopping Center

However, a general understanding of how shopping centers are created is unquestionably of value to anyone charged with operating a center, so there follows a summary exposition of the procedures followed in bringing into being a typical shopping center.

A shopping center developer tries to find the best location for the kind of center he wishes to develop. The "best" location is the one within a trade area that will produce more traffic and sales than any other location for a comparable shopping center within that trade area.

To fix upon a location, theoretically a developer should weigh the relative merits of all available sites in the trade area and then select the best. In the real world, however, sites can seldom be selected as if they were cans of peas on a shelf. A potential site may come to a developer's attention in a variety of ways, and, once having found a site, a developer is unlikely to find alternative sites readily available within the trade area.

Consequently, economic analysis of the potential use of a piece of land as the site for a shopping center is generally in the nature of verification, modification, or negation of a developer's preliminary judgment. Experienced developers are able to evaluate sites with fair accuracy, using rules of thumb based on their experience with somewhat similar sites and trade areas.

Economic analysis begins with tentative delineation of the boundaries of a trade area for a potential shopping center of an assumed size. The larger the center, the larger the assumed trade area. The industry has not yet agreed upon a hard-and-fast method of delineating a trade area, but in broad terms it is that territory from which 85 to 90 percent of retail trade will come on a continuing basis.

Once a center is in operation, it is relatively easy to measure the extent and composition of its trade area. Making that determination when planning a center, however, requires the application of judgment as well as objective measurements. Hence, equally competent analysts, using the same data, may reach different conclusions about the trade area for a potential center.

Ideally, the data desired about a trade area include: total number of people categorized by age, sex, ethnic characteristics, income, educational level, and occupation; their ownership of homes, automobiles, major appliances, and other capital household goods; and their expenditures for various types of merchandise and services. The data should also include frequency of visits, days and hours of visits, and mode of transportation to specific stores and shopping centers. Analysts obtain as much detailed information as they can from published sources. Data on population, housing, economic status, and shopping habits are available from both government and private sources.

In the United States, the basic source of population data is the U.S. Census of Population and Housing, taken every ten years, from which information is grouped in a number of useful ways. Data on small, permanently established geographical areas, called Census Tracts, are considered very useful in trade-area analyses for projected shopping centers. In Canada, similar census information is available from the Dominion Bureau of Statistics.

Additional information may be obtained from planning commissions, Chambers of Commerce, newspapers, TV and radio stations, banks, trade unions, trade associations, industrial development committees, and business schools. Post Office drop figures; sales-tax payment records; and data from telephone, electric, water, and gas utilities, and garbage pickup and building-permit figures also provide useful information for analysts.

The objective of an economic analysis is to provide information that assists a developer in establishing whether his project is economically feasible. The analysis delineates the trade area, estimates current and future total retail trade, assesses actual and potential competition, and computes the sales potential of a projected center in that trade area.

Analysts are also likely to investigate the perimeter of the probable trade area to determine where people faced with multiple choices are likely to shop.

Although the analysis is used by the developer primarily as an aid in his decision to build a center on a proposed site, it may also guide him in determining the size and character of the center. The analysis may also be useful in demonstrating to financing organizations and to potential tenants that the proposed shopping center is feasible from their respective points of view. An experienced developer, convinced from the outset that he can build a successful center on a proposed site, may nevertheless authorize an extensive economic analysis in order to provide evidence acceptable to financing organizations and potential tenants.

Before a developer goes ahead with site acquisition (assuming he does not already own the property), he works out a detailed state-

```
                    XYZ SHOPPING CENTER
             Pro Forma Income and Expense Statement
                         (First Full Year)
Income:
   Minimum Rent                                    $.....................
   Estimated Overage Rent                           .....................
   Miscellaneous:
      Public Telephones          $.....................
      Kiddie Rides                .....................
      Other Concessions           .....................       .....................
      Common Area Payments                                     .....................
   Total Income                                     $.....................

Expense:
   Real Estate Taxes             $.....................
   Insurance                      .....................
   Maintenance                    .....................
   Common Area                    .....................
   Promotion                      .....................
   Legal and Auditing             .....................
   Management Fee                 .....................
   Vacancy                        .....................
   Miscellaneous                  .....................
   Total Expense                                    $.....................

Cash Flow Before Debt Service                       $.....................

Mortgage of $..................... @.........% for.........years
   Constant annual payment.. @.........%                      .....................
   Net Cash Flow                                    $.....................
```

Figure 9

ment of projected expenses and income, known in the industry as the
pro forma (Figure 9).

To produce the pro forma, the developer estimates the costs of
land, financing, architectural, legal and other services, construction,
and leasing, public relations and advertising activities, center management, real estate taxes, and insurance. In sum, he estimates all
costs of planning, developing, building, and operating the center. Then
he must develop estimates of income, primarily from rents to be paid
by tenants.

From these estimated expenses and income, the developer computes the anticipated net income for the shopping center. From that
item, the presumptive value of the completed, operating shopping
center may be calculated through application of a capitalization rate.
The net income multiplied by 100, and the product divided by the

19

capitalization rate, equals the presumptive value. The capitalization rate varies with the availability of money, the going interest rate in the center's geographical location, the relative amount of risk estimated by a lender (based in large part on the quality of the leases eventually produced by the developer), and the overall bargaining position of the developer. A typical capitalization rate as of this writing is 8 to 9 percent. The higher the risk, the higher the capitalization rate; hence, the higher the risk, the lower the presumptive value based on a specific estimated net income.

The anticipated income is based on a leasing plan that represents the developer's estimate of the amounts of space to be rented to specific tenants. The rent to be paid may vary with the amount of space to be rented by a tenant, the tenant's financial standing, the sales histories of other stores operated by the tenant, the relative demand for space by retailers in each line of trade, the location within the center of the space to be leased, the length of the lease, and the general demand for space in the trade area.

Most leased space in shopping centers is contracted for on the basis of a percentage of sales or a guaranteed minimum rental, whichever is higher. Additional payments, generally accepted as equitable today, include pro rata contributions to the maintenance and operation of common areas, real estate taxes above a stated level, and contributions to a merchants' association if one is formed.

If a developer does the leasing job properly, his center will have the optimum mix of tenants in relation to the service they can render for the community, the income they provide to the developer, and the security they guarantee for the financing organization or organizations.

Only the barest essentials of the process of developing a center have been outlined here. The complexity of the process will vary with the size of the center, but in every case the same criteria apply, namely: careful selection of a location in the light of all known facts; formulation of a pro forma statement of expenses and income; and development of a tenant mix and implementation of a leasing plan that will maximize income for the developer, security for the financing sources, and service for the community.

Ownership and Financial Structure

The ownership and financial structure of shopping centers vary from extremely simple to extremely complex. It is important that the manager of a center understand exactly what the owner's objectives are. Not all owners have the same objectives; to an extent, this may also apply to those who share the ownership of a center.

The equity holders own the center, but the mortgagees or other lien-holders have quasiproprietary rights that must be understood and respected. The complications of ownership are not related to the size or age of a center. They are too numerous and, in some instances, too complex to be set forth here in detail. Some of the more common arrangements, however, are as follows.

Simplest of all is full ownership by a single person, with no debts attached to the property, but this is an extremely rare circumstance. Single ownership is not uncommon, but in almost every such case there is also a mortgage-holder having certain latent rights that cannot be ignored.

A partnership of two or more owners has essentially the same characteristics from the standpoint of an outside manager except that, potentially, the partners may disagree. This is probably the most common form ownership takes, although the incidence of corporate ownership has been increasing in recent years.

As has been noted earlier, the shopping center industry suffers from a certain amount of semantic confusion, and among the more common practices is the use of the terms "owner" and "developer" as synonyms. Sometimes they are, but more frequently they are not, and in this book an attempt will be made to apply them selectively according to the function implied. The difference may be illustrated by some examples.

If Jack Jones, as individual, partnership, or corporation, conceives the plan for a center, supplies the equity money, and carries the project through to completion, he is both developer and owner, although his active role shifts from the former to the latter at the time the center becomes operational.

If Jack thereafter sells his entire interest to Joe Smith, who thus becomes owner, Jack may still be properly referred to as the developer even though he no longer has any interest in the center. Joe, however, acquires no claim to the appellation of developer.

If, in the beginning, Jack Jones forms a joint venture with Joe Smith, under the terms of which Jack has a 10 percent ownership interest in return for directing the development of the center, and Joe has a 90 percent interest for supplying the money, common usage will categorize Jack as developer and Joe as owner even though there is a partial overlap in the roles.

Broadly defined, "developer" applies to the entity, individual or otherwise, that functioned as entrepreneur in planning and executing the project; "owner" refers to the entity receiving the profits, or bearing the losses, from the operating property. There are no industry statistics available on the number of existing shopping centers in which the developer continues to function as an owner, but observation indicates that the incidence of a dual role declines as the center ages. There is a particularly sharp drop-off after the seventh or eighth year, due to the workings of accelerated depreciation, and it appears probable that relatively few ten-year-old centers remain in the hands of the original owners.

If the owner is a corporation, it is subject to somewhat different tax treatment than individuals—a fact that must be taken into consideration by the management when certain financial decisions are made. Furthermore, corporate ownership can take one of two forms. The publicly owned corporation is concerned with profit, sometimes referred to as "reportable gain," as well as cash flow; and sometimes such a corporation is willing to accept a lower net cash flow in a trade-off for a higher reportable gain. The privately held corporation is generally anxious to maximize cash flow, unless it is planning to "go public" or to engage in a merger/acquisition situation. In that case, it may wish to maximize reportable gain in anticipation of the need to provide an earnings base from which a sale price of the company can be computed. Although these are largely matters of accounting systems, they do sometimes have a bearing on operating decisions. This aspect of ownership is discussed more fully in Chapter 3, on financial planning, budgeting, and control.

It is not unusual for the land to be owned by one entity, individual or corporate, and the buildings by a separate entity. In that case, the second entity holds a long-term net lease on the land for which it pays ground rent as a fixed sum, as a percentage of income, or a combination of both. Such an arrangement tends to complicate the financing, and it is essential for the manager to have a clear understanding of the several contractual agreements in effect. A major factor to be considered is whether the land is subordinated to the mortgage—in effect, whether the land is "put into the pot" as security in addition to the buildings erected upon it.

22

When a center includes major department stores, it is common (but not universal) practice for the department stores to own their own buildings and also usually (but again, not always) some part of the land within the center's perimeter. A department store owning its own building may: (1) lease from the center owner the exact parcel on which its building stands, called "the pad"; (2) it may own the pad; or (3) it may own a part of the entire site in addition to the pad.

When three or four department stores each own a share of the site, the developer owns the portion occupied by the satellite stores, and the structures are all physically tied together, things get pretty complicated. Add to this fact that each party will want to finance its investment with a separate mortgage. The result is a real-estate development in which as many as ten entities hold long-term, effectively inseparable interests. What makes this possible is the understanding by all concerned that the commercial success of the enterprise depends on the finished product functioning as a unit, presenting to the public a single face.

This joint effort is cemented by a master agreement, entered into by all the parties, that sets forth in precise terms the rights and obligations of each party. Such an instrument is sometimes identified as a Construction, Operating, and Reciprocal Easement Agreement (COREA), but is commonly referred to as a Reciprocal Easement Agreement (REA). A shopping center manager must thoroughly understand this formidable document. The manager is usually employed by the owner of the satellite-store portion of the center and is responsible to that owner. But the manager's duties include all of those centerwide activities for which his employer is in turn responsible to the other parties under the REA.

There is a miscellany of other types of ownership, such as foundations, pension trusts, insurance companies, endowment funds, and real estate investment trusts, most of which have minor quirks in their investment objectives. By and large, however, they fit into either the individual or the corporate mold, or a combination of the two.

Almost all shopping centers are financed by means of a first mortgage held by an insurance company, bank, pension trust, or other institutional lender. It is generally a long-term mortgage, and typically calls for monthly or quarterly payment of a constant amount sufficient to meet the interest accruals and retire the principal, or most of it, within the term. Some large centers, particularly those recently constructed, have more complex financial structures involving two or more

23

layers of debt, and frequently providing the mortgagee with a share of the income in addition to the interest; or sometimes granting the lender a portion of the equity, either immediately or to be acquired at a later time. Such arrangements exist in great variety and will not be detailed further in this book, but it should be stressed that a center manager must familiarize himself with all the details of financing likely to affect his method of operating the center.

From a management standpoint, the essential fact is that the manager must be aware of the existence of some form of debt financing. He must be sure he understands the implications as they bear on operations, both day-to-day and for the longer term. Generally, the controls or restrictions exercised by a lender are designed to prevent a lessening or impairment of the value of the property pledged as security for the loan. Typically, this means a prohibition of acts, or failures to act, that may result in physical deterioration, or of leasing practices that may weaken the income stream. Usually the mortgage instrument also calls for the owner to submit fairly detailed annual operating reports.

Suggested Readings

This chapter is designed to provide an overview of the shopping center field as a background for the specialized chapters to follow. For those interested in more thorough coverage, there is presented at the end of each chapter a list of other publications that discuss in detail the planning and development process developed here in outline form.

QUESTIONS FOR DISCUSSION

1. *Discuss the author's definition of a shopping center.*

2. *What is the industry's standard unit of measurement for size of shopping centers?*

3. *Distinguish between "owner" and "developer" of a shopping center. Explain how overlapping of functions may take place.*

4. *Give an example of each of the three types of shopping centers, discussing its functional and occupancy characteristics.*

5. *Discuss the factors to be considered in a shopping center economic feasibility study.*

6. *Explain the entries of the pro forma statement.*

7. *Assume the net cash flow in your pro forma statement is $120,000 and the capitalization rate in your community is 10.*
   a. Compute the presumptive value of your proposed shopping center.
   b. Why is the presumptive value important to you as a builder?
   c. Why is the pro forma of interest to the center manager?

8. *Give an example of a simple and of a complex shopping center ownership and financing arrangement.*

9. *Discuss the various ways of financing a shopping center.*

10. *Define and explain a Reciprocal Easement Agreement.*

RECOMMENDED READING LIST

Applebaum, William and S. O. Kaylin. **Case Studies in Shopping Center Development and Operation.** New York: International Council of Shopping Centers, 1974. 280 pp.

Applebaum, William. **Shopping Center Strategy—A Case Study of the Planning, Location and Development of the Del Monte Center.** New York: International Council of Shopping Centers, 1970. 202 pp.

Davis, Milton. **A Lender's View of Unsubordinated Ground Leases.** New York: International Council of Shopping Centers, 1971. 6 pp.

Garrett, Robert L., Hunter A. Hogan, Jr., and Robert M. Stanton. **The Valuation of Shopping Centers.** Chicago: American Institute of Real Estate Appraisers, 1976. 45 pp.

Gettel, Ronald E. **Real Estate Guidelines and Rules of Thumb.** New York: McGraw-Hill Book Company, 1976. 234 pp.

Gruen, Victor. **Centers for the Urban Environment.** New York: Van Nostrand Reinhold Company, 1973. 320 pp.

Gunning, Francis P. **A Lender's Examination of Shopping Center Leases.** New York: International Council of Shopping Centers, 1970. 8 pp.

Gunning, Francis P. **New Techniques in Financing.** New York: International Council of Shopping Centers, 1969. 6 pp.

Gunning, Francis P. **On Submitting Mortgage Applications.** New York: International Council of Shopping Centers, 1969. 8 pp.

Gunning, Francis, P. **The Wrap-Around Mortgage . . . Friend or U.F.O.?** New York: International Council of Shopping Centers, 1972. 12 pp.

Kaylin, S. O. **How to Create a Shopping Center.** New York: Shopping Center World Books, 1973. 64 pp.

Klein, Philip E. **Feasibility of Shopping Center Development.** New York: International Council of Shopping Centers, 1976. 6 pp.

Kusnet, Jack and Owen T. Smith. **Modern Real Estate and Mortgage Forms: Construction and Development Forms.** Boston: Warren, Gorham & Lamont, 1975. 500 pp.

Levin, Michael S. **Measuring the Fiscal Impact of a Shopping Center on Its Community.** New York: International Council of Shopping Centers, 1975. 32 pp.

McKeever, J. Ross, Nathaniel M. Griffin and Frank H. Spink, Jr. **Shopping Center Development Handbook.** Washington: Urban Land Institute, 1977. 290 pp.

McMahan, John. **Property Development: Effective Decision Making in Uncertain Times.** New York: McGraw-Hill Book Company, 1976. 432 pp.

Parking Requirements for Shopping Centers. Washington: The Urban Land Institute, 1965. 24 pp.

Pearlstone, Jack H., Jr. **Deck Parking at a Regional Shopping Center.** New York: International Council of Shopping Centers, 1971. 4 pp.

Rams, Edwin M., ed. **Analysis and Valuation of Retail Locations.** Reston, Virginia: Reston Publishing Company, 1976. 464 pp.

Redstone, Louis G. **New Dimensions in Shopping Centers and Stores.** New York: McGraw-Hill Book Company, 1973. 323 pp.

Smith, Roger S. **A Professional Approach to Buying and Selling Shopping Centers.** New York: International Council of Shopping Centers, 1975. 12 pp.

Telchin, Charles S. **How to Improve Developer-Tenant Planning and Construction Coordination.** New York: International Council of Shopping Centers, 1977. 16 pp.

Wiedemer, John P. **Real Estate Finance.** Reston, Virginia: Reston Publishing Company, Inc., 1974. 331 pp.

CHAPTER 2

Organizing for Management

a shopping center is a meld of two types of entrepreneurship: physically it is a real estate investment; in terms of function it becomes a business investment. The quality of management it receives greatly affects how well it performs as an economic whole. Before considering the enterprise as a whole, let us first examine the two aspects separately.

All multi-occupancy, income-producing real estate requires constant housekeeping and maintenance attention. For the shopping center this is especially true for two reasons: it is subjected to the wear and tear of many visitors coming and going over long hours of every day; and to continue drawing that daily throng of patrons it must unfailingly present an attractive appearance. In every metropolitan area, the shopper has a wide choice of retail facilities, including downtown and other dispersed store groupings as well as those in several organized centers. Although the basic shopping purpose is accomplished inside a store, the shopper is influenced, consciously or unconsciously, by the quality of the store's surroundings. A littered parking area and shabby buildings do not invite repeat business.

A less obvious but equally important characteristic of the shopping center as a real estate investment is its tendency toward rapid obsolescence. The industry is still too young for any significant statistical data to have become accumulated, but there is some evidence to indicate that the average life expectancy of the improvements is relatively short as compared to some other forms of income property. Part of management's function is to keep abreast of pertinent technological and societal developments and to formulate prudent additional capital investment programs designed to arrest—or, at least, to slow—creeping obsolescence.

Percentage Leases Provide Potential for Appreciation

Turning now to the business investment aspect, nearly all of the center's potential for appreciation of value resides in the percentage leases. The standard pattern has always been for the tenants to pay rent on the basis of a percentage of their sales volume or a guaranteed minimum amount, whichever is the greater. Exceptions to the pattern have become progressively fewer; today they are rare and are confined to special situations. Of course, with some businesses, such as travel agencies or the customer-service offices of utilities, there is no meaningful volume figure on which to base a percentage. In some other cases in which the tenant is unwilling to assume a fixed obligation, the rent is charged on a straight percentage basis, with the rate customarily somewhat higher than it would be if a guarantee were included.

The leverage inherent in the percentage lease is best demonstrated by a simple example. Mr. A acquires a shopping center for a purchase price of $1,000,000 and finances it with a $750,000 mortgage, leaving him with a cash investment of $250,000. Assume, for simplicity, that the mortgage calls for payment of interest only and does not require any amortization of principal. Further assume that the total cash expenses of operation, maintenance, taxes, insurance, interest, and management are $175,000 per year; that the tenants have a combined annual sales volume of $4,000,000; and that their percentage leases average out at 5 percent. The first year's results will be

Rental income	$200,000
Less operating expense	−175,000
Net cash income	$ 25,000

and Mr. A will have a 10 percent rate of return, before income taxes, on his $250,000 investment.

Assume now that next year the tenants as a whole experience a 5 percent increase in sales, resulting in a combined volume of $4,200,000. The increased activity in the stores will not affect the operating expense of the owner, and the financial result will become

Rental income	$210,000
Less operating expense	−175,000
Net cash income	$ 35,000

and Mr. A's rate of return is now 14 percent.

Following Mr. A's fortunes for still another year, let us assume there is no additional growth in sales and the volume for the third year remains at $4,200,000. Let us also assume that, during the preceding two years, he has negotiated lease renewals resulting in a 5 percent improvement in the average percentage rate, raising it from 5 percent of sales to 5.25 percent; and let us further assume that he has been able to effect economies that produce a 5 percent reduction in the operating expense, from $175,000 to $166,250. Given that set of circumstances, the third year's operating result will be

Rental income	$220,500
Less operating expense	−166,250
Net cash income	$ 54,250

and Mr. A is now receiving income at an annual rate of 21.7 percent on his invested capital.

However, before we are overwhelmed by the euphoria of Mr. A's accelerating rise to riches, let us prudently pause to reflect that, financially speaking, Mr. A and his shopping center live on a two-way street. Had sales volume gone down 5 percent, expenses gone up 5 percent, and two tenants paying a total rent of $10,000 per year moved out, Mr. A's investment would appear less promising, as follows:

Rental income	$ 180,500
Less operating expense	−183,750
Net cash LOSS	$(3,250)

Variables: Sales, Rental Terms, Expenses

The point of the illustration is that there are three vital elements of the operation to which management skill can be applied—the total volume of sales, the rental terms of the leases, and the expenses. The three elements are synergetic to an extent found in few other types of business. The greater the volume of sales the more profitable the stores are to the tenants, and the more profitable they are the easier it is to upgrade the leases, either by renewal negotiation or by replacement with more productive tenants. Upgrading includes both better rental terms and assumption by the tenant of a greater share of the operating expenses. Each increment of rental income and recovered expense becomes an immediate net addition to profit; and since the equity investment is in most cases highly leveraged with borrowed money, the effect on rate of return is highly beneficial.

The preceding illustration utilized dollar amounts applicable to a neighborhood center in the range of 50,000 to 60,000 square feet of GLA; multiplied by ten, they would describe a moderate-sized regional center of about 500,000 square feet. On that scale, the amounts become large enough to demonstrate why shopping center management has become a well-compensated occupation.

Three Roles of a Manager

The manager's role in attending to the physical condition of the shopping center is not materially different from his role in performing the same function for any other form of commercial real estate. His responsibilities in the area will be considered in subsequent discussions, principally in Chapter 7.

The manager's role in negotiating—and, thereafter, administering—the agreements with tenants differs from standard real estate practice only in that it calls for an unusually thorough understanding of store operations and, more important, a solid grasp of the economics of retail distribution. This too will be discussed later, particularly in the chapters devoted to tenant relations and to re-leasing.

The manager has a third role, however, that is almost unique to the shopping center: he is, in a way, fulfilling the job of executive director for a chamber of commerce. The ways in which that role is performed are presented in some detail in the chapters on community relations, promotion, and publicity. However, it is appropriate to summarize at this point since it is generally one of the basic criteria considered by owners in employing—and thereafter evaluating—a manager.

A shopping center may contain one hundred individually owned businesses, many of which seek customers having widely varying needs, and some of which are in direct competition with one another. However, in its approach to the community from which it derives a living, and with which it must live in harmony, the center—particularly the larger center—must function as a unit.

To take such an approach necessitates an internal organization, usually embodied in the form of a merchants' association, that will promote the common cause by speaking to the community with a single voice. The principle, and it has been demonstrated beyond question, is that a patron attracted to the center for any purpose, if only to walk around looking at the other people, will probably make some kind of purchase, if no more than a bag of popcorn. And even if no immediate sale is made, the individual has at least been exposed to the attractions of the place for future use.

In a great many centers, including practically all of the larger ones, it is mandatory that every tenant belong to the merchants' association and pay dues on some specified basis. With few exceptions, retailers are prepared to cooperate in the execution of programs designed to strengthen the competitive position of the center as a whole in its trade area. However, the organization and continuing leadership of such an activity inevitably devolves on the center management, and with rare exceptions the effectiveness of the programs will reflect the skill with which that leadership is exercised.

A further responsibility, which will go by default unless assumed by the owner or his agent, the manager, is the public relations function of maintaining needed contacts with the numerous forces that control and shape the center's environment. Included are such obvious government agencies as the police and fire departments, and such social forces as schools and churches. Their approval or, more important, disapproval of the way the center is operated can affect its competitive position in many, ofttimes subtle, ways.

Tieing together the separate merchandising efforts of the tenants into a unified whole for presentation to the consumer is the distinguishing characteristic of the shopping center as a business investment as well as a real estate investment. It is true that a shopping center can function for years with minimal attention from the owner. In the last two decades, however, it has become evident that the extent to which any center, large or small, reaches its potential is a direct reflection of the quality of management it has received.

Two Basic Management Methods

The methods employed in the management of shopping centers

vary widely but can be divided into two categories for the purpose of discussion. The first is controlled directly by the owner, employing his personal attention in smaller centers or via his employees in larger ones. The other method is by means of a contractual arrangement, on a fee basis, with a professional manager that is either an individual or a real estate company.

The procedures followed by the owner-manager may vary greatly, depending on the size of the operation. At one end of the scale is the neighborhood center operated by an owner with an office on the premises, or nearby, from which he can give day-to-day attention to his investment. At the other extreme is the publicly held corporation owning a dozen or more regional centers spread around the country, and usually also involved in other real estate and business activities.

The owner-manager of a neighborhood or community-type center is usually engaged in a related activity (such as real estate, law, construction, or insurance) and thereby brings to the enterprise a certain amount of know-how. Typically, he has no payroll employees but contracts all housekeeping and maintenance work with firms specializing in that field. He may work directly with the merchants' association in developing promotional programs, but in the larger centers he is more likely to use the services of a professional advertising firm or a free-lance promotion specialist. The quality of management provided in this manner varies from excellent to poor, depending on the individual's level of expertise and the diligence with which he applies it.

At the other end of the scale, the methods used by the multi-center owners tend to be determined by the size of individual properties and, to some extent, by their geographic dispersion. Size is the determinant of the number, if any, of on-site direct payroll employees. Geographic concentration, or the lack thereof, has some effect on the degree of concentration of supervision by the central office.

There is no rigid line at which the size of a center becomes large enough to justify an on-site manager, but observation establishes that they are rare in centers of less than 400,000 square feet and are generally present in those of more than 600,000 square feet. Sometimes, a single individual can be "on-site" manager for two or three intermediate-sized regional centers that have the same ownership and are grouped within the same metropolitan area. This, however, calls for an individual of unusual ability, and it has not often worked out well. A center's capacity for supporting an on-site manager critically influences whether other on-site personnel are also employed—or whether an outside management service is contracted for on a fee basis.

As a general rule—and there are exceptions—multicenter owners tend to concentrate either on centers large enough to support an on-site payroll operation, or on developments below that size level. In the former group, the degree of centralization of authority is generally somewhat related to the number of centers and other commercial properties involved. Typically, the owner of two or three large regionals, and no other major real estate holdings, will be likely to staff each one with an experienced manager and give him a good deal of autonomy. Conversely, the companies owning the larger groups of big centers almost invariably develop strong central organizations of specialists in various phases of the operation, and treat the on-site manager's job as more of a training position.

The pattern of centralization is largely the same among firms owning several centers too small and dispersed to justify direct employment of any on-site personnel. If the number of properties is quite limited, they will probably be operated individually by fee managers whose contracts provide for a wide jurisdiction, with relatively thin supervision by the owner. When numerous centers are involved, and particularly if they happen to be geographically bunched, the opposite is usually the case. The management contracts will provide for more limited authority and there will be more frequent visits by supervisors from the central office.

The various methods of management cannot be broken down by size of center. Informed observation, however, leads to the belief that, in the more-than-600,000-square-feet-of-GLA class, some degree of direct owner participation is all but universal; the role varies from that of a general overseer to that of an active day-to-day operations manager. The reason for this is probably the size of the investment and the tendency for large centers to remain in the ownership of the original developer for long periods of time.

There also appears to be a high incidence of ownership-management in the less-than-75,000-square-feet-of-GLA group, although the evidence of this is less conclusive. In this case, the condition is probably due to the relative simplicity of operation; moreover, these centers' small size makes them unattractive to professional management firms except for a disproportionately high fee .

In view of the estimated distribution by size noted in Chapter 1, it may be hypothesized that, of the approximately 17,000 centers in the United States, between seven and eight hundred, or about four percent of the total, are operated by on-site salaried managers. The remainder are in the hands of owners, or contract managers, or a combination of the two. Among the very large number of fee managers so engaged it appears that few, if any, engage in shopping center management as their principal source of income. In the main, managers are real estate professionals conducting a general brokerage and management business.

A large number of intermediate-sized centers are in the hands of absentee owners who place the responsibility for the supervision of their investment in the hands of a manager. As previously noted, the manager can be an individual realtor, a management firm, an attorney, or other person thought to be qualified to give the property expert attention. His activities may be confined to a single center or may encompass several centers as agent for various owners; his work also may involve the services of one individual or of a sizable staff that includes experts in specialized fields.

The compensation paid by owners for management services is, as has been implied, of two kinds: salaries or wages paid to direct employees, and fees paid to contract managers. Generally, compensation is all one way or the other, the principal exception being the chain ownership of small centers whose day-to-day operation is in the hands of fee managers under the supervision of salaried personnel working out of the owner's central office.

Compensation for Employee-Managers

Salaries, and other forms of compensation such as bonuses, expense accounts, company cars, etc., paid to employee-managers are, of course, a matter of employer-employee agreement in the individual case, and vary widely. During the past ten years, compensation has increased rather sharply, reflecting both the increased construction of large centers and the heightened awareness within the industry of the importance of competent management. As of the time of this writing, there is a strong demand for qualified management personnel at all levels, and it appears that condition will continue for some time.

Compensation for Fee-Managers

Compensation for fee-managers also varies considerably, both in amount and the method of computation. Some general guidelines may be helpful in understanding how the arrangement works. In most cases, the management fee is computed, month-to-month, on the total rental income, and will range from a low of 2 percent to a high of 6 percent, depending on a number of variables in the individual case. The controlling variables, not necessarily in order of importance, are:

Size of centers, with the rate tending to go down as size goes up.

Scope of responsibility, which can vary considerably. In the case of the chain operation supervised from a central office, referred to above, the fee-manager's responsibilities are usually minimal, often not much more than collecting the rent, seeing that the premises are kept clean, patching a roof leak, and calling the owner's office if anything else happens. On the other hand, should the owner be an estate handled by the trust department of an out-of-town bank, the manager would have almost total responsibility for the center.

Extent of reimbursement, which is fairly standard but can have minor variations. The usual practice is for all out-of-pocket expenditures for goods or services made solely for the owner's benefit to be reimbursed on a dollar-for-dollar basis, with any discounts or commissions on purchases passed on to the owner. Wages, including fringes, of all personnel performing actual services on-site, full- or part-time, are considered reimbursable expenses, so that the owner is never in the role of being legally an employer. Ordinarily excluded from the reimbursable category are salaried employees and office personnel who constitute part of the manager's general overhead. Their services, and those of the principals of the management firm, are considered as covered by the fee.

Lease negotiations, both renewals and replacements, are not always included in the management fee. If excluded, they become additional compensation on a commission basis, usually related in some manner to the going rate among community real estate brokers, and a split-commission arrangement among several brokers is often required.

Planning, contracting, and supervising major repairs is commonly subject to additional compensation, but the distinction between routine repairs and those to be considered as major has no uniform definition and is as spelled out in the contract. The additional fee in such cases is either a percentage of the cost or a fixed sum, and it is generally established on a case basis rather than stipulated in the management contract.

The stated management fee may also be influenced by the presence of some form of incentive arrangement providing for a flexible rate, or annual bonus, linked to the attainment of certain specific operating results.

An intangible variable affecting the fee percentage rate can be the respective evaluations by the two parties as to how difficult the job will be. An older center with a lot of deferred maintenance, a weak leasing structure, and some new competition in the area would call for a higher management fee than a new one in a less precarious position.

Management contracts are usually renewed annually and tend to be quite stable, with termination more likely to result from change of ownership than dissatisfaction on the part of either party. The quality of management provided on a fee basis is necessarily somewhat uneven and there is no truly objective test that an owner can apply. Poor management is likely to become evident fairly quickly, but the difference between "adequate" and "good" is difficult to evaluate over the short term. Here again is the business-investment characteristic that tends to reward an owner in proportion to the attention he gives it. A little judicious prodding by the owner can sometimes make the difference between his property receiving good management or only adequate management.

As we have seen, the shopping center manager is an amorphous entity that cannot be precisely defined. Throughout the remainder of this book, the words "manager" and "management" will be used as generic terms unless identified as having a specific form in that particular usage. The terms will also be understood as applying either to individuals or to groups of persons functioning as a team, and to both men and women.

QUESTIONS FOR DISCUSSION

1. *Discuss the physical and functional management of shopping centers.*

2. *Explain the two basic approaches to the management of shopping centers.*

3. *What is the desirability of an "on-site" salaried manager?*

4. *Discuss the low percentage of "on-site" salaried managers.*

5. *Why are owner-manager shopping center management operations concentrated in very large and very small centers?*

6. *Discuss the variables controlling compensation of fee-managers.*

36

7. *Discuss the three roles of a shopping center manager*

8. *Why is the role of a center manager characterized as that of an "executive director for a chamber of commerce" and not that of an executive director of a business firm?*

9. *The owner's return on investment is based on the flexibility of sales rent income and operating expense variables. Explain how this flexibility affects the owner's return.*

10. *Explain why shopping center management has become an important and well-paid field.*

RECOMMENDED READING LIST

Dean, Michael A., Frederick M. Nicholas and Robert Caplan. **Commercial Real Property Lease Practice.** Berkeley: California Continuing Education of the Bar, 1976. 426 pp.

Gunning, Francis P. **A Lender's View on Operating Agreements.** New York: International Council of Shopping Centers, 1970. 12 pp.

Percentage Leases. 13th edition. Chicago: National Institute of Real Estate Brokers, 1973. 100 pp.

Randolph, Robert M. **Planagement—Moving Concept into Reality.** New York: American Management Associations, AMACOM Division, 1975. 212 pp.

Reilly, John R. and Eliot R. Cutler. **The Antitrust Aspects of Restrictive Covenants in Shopping Center Leases.** New York: International Council of Shopping Centers, 1976. 36 pp.

Review of Court Decisions Relating to Commercial Restrictions in Shopping Center Agreements. New York: International Council of Shopping Centers. 8 pp.

The Shopping Center Industry and Antitrust Laws. New York: International Council of Shopping Centers, 1972. 53 pp.

Antitrust Update: The Shopping Center Industry and Antitrust Laws. New York: International Council of Shopping Centers, 1974. 41 pp.

CHAPTER **3**

The Manager's Relationship to the Owner

We have already seen that the ownership of shopping centers takes disparate forms and that the methods of management are equally diverse. Since there is no typical owner or typical manager, it follows that there is no typical owner-manager relationship.

What follows, therefore, is a synthesis of the great variety of relationships that do exist within the industry. Some of the explanations and recommendations will be appropriate to a wide band of the spectrum, whereas others will have limited application. It is hoped that the reader will be able to interpret the principles advanced and adapt them to real situations.

Understanding the Owner's Objectives

To establish a sound relationship, the manager must first obtain a clear understanding of the owner's objectives. This is not always simple.

If the owner is a large corporation and the manager an employee, it is almost certain that the company goals are spelled out and the manager's responsibility for achieving them is well-defined. The same condition will probably also prevail in the case of a contract manager providing local management for an owner of several centers who has a central staff.

38

The problem arises when the manager reports to an owner to whom the shopping center is an incidental investment rather than a principal business. In this situation, which is probably true for a majority of all centers not directly owner-managed, the financial results sought must be meshed with the owner's overall investment planning, which can vary considerably among owners.

An owner's directive to "manage it as though it were your own property" is a comforting expression of confidence, but it leaves the manager with some unanswered questions. In today's business world, few decisions can be made without due consideration of the tax consequences; and in that respect the center is rarely a separate entity to be viewed by itself. Rather, it must be operated within the context of the owner's overall income and tax considerations. This does not imply that the manager needs to know all the owner's affairs, but he will do a better job if he has something more to go on than a generalized "run it the best way you know how."

Three Basic Interests

In a broad sense, all owners of shopping centers are interested, to varying degress, in three things:

1. The greatest amount of income from the invested capital that can be achieved without damaging the property's future productivity.

2. Appreciation of the market value of the investment.

3. Pride of ownership.

The three directions of interest are closely interrelated. Since many day-to-day operating decisions involve some kind of trade-off between two, or possibly all three, it is important for the manager to understand their relative importance to the owner. There is even a distinction to be made within one of the categories of interest—that of income. The basis for computation of income taxes—federal, state, and city—varies so widely among owners that there is no such thing as a typical or usual situation. A further complication is that what constitutes income is not clearly defined in the language of the industry.

Reportable Income

To most individual owners, partnerships, and nonpublic corporations the word "income" is synonymous with "cash flow." A publicly held corporation, however, is also concerned with what is commonly called "reportable income," the figure on which income tax is computed. Reportable income, after deduction of income tax, also trans-

39

lates into "earnings per share" from which dividends can be paid, and earnings per share is a major determinant of the market value of a stock.

Expressed in the simplest terms, reportable income equals cash flow minus depreciation charges and plus payments of principal on debt (usually referred to as "amortization"). In symbolic terms, the equation reads:

$$RI = CF - D + A$$

where RI = reportable income
CF = cash flow
D = depreciation
A = amortization

Another way of expressing the equation is $CF = RI + D - A$.

From the above equations, one may see that reportable income increases as amortization increases and as depreciation decreases. Conversely, cash flow increases as depreciation increases and amortization decreases.

Hence, an owner may elect to elevate the reportable income at the expense of depressing the cash flow, or he may make the opposite decision. The manager should be sure that he is aware of which decision the owner has made.

Immediate vs. Future Income

Another trade-off decision made by the owner is important to the operating procedures of the manager: the choice between immediate and future income. One owner may choose to obtain maximum current cash flow; another may prefer to forgo the immediate income in favor of building up the equity value in anticipation of a later sale and the more favorable tax treatment accorded a capital gain.

Pride of ownership is an intangible; it cannot be measured in monetary terms. However, it is a very real factor to be taken into account by a shopping center manager. To some owners, the center is essentially an abstraction, existing only in the form of its financial statements; to others it is a product of their own creation, nearly as dear to them as their own children. Between such extremes, owners' conceptions of what might be called the quality level of appearance to be maintained in their centers vary considerably.

Incidentally, in pondering the correct level of housekeeping and maintenance he should strive for, the manager must keep in mind the difference between the quality implicit in the type of center and the standard that may result from the owner's caprice. A center occupied mainly by stores catering to shoppers of above-average income calls for a higher level of visual amenities than one concentrating on the sale of popular-priced merchandise. Most owners understand this, but the manager should not hesitate to question an owner's judgment if he feels that budgetary limitations are forcing a lower standard than is likely to be acceptable to the center's shoppers. Indeed, it can be a matter of a manager's self-preservation to protest such a course. Displeased customers cause unhappy tenants, who in turn cause dissatisfied owners—and dissatisfied owners tend to think about a change in management.

The quality of appearance stemming solely from pride of ownership, or lack of it, is an owner's prerogative. It is up to the manager to achieve an understanding of what is desired and to act accordingly. However, when he thinks the results are too far above or below the norm, he may find it a good idea to register his dissent in writing. This can serve two purposes: it establishes that the condition of the center is not due to the manager's inattention; it also provides some measure of job-insurance against future recriminations.

Once the owner and manager understand each other's objectives, it then remains to provide an adequate system of communication. This is far from easy, for there is quite a different set of problems in reporting activities within, say, a 40,000-square foot strip center and its eight tenants and those at a 1,000,000-square foot regional center with its 120 tenants.

What Reports Are Needed?

There is no way to establish a uniform system of reports that could be recommended for general use within the industry. However, the common informational reports can be categorized and described in general terms, and overall formats can be suggested, with the understanding that they can vary widely in the extent of detail presented.

In general, an owner is interested in being furnished with two types of information concerning his property. He needs current, accurate financial reports in the degree of detail appropriate to the size and complexity of the center. As a part of such reports, he wants adequate forewarning of unusual expenditures that will call for advance cash planning. To supplement the financial data, most shopping center owners also like to be kept informed of events, both internal and ex-

41

ternal, that may affect the future well-being of the center.

To prepare good financial reports, the manager must maintain adequate internal records and accounting procedures. In fact, this is his most important responsibility. Management records should provide for three things:

1. Control and accounting for cash and other physical property.

2. Figures necessary for preparing tax returns.

3. Production of data useful in determining policy and making decisions.

These three purposes are common to all income-producing real property, but the last one is applied in a particular manner in shopping centers, where continual monitoring of tenants' sales performance can be highly significant. The uses of these data will be touched on shortly.

The Urban Land Institute has published a *Standard Manual of Accounting for Shopping Center Operations,* designed specifically for the industry with industry requirements in mind. It provides a system of income and expense accounts that is flexible enough to meet the needs of the individual center, large or small. Unless an owner has compelling reasons not to adopt this standardized accounting method, it is worth considering its use even for small centers. It permits comparison of specifically defined items, from period to period, from center to center, and, eventually, from center to industry-wide experience.

Important among the income accounts, of course, is overage rent, the amount exceeding the minimum guarantee, which is based on the percentage arrangements in the leases. Administering that provision requires obtaining from the tenant a statement of sales volume at whatever intervals are called for in the document. A useful supplement to the periodic financial reports to the owner is a tabulation showing individual tenant sales volumes and consequent rent accruals for the preceding period, with a percentage figure indicating the increase or decrease from the same period of the previous year. Both the sales and rent figures are more meaningful for purposes of evaluation if they are also expressed in terms of dollars per square foot of GLA.

Attempting to secure sales figures on a monthly basis from the home offices of chain tenants is generally futile. Informal reports, however, adequate for the purpose, can be obtained from store officials if the manager is willing to share other data with them. Retailers are invariably interested in knowing how they are doing relative to their environment and to their competitors. In fact, it is excellent tenant relations to circulate a monthly bulletin showing the center-wide variation, expressed as a percentage, from the comparable last year's period. This provides each tenant with a benchmark for measuring his own progress. In a small center, the composite figure must necessarily be on an overall basis, but in a large one it can be broken down into approximate categories so that the shoe merchant, for example, can evaluate his results within the framework of the total shoe volume in the center.

The historical record of every tenant's performance, placed in a context that permits ready comparison of each with each and with the group as a whole, is an essential tool for management *(Figure 10)*. This record largely controls the decisions on which tenants should be replaced, which ones enlarged, and which contracted. And obviously it is something to be studied carefully in preparing for a lease-renewal negotiation.

These records can also be persuasive when talking with a tenant whose performance does not appear to be consistent with the potential of his location. This is particularly true when it is deemed necessary to go over a local store manager's head and discuss the matter with his superiors.

On the expense side, especially in a large center, it is desirable to record maintenance and repair expenditures in a systematic manner that permits immediate identification of problem areas—this becomes increasingly important as a center ages. For example, if there is more than one building, roof repairs should be coded in a manner that will automatically flag the probable sequence in which roof replacement will be necessary, and financial planning can proceed accordingly. Similarly with parking lot or mall-surface repairs. A clear identification of where the repair money has been spent helps to guide the decision on when and where to stop patching and start replacing.

The program of owner reports for which a manager is responsible in cyclical in nature and is geared to the fiscal year on which the center operates. For our purposes, it will be assumed that owner and manager are geographically separated and that personal meetings are infrequent, with communication largely by mail. When this is the case (and in most other cases, for that matter), the two primary communications from manager to owner are the proposed operating budget, presented before the start of the year, and the annual report compiled after the

43

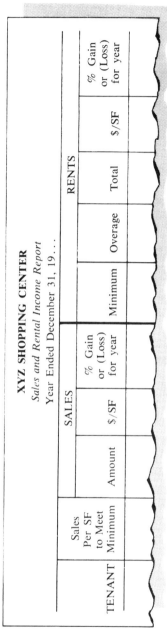

Figure 10

year has ended. The latter is essentially a mechanical task of recording in proper form what has already taken place. The former, however, represents an important exercise of managerial skill, and both its content and format should be carefully considered.

Submitting the Annual Budget

In submitting the annual budget for the owner's approval, the first rule is that it be done in a timely manner—typically, at least one month before the start of the fiscal year.

Rule number two is that the bare figures be adequately explained if there is any question that they might not be self-explanatory—particularly when they involve unusual expenditures.

Sometimes, an appropriate third rule would be for a manager to be ready to debate changes proposed by the owner if they go contrary to the manager's professional opinion of what is most advantageous for the center.

The suggestions advanced here are placed in the context of an owner-manager relationship in which the manager's role is to present a detailed operating plan for the owner to consider. With minor variations, the procedure is the same whether the manager is an employee or a fee contractor. It can also be a valuable exercise for an owner acting as his own manager, for it will, in effect oblige him objectively to review his past performance and establish a thought-out plan for the year to come.

All large centers, and a great many small ones, should have two annual budgets—one for operations and another for capital expenditures.

The operating budget includes all income other than sale of capital assets, offset by all items of expense, including depreciation and interest on debt, but not payments on debt principal or added investment. The difference between income and expense, as finally determined at year end, becomes the operating profit, or loss, for computation of ordinary income tax.

The capital budget includes income from sale of assets, broken down as to gain or loss against book value, payments on the principal of a mortgage or other debt, and the year's outlays for repairs or additions to be capitalized for depreciation over future years. The net gain or loss on sale of assets establishes the capital gain tax, if any, which also figures in the year's tax liability. As is the case with an operating budget, all numbers used in the capital budget are as-estimated going in and as-actual in the year-end report.

It is helpful if the operating budget to be submitted to the owner contains four columns of dollar amounts for each item of both income and expense, in accordance with the abbreviated format shown in *Figure 11.*

By showing on an item basis the as-reported figure for the last fiscal year, the budgeted amount for the current year, and the estimated actual for the present year, the background is established from which to project a dollar amount for the forthcoming year. If the budget is prepared during the eleventh month, the cumulative results of the first ten months should be available. If he has kept a running tab on tenant sales volumes, a competent manager should be able to forecast the year-end figures with a fair degree of accuracy.

Except, of course, for a brand-new center, the record of the past is an excellent guide for the future because it indicates patterns and trends. It is not, however, a guide to be followed blindly; the dollar amount allocated to each item of both income and expense must be weighted with the realistic probabilities of the coming year. The income portion of the budget must allow for potential changes in tenancy, for new elements of competition, for the economic well-being of the community, and for inflation. On the expense side, the only

45

PROPOSED OPERATING BUDGET			
Fiscal Year Beginning January 1, 19			

Income and Expense	*Last Year Actual*	*Current Year*		*Next Year Proposed*
		Budget	*Est. Actual*	
Income:	$	$	$	$
Minimum Rent				
Overage Rent				
Other Charges To Tenants				
Other Income				
Total Income				
Expense:				
Common Area Maintenance				
Other Maintenance & Repairs				
Advertising & Promotion				
Interest				
Depreciation				
Real Estate Taxes				
Insurance				
General & Administrative				
Miscellaneous				
Total Expense				
Net Income (Loss)				
Add: Depreciation				
Deduct: Amortization of Debt				
Other Capital Costs				
Net Cash Flow				

Figure 11

items that can be precisely foreseen are interest and depreciation, with all others requiring the same individual consideration.

When the year-end result is disappointingly different from the budgetary forecast, the variance is more likely to be caused by an overrun of expense than an overestimate of income. To avoid such overruns there are a number of precautions a manager can take of a more sophicated nature than simply padding the budget. For example, his contacts at City Hall can provide a reasonably close estimate of next year's real estate taxes. Insurance rates do not ordinarily change significantly without some advance indications, of which an alert agent or broker is aware. Changes in wage rates tend to cast their shadow before them, at least for the near term, as also do utility rates. Contractors supplying services are not usually prepared to set firm prices very far into the future, but discussions with them sometimes produce a sense of what they have in mind.

The real problems, particularly for an older center, are the small repairs that pop up so frequently and are budgeted on a lump-sum basis. For this purpose, there is no substitute for a thorough, first-hand knowledge of the property, and its maintenance records, by the individual responsible for making the annual estimate. An experienced manager may develop a certain intuition about his property. Lacking that facility, a manager's best course is to relate physical condition of the center to the level of repair expenditures in past years. If the property appears to be in generally good condition, it is indicative of an adequate repair program; if the overall appearance is shabby and run-down it means a day of reckoning is near.

In general, shopping center operating budgets and annual financial summations in the United States and Canada more often err in being too skimpy for effective management guidance than too detailed. Once soundly established, an accounting system and a reporting format are good for the life of the property. It cannot be over-emphasized that accurate, detailed records are an indispensable ingredient of a good management program. Financial reporting is the skeleton around which the whole system of communication between manager and owner is formed and, within sensible limits, there is no such thing as too detailed a breakdown in the budget presentation.

The Pro Forma vs. the Operating Statement

In designing the form of financial reporting to be used in a new center, it is important to understand the difference in purpose between the pro forma statement prepared prior to construction and the operating statement for the finished product. The pro forma is intended solely to establish to the satisfaction of a developer and a prospective mortgagee that the project, if completed in accordance with the stated assumptions, will be a financially viable enterprise. In the interests of simplicity and brevity, some relatively minor phases of proposed operation are frequently included as a net income or expense item. Examples are such things as the operation of community rooms, the resale of utilities to tenants, or the difference between the common area maintenance expense and the anticipated recovery from tenants.

In actual operation, netting income or expense is not a good practice and should be used only for trivial matters. In activities such as those noted above, and including real estate tax sharing, maintenance services furnished tenants, and contributions of services in lieu of cash to a merchants' association, it is preferable to identify separately every dollar of income and every dollar of expense as to where it came from or where it went. Such a method minimizes the risk of losing track of some of the expense dollars that should be charged against the appropriate income source. As an incidental benefit, the procedure tends to facilitate the annual preparation of income tax returns.

As noted in the second chapter, a significant characteristic of the shopping center is the rigidity of its expense structure, a fact clearly evident on detailed analysis of the expense budget of a typical center. Big items such as payments on debt, real estate taxes, and insurance are not subject to short-term control. Therefore, only a relatively small segment is available for the practice of economy through improved efficiency or outright elimination of an activity. The really controllable portion of a typical expense budget will rarely exceed 20 percent of the total, and is more likely to be around 10 percent. Thus, a saving of 5 percent in, say, one-fifth of the expense comes to 1 percent of the total budget. This is not to say that the search for more efficient ways to do things is not important, but rather to emphasize that the more likely route to increased profit is via the income portion of the operation.

Capital and Operating Budgets Interrelated

Preparation of the capital budget for a shopping center must proceed concurrently with the operating budget since the two are closely interrelated. The two frames of reference, however, are somewhat different, and a manager needs to keep the distinction clearly in mind as he approaches the task. The operating budget is focused essentially on the year immediately ahead, while the outlook of the capital budget must range from the next several years to the remaining economic life of the center. Capital expenditures in a completed, operating shopping center generally fall into either of two classifications— preservative or income-producing. The economics of the two are quite different.

Preservative expenditures are, as the designation indicates, incurred to sustain what is already there and to protect the existing income from being diminished. Installing a new roof or replacing a worn-out jeep obviously do not generate new income, and except for the short term they are not discretionary. The judgment factor in the budgeting process has to do with the time when an expenditure should be made, and that decision is discussed at some length in the chapter on maintenance. As noted there, the economics of preservative capital expenditures are further complicated when the cost, or a portion of it, will be borne, directly or indirectly, by the tenants via the common area maintenance charge.

The economics of income-producing expenditures are akin to the development process described in Chapter 1, and the prebudget arithmetic follows the same pattern of determining cost and then relating it on a pro forma basis to the estimated income and operating expense. Such proposals are generally entirely discretionary, and are accepted or rejected by an owner on the basis of his investment criteria. They do not necessarily produce more gross income, and may, in fact, achieve their result by reducing expense. For example, a rubbish compactor might pay for itself over a period of time by way of reduced hauling charges. Under certain conditions, capital programs that are primarily of an expansionist nature can also have preservative side-effects that warrant consideration in evaluating their investment potential. Some thoughts along that line will be presented in Chapter 12 in the section entitled "Defensive Expansion."

The principal budgetary planning of a shopping center manager, however, is likely to concern the more mundane aspects of preservative capital and how the requirements can be met to the best advantage of a particular owner. As an example of how the process might work, consider the following hypothetical situation.

A small shopping center for which $10,000 is a significant sum in the annual cash flow must replace its old parking lot sweeper. The center is owned by an individual whose total income is in the 50% tax bracket. The management responsibility is to finance the new sweeper in a manner that has the least impact on the owner's spendable income, i.e. his after-tax cash.

The center's lease clause defining the common area expense provides for the inclusion of equipment rental and of depreciation charges on any that is owned, but excludes all capital charges. Because of the ceilings and offsets in the present leases the owner is recovering from the tenants only 60 percent of the total common area expense and must absorb the remaining 40 percent. However, that condition is being rectified as rapidly as lease renewals permit, and it is estimated that within the next five to six years all except 10 percent of the common area expense will have been shifted to the tenants. However, it will be twelve years before that last 10 percent can be eliminated as an owner expense.

Given that background, the manager has obtained from the equipment dealer three options:

Plan 1. Buy the machine for $10,000 cash.

Plan 2. Buy it on an installment basis with $2,000 down and the remainder in four annual payments of $2,000 each plus 7 percent interest on the outstanding balance.

Plan 3. Lease the equipment on a twelve-year contract at an annual rent of $1,800, completely net.

In considering which of the three alternatives will best meet the owner's needs as he understands them, the manager assumes that Internal Revenue Service will accept an eight-year life for depreciation purposes but that with proper maintenance the machine will remain serviceable for at least twelve years. He further assumes that the owner's share of common area expense will for the next five years decrease from the present 40 percent to 10 percent at an average rate of 6 percent per year.

The solution to the problem lies in preparing a twelve-year projection for each of the alternatives and then discounting the resulting cash flows in accordance with that particular owner's standard of the time-value of money. In making the projections, several variables will enter into the calculations, and the following examples all assume the acquisition takes place at the start of a fiscal year.

Under Plan 1, the owner will lay out an immediate $10,000 in cash and during the first year charge $1,250 depreciation to the common area account, of which he will recover $750 (60 percent) in cash from the tenants. The remaining $500 becomes a noncash operating expense having the effect of reducing his income tax by $250. Applying the tenant recovery of $750 and the tax saving of $250 against the capital outlay of $10,000 results in a first-year negative cash flow of $9,000.

In the second year under Plan 1, the owner will recover $825 (66 percent) from tenants and be left with a noncash expense of $425 for a tax saving of $212, with the two items combining for a positive cash flow of $1,037. In each of the sixth, seventh, and eighth years, assuming the pass-through to the tenants is by then up to 90 percent, the owner will receive from that source $1,125 plus a tax benefit of

$62 for a positive cash flow of $1,187. Following the eighth year, when it has been fully depreciated, the sweeper will no longer be a factor in the cash flow until it again becomes time to replace it.

Looking now at Plan 2, the first year will call for a capital outlay of $2,000 plus $560 for interest on the unpaid balance of $8,000. The interest, however, is an expense item having the effect of reducing income tax by $280, so that the actual cash outflow on account of the purchase is $2,280. The annual depreciation charge of $1,250 will be the same as for Plan 1, as will also be the $750 recovery from tenants and the $250 tax saving from the $500 of unrecovered depreciation expense. The end result is a $1,000 offset against the $2,280 purchase cost and a negative cash flow for the first year of $1,280.

The numbers for the second year under Plan 2 will take this form—

Installment payment		$2,000
Interest on $6,000 @ 7%	$420	
Less 50% tax benefit	210	
		210
Total cash outflow		2,210
Offsets same as for Plan 1		
From tenants	825	
Tax saving	212	
		1,037
Net negative cash flow		$1,173

If the sweeper is leased under Plan 3, no capital asset will be created and consequently no depreciation charge established. The annual rental of $1,800 will become a cash expense of the operation subject to recovery from the tenants in accordance with the aggregate of the lease obligations. In the first year the unrecovered portion of 40 percent of total would be $720, which after the 50 percent tax offset would leave the owner with an out-of-pocket loss of $360. That amount would progressively decrease until in the sixth and succeeding years it would become $90 annually.

Filling in the blank years of the preceding examples produces the following comparisons, with the bracketed figures indicating a net cash loss.

Year	Plan 1	Plan 2	Plan 3
First	$(9,000)	$(1,280)	$(360)
Second	1,037	(1,173)	(306)
Third	1,075	(1,065)	(252)
Fourth	1,112	(958)	(198)
Fifth	1,150	(850)	(144)
Sixth	1,187	1,187	(90)
Seventh	1,187	1,187	(90)
Eighth	1,187	1,187	(90)
Ninth	—	—	(90)
Tenth	—	—	(90)
Eleventh	—	—	(90)
Twelfth	—	—	(90)
	$(1,065)	$(1,765)	$(1,890)

Plan 1 would obviously be most advantageous to the owner if it were to be assumed that money had no time-value, but when such a value is assigned, even though it be relatively low, the sequence is reversed and Plan 3 becomes the choice. The purpose of this detailed examination of a relatively minor decision is to illustrate the requirement that every preservative capital expenditure be approached from the viewpoint of its effect on cash flow, and a dominent aspect of cash flow, both in and out, is timing.

Discounted Cash Flow

The significance of evaluating future cash flow is in no sense limited to preservative capital; it is equally important in arriving at decisions regarding investment of funds for expansion or alteration designed to produce additional income. The accepted procedure is to weigh the future value of the anticipated stream of income against the present value of the cash outlay required to set it in motion. The method consists of preparing what is commonly called a discounted cash flow (DCF) projection.

If the variables are numerous and complicated, as they frequently are, an accurate DCF projection calls for some specialized training and preferably the aid of electronic calculating equipment. However, an understanding of the concept and a working knowledge of the required inputs are essential parts of a shopping center manager's capability. Sometimes, in matters of multiple choice, a few comparatively simple calculations on first approach will earmark those alternatives appearing to warrant in-depth study.

The principle is that, to an active businessman or investor, a dollar in hand is of greater value than one to be received at a future time, and the future value progressively diminishes as receipt is further deferred. For example, to the individual anticipating a 10 percent rate of return on his employed capital, a dollar to be received after a year is worth only 90 cents as compared with one now available. If he must wait two years, the value shrinks to 81 cents, and so on at successive annual discounts of 10 percent. In making a DCF projection, there is no such thing as a standard discount rate. Owner A may accept an 8 percent rate while Owner B considers his capital as worth 16 percent, and what either owner accepts this year may be different next year.

When it is a matter of paying money out, as in the case of the parking lot sweeper, the process becomes reversed; the longer the pay-out can be deferred the better. An immediate lump sum payment of $75 becomes more costly in terms of cash management than a $100 payment spread over several years. The mathematical process of running a DCF on the proposed investment is simply a means of comparing the time-values of the money involved in the various alternatives.

As was emphasized in the first part of this chapter, supplying good, professional management service is dependent on manager and owner sharing an understanding of objectives. In order to do so, it is important that the manager be aware of how his client, or employer, perceives the time-value of money, since that will color many decisions.

When agreement has been reached with the owner on the annual budget, the manager then must prepare a monthly forecast of cash flow to form the basis of his money-management for the year ahead. The term "cash flow" as applied to this monthly forecast has a somewhat different meaning from the same term as used previously in this chapter. In the present context, cash flow is simply the difference between money taken in and money paid out in the period. The monthly forecast is necessary because of the uneven flow of both income and expense during the annual cycle. Expenses in particular are likely to have occasional peaks, which must be anticipated; cash must be available to meet them when due. Real estate taxes are typically paid in one or two installments during the year, insurance premiums usually are billed annually or semiannually, mortgage payments are frequently on a quarterly schedule, and repair bills are due at odd intervals as the work is performed. To a lesser degree, income is also susceptible to intermittent peaks as percentage rents become due on an annual or

CASH FLOW FORECAST						
Income and Outgo	Jan.	Feb.	Nov.	Dec.	Total

Income:
  Same as Budget except—
  Add: Sale of Assets
	$	$	$	$	$

Outgo:
  Same as Budget except—
  Delete: Depreciation					

Add: Amortization of Debt Other Capital Costs					
Net Income (Outgo)					

Figure 12

other than monthly schedule.

To prepare a schedule of the type illustrated in *Figure 12,* the manager must judge when the estimated total annual income will be received and when the total expenses will be paid out. He calendars these estimates by months, breaking them down by items in conformity with the budgets, both operating and capital. Generally, he does not have much control over the flow of income on a month-to-month basis, but to a limited extent he can regulate the outgo on a short-term basis by the timing of processing the center's accounts payable.

An important part of a cash-management program is to ensure that all of the pass-through expenses, recoverable from tenants in accordance with lease agreements, are in fact recovered with the shortest possible interval between actual expenditure and receipt of reimbursement. For instance, if the center's real estate taxes are payable on July 1, it is good practice to assess the individual tenants for their share as part of the June 1 rent billings.

Budget Billing

The precise wording of leases usually identifies the tenant contributions to common area maintenance expense as a reimbursement of actual outlays by the landlord, but what is called "budget billing" is widely accepted by tenants as both equitable and preferable. In this method, the manager distributes copies of the applicable portion of the annual expense budget and thereafter bills one-twelfth of the total for eleven months, with a final year-end charge adjusted for the by-then-established deficit or surplus.

A prudent manager will review the cash forecast at least quarterly and adjust it for the balance of the year if it has become obvious that things are not going as planned. Of all the many points at which a manager cannot afford to have his head in the sand, this is one of the more important.

The monthly cash flow chart is of great interest to an owner because this is the key document determining the pay-out of cash to him, a subject always dear to his heart. The working bank account in which the manager deposits receipts, and on which he draws the checks to pay obligations, should have an adequate balance at all times, but very few owners prefer to let surplus funds accumulate there. In most cases, owners expect to receive the pay-out in one of two ways. Some seek a uniform monthly or quarterly remittance in an amount calculated to level off the irregularities of actual receipts and disbursements; others prefer to drain the account each month, leaving only the balance necessary to meet the next peak.

This is possibly an appropriate place to interject the admonition that it must be a cardinal principle of the contract or fee manager that he never commingle the shopping center money with his own funds. There should be a separate bank depository, clearly identified as being an agency account and used for no other purpose. The prudent manager will also insist that his accounts be subject to periodic outside audit.

How frequently interim operating reports should be submitted, and, particularly, the amount of detail they should contain, varies. Most owners want a monthly report, but some are satisfied with quarterly or semiannual statements. When it comes to detail, there tends to be some correlation between size of center and quantity of information desired.

The monthly report for a medium-sized strip center can usually be prepared by using the same itemization as for the annual budget, with no greater breakdown of income and expense than was shown for that purpose. It goes without saying that the monthly reports should be prepared as promptly as the clerical process permits, and every effort should be made to forward them on the same date each month.

For large centers, additional details are usually required, especially for those parts of the operation that present problems, that relate to plans for major change or expansion, or that are called for in agreements with lenders.

The elaborateness of the financial data included in the interim reports, monthly or otherwise, is up to the owner, but the manager should attempt to keep it appropriate to the size and complexity of the operation. A factor sometimes important in this regard is the nature of the bookkeeping and accounting system in use. When electronic data processing can be used, it is possible readily to furnish detailed data to an extent that would be extremely burdensome in a manual system. It is possible to produce a number of interesting statistics about the operation on a monthly, or even daily, basis if enough time is expended in collecting and processing the necessary data.

Cost-Benefit Analysis of Data Gathering

There is, however, a difference between what is only interesting and what is also useful as the basis for decision-making. Particularly in a large center, the whole information-gathering and -distributing process should periodically be subjected to a rigorous cost-benefit analysis and pruned accordingly.

The principal point of difference in the content of interim reports is generally related to the nature of the ownership. The public corporation must issue quarterly reports of its earnings, which means that both income and expense must be stated on an accrual rather than on a cash basis. This, in turn, requires the use of various accounting conventions in order to spread the cyclical peaks and valleys throughout the year with no relationship to the actual flow of cash. For such corporations, shopping center managers, both fee and employee, customarily prepare monthly or quarterly operating reports in accordance with a format tailored to fit a particular owner's system.

Among individual and private corporation owners, particularly in smaller centers, interest is customarily focused on the cash situation. Therefore, monthly reports are keyed to the monthly cash forecast prepared before the start of the year, following agreement on the annual budget. Since the forecast deals only in cash items excluding depreciation but including amortization of debt and capital expenditures, it becomes, in effect, the operating plan for the year. If an excess of income over outgo is indicated, it points to the surplus available for other purposes at the end of, or during, the year. If a deficit

MONTHLY CASH FLOW REPORT *Month of*						
	Current Month			Year to Date		
Income and Outgo	*Budget*	*Actual*	*Over (Under)*	*Budget*	*Actual*	*Over (Under)*
Income: Same as Cash Forecast Total Income	$	$		$	$	$
Outgo: Same as Cash Forecast Total Outgo Net Income (outgo)						

Figure 13

is displayed, it establishes the point during the year at which additional cash must be provided from a reserve fund, by borrowing, or from some other source.

A monthly report in the form illustrated in *Figure 13* should be adequate for most centers, and is just as desirable for an owner-manager as for a manager's communication to a remote owner. It is important, of course, that the itemization of income and expense, depicted here in greatly abbreviated form, be identical in the annual budget, the monthly cash forecast, and the interim report, with an explanatory footnote of any extraordinary sum that shows up on the "Miscellaneous" line. By showing budgeted, actual, and variance figures for both the reported month and the year to date, the direction in which the operation is moving relative to the anticipated annual cash flow is clear. The variance may be shown only as a dollar figure over or under the forecast amount, but a useful addition is also to show it as a percentage. Sometimes, instead of the reversed use of parentheses on the words "over" and "under" as depicted, "better" and "worse" are substituted—a greater than planned income is better and an expense overrun is worse. The "better/worse" usage is desirable particularly when the reports are likely to be circulated among persons not accustomed to reading financial reports.

In addition to reconciling the actual results with the budget, the year-end financial reports *(Figure 14)* should contain the supplementary information required by an owner for income tax purposes. Essentially, that consists of identifying the sums paid out for reduction

ANNUAL OPERATING REPORT

| Income and Expense | Last Year | Year Ended December 31, 19 ... | | | |
		Budget	Actual	Over (Under)	Current Budget
	$	$	$	$	$
Same as Proposed Operating Budget					

Figure 14

of debt and for capital improvements, and the computed amount of depreciation charges on the real and personal property. In simplified form the added information can be tacked on to a summary of the year's cash flow using the same format as the monthly reports.

The essential information is in the three central columns showing budget, actual, and variance for the reported year. Showing last year's results and next year's budget simply provides a panoramic view without having to use three separate documents. For study purposes, a sixth column might be added in which the income and expense items are expressed in terms of dollars per square foot of GLA (gross leasable area). Such a breakdown permits reasonably meaningful comparisons with other shopping centers held by the owner or included in the manager's portfolio, or with industry norms as published in the Urban Land Institute's *The Dollars and Cents of Shopping Centers.*

A useful auxiliary to the annual budget is a work-sheet outline of tentative budgets for two or three years ahead, adjusted and extended each year as the immediate one is put in final form. A forward look of this kind is particularly helpful in planning capital expenditures to be spread over several years.

58

As has been noted, most owners do not favor letting any more cash accumulate in the shopping center's bank account than is necessary for the efficient operation of the business. On some occasions, however, large surpluses are unavoidable, such as when there are impending large expenditures at uncertain dates and the owner is not readily available. When this or some other condition requires holding significant amounts of idle cash, a procedure should be established for putting the money to work. In communities where short-term bank savings accounts are available, the surplus can be thus stored separately from the center's own working account or the manager's agency account. Where such a resource is not available, the situation can be handled by the manager being authorized to purchase and cash short-term commercial paper for the owner's account.

Remarks on "Remarks"

An important part of the monthly reports prepared by a contract manager is the "Remarks" section. In most cases, the owner is not in direct touch with the center and is dependent on the manager for general information as well as financial data. A few comments each month on events that may affect the future conduct of the business are invariably welcome and minimize the chance of an unpleasant surprise. Owners are always interested in a planned, stable operation with adequate advance warning of developments that might create a problem. Such things as an important tenant being unlikely to renew his lease, the possibility of an unplanned major repair, or a highly critical report following a visit by the insurance inspector usually cast their shadows before them, and if passed on to the owner enable him to adjust his thinking accordingly in advance of the event itself.

Where the manager is a direct employee, which is likely to be the case in most regional-size centers, he can assume that the scope and format of his monthly reports, and most of the other paper work, will be prescribed by the central office of the corporate or partnership owner. And if the owner happens to be a public corporation, the manager can expect to be up to his elbows in reports a good share of the time. His hope for survival in a sea of paper lies in his ability to systematize the collection and transmission of data in a manner that makes it largely a clerical assignment. At least a rudimentary understanding of accounting principles is necessary for this and most other aspects of financial recordkeeping.

Supplementing the periodic reports, a manager is also obligated to keep the owner informed promptly of any unusual happening likely to have an impact on the center's fortunes. A fire, civil disturbance, damaging windstorm, demise of a tenant, either corporeally or financially, are all events the owner is likely to learn of through news sources and to be concerned about. A succinct advance report, oral or written, of the facts and potential consequences is always welcome and is evidence of alert management. It is a safe assumption that it is impossible to overinform an owner about things that either do, or might, affect his property, keeping in mind that a condition appearing obvious to the man on the spot may be news to one remote and having other matters on his mind. Never overestimate the amount of information an owner has or underestimate his level of interest.

The total community with which a shopping center manager deals is made up of many segments in addition to the owner. His own employees, the tenants and their employees, the shopping public, and the society in which they live all have a claim on his attention and responsiveness. Paramount, however, should be the interests of his employer, whether by payroll or contract, whose affairs have been placed in his hands for management. In addition to the business ethics involved, there is also the pragmatic consideration that the owner is the one whose dissatisfaction can take the form of direct action.

QUESTIONS FOR DISCUSSION

1. *Why is it important for the shopping center manager to have a clear understanding of the owner's objectives?*

2. *What are the three basic interests of owners of shopping centers in which center managers must likewise have an interest?*

3. *Explain the reportable income versus cash flow decision of shopping center owners.*

4. *What is the shopping center manager's most important responsibility to the owner?*

5. *State the three rules for submitting a center's annual budget and explain the reasons for them.*

6. *Explain a discounted cash flow projection and how to prepare it.*

7. *Differentiate between preservative expenditures and income-producing expenditures.*

8. *Discuss the line item entries in the Cash Flow Forecast, Monthly Cash Flow and Annual Operating Report.*

9. *What advantage are the numerous center reports to the owner and shopping center manager?*

10. *Why is the "Remarks" section of the center manager's monthly report of significance to the owner?*

RECOMMENDED READING LIST

Library of Shopping Center Forms for Management and Operations. New York: International Council of Shopping Centers, 1977. 57 pp.

McKeever, J. Ross, ed. **The Dollars and Cents of Shopping Centers: 1975.** Washington: The Urban Land Institute, 1975. 325 pp.

Probing Potential in New and Existing Shopping Centers: A Property Manager's Blueprint. Chicago: Institute of Real Estate Management, 1972. 63 pp.

Standard Manual of Accounting for Shopping Centers. Washington: The Urban Land Institute, 1971. 39 pp.

CHAPTER 4

The Manager's Relationship to the Tenants

Somewhere in every shopping center lease there is, or should be, a clause that says, in substance:

> Nothing contained herein shall be deemed or construed by the parties hereto, nor by any third party, as creating the relationship of principal and agent or of partnership or of joint venture between the parties hereto, it being understood and agreed that neither the method of computation of rent, nor any other provision contained herein, nor any acts of the parties herein, shall be deemed to create any relationship between the parties hereto other than the relationship of landlord and tenant.

Having thus established that neither the landlord nor the tenant is responsible for the other's debts, nor for his negligent or wrongful acts, the structure of the lease acts to establish a broad community of interest between landlord and tenant, and collectively among the tenants. The workings of the percentage rent provision give the landlord a direct, immediate stake in the effectiveness with which the tenants, individually and as a group, are able to attract and hold public patronage; and the common area maintenance operation is essentially a cooperative endeavor carried on under the direction of the manager. The mutuality of interest, however, is not total either between landlord and tenant, or between tenant and tenant, and an understanding of the differences helps smooth the manager's path in his day-to-day dealings with the tenants.

Store Hours: a Divergence of Interest

A frequent point of difference in recent times has been the matter of store hours—a divergence of interest that often is inherent in the workings of the percentage lease. The landlord's income is related to the gross sales volume, but his operating expense is typically almost unaffected by hours of operation. The tenant, on the other hand, is faced with a different set of economics: many of his operating expenses are directly related to the amount of time his store is open. Usually, his weekly sales volume will not increase in direct proportion to additional store hours but will, rather, tend to have a declining ratio as more and more hours are added. For example, lengthening weekly hours by, say, 10 percent will rarely increase total weekly volume by a like amount, the additional business being more likely to be in the 7 to 8 percent range. If a second 10 percent of open hours is added, the weekly volume increase will probably drop to around 5 percent, and so on to the point of a vanishing return. Since a significant portion of his expense is incurred simply by being open, the tenant can find himself losing money at an accelerating rate as the volume per hour declines.

Furthermore, the effect is not uniform among all types of retail businesses. A supermarket, for instance, has a comparatively low ratio of payroll expense to volume of sales and the operation involves a good deal of stocking and similar housekeeping activity, which can keep the personnel productively employed when customer traffic is slow. On the other hand, a store handling better women's wear typically has a high selling expense and cannot afford to have relatively well-paid salespeople standing around talking to each other.

Another characteristic difference among store types is attributable to the shopping habits of their customers. Stores dealing in convenience goods, such as food and drugs, are commonly patronized at all hours of the day and evening. In many communities, however, the better women's wear and the fine jewelry shops would do little business if they were open on Saturday night, and less on Sunday. For such retailers, the payroll expense could well consume the entire gross margin on sales made during those periods.

The store-hour situation has sometimes become a major landlord-

63

tenant bone of contention. It epitomizes a type of problem that tests a manager's ingenuity in reconciling the sometimes conflicting interests of lessor and lessee,

There never has been a standard pattern of hours-open in the shopping center industry. Prior to about 1960, center hours approximately coincided with whatever was usual in the community—typically, six days plus two evenings, for a total of 45 to 55 hours per week. In the 1960's the large discount stores, with their long operating hours, began to proliferate in suburban metropolitan areas and exert an irresistible competitive pressure on other retailers, particularly department stores.

For this and such other reasons as changing life-styles, the past ten years have seen a steady increase in the number of hours retail stores are open. As shopping center density has increased, the center managements have, for obvious reasons, aggressively fostered the concept of longer hours. Today, schedules of seven days a week totaling 75 to 80 hours are common.

The retailer in a downtown or outlying suburban business district is in a position to maintain store hours based on the economics of his own situation, but as part of the organized community of a shopping center there are other considerations. The basic merchandising concept of a shopping center is that the whole is greater than the sum of its parts; that is, the synergetic action of a varied assortment of stores will attract more shoppers than the individual units could do, and all will benefit from the resulting interchange of customers. That this principle is well understood by progressive retailers is evidenced by their presence in shopping centers, where the occupancy costs are generally significantly higher than in alternative locations. Therefore, when a tenant elects to maintain store hours different from the center standard, it is rarely a matter of natural orneriness. It is more likely to result from a careful income and expense analysis, and a change in his decision is more often brought about by an intelligent discussion than by a curt letter. This and some similar internal-relationship problems will be discussed later in the chapter.

Another phase of the operation in which the interests of landlord and tenant do not run exactly parallel is the matter of advertising. If the owner interests himself in the matter—and not all do—he will favor a strong advertising program maintained by the tenants. Not surprisingly, the tenants reciprocate the feeling, but put the financial shoe on the other foot. The matter of balancing the respective interests in the field of publicity and promotion will be treated at greater length in Chapter 6.

Latent in the whole situation, of course, is the basic vendor-vendee relationship, with the inherent belief by the owner that he is receiving inadequate compensation for the use of his property, and the frequently equally firm conviction by the tenant that he is paying an exorbitant price. Ideally, this difference of opinion surfaces only at lease-renewal time, but the manager must keep in mind that it exists and will sometimes serve to exacerbate an otherwise minor dispute.

Two Roles for the Manager

In conducting his day-to-day affairs, the manager is cast in two roles: first, as the administrator of the contractual agreements embodied in the lease and, second, as leader and collaborator in the effort to secure the public patronage on which depends the prosperity of landlord, tenant, and manager. In fulfilling his responsibilities in both roles, and particularly the first, the manager must maintain a clear picture of his relationship to the other participants in the enterprise.

The owner is the manager's client or employer, as the case may be, and the owner's interests should be paramount in all the manager's dealings with other parties. The tenants are the owner's customers and the manager deals with them as the agent or representative of the owner. The shoppers have a dual role: while in the public areas of the center they are essentially guests of the owner, but upon entering a store they become customers of the tenant. The manager's employees are extensions of himself and are bound by the same rules of conduct. The store employees are similarly extensions of the tenant and should be dealt with through the tenant. In some shopping centers, the merchants' association employs and pays a promotion director, and the amorphous relationship between such a person and the center manager is discussed in Chapter 6.

In his role as administrator of the lease, as distinguished from renewal negotiator (which is treated in Chapter 8), it is essential that the manager know exactly what the agreements are, understand the intentions of the parties in entering into them, and have a clearly thought-out policy covering eventualities not precisely spelled out in the document. The overwhelming majority of commercial tenants are reasonable people and, being businessmen themselves, understand and accept a businesslike approach to any common problem. A managerial vice to be avoided in dealing with tenants is procrastination—when indulged in, it has a tendency to turn molehills into mountains. A thorough knowledge of the lease helps to minimize that danger.

Tenants invariably respect decisiveness on the part of a manager. When a tenant presents a request he is entitled to a prompt response. If the tenant's request is refused, the appropriate reasons should be given; if it must be referred to higher authorities, it is the manager's responsibility to follow through to prevent unreasonable delay of the final answer. Of course, supplying quick answers emphasizes the importance for the manager of knowing the lease. He can thus avoid the embarrassment of being forced to reverse a negative reply after having his nose rubbed in the fine print. It is also important that the manager not let decisiveness become brusqueness; he must keep in mind that very few tenants are accustomed to making frivolous requests, and that even the ones who do are entitled to a courteous hearing.

Computing and Collecting Money Due

Of all the responsibilities to be discharged by a shopping center manager, high priority must be given to computing and collecting all of the monies due the owner. The scope of his activity can vary considerably in ways other than those related to the physical size of the center, and here seems to be an appropriate point at which to identify the more common forms of income and methods of computing them.

Common to all centers is guaranteed rent, whether expressed as a minimum or a fixed amount, which is invariably stipulated as being payable in advance on the first day of each month. This involves no requirement for computation, but it does sometimes present a collection problem. When a tenant is chronically slow in paying, it signals one of three things—financial weakness, a poor accounting system, or a deliberate use of the landlord's money for working capital purposes (not unknown even in the best of families). Any one of the three conditions warrants a manager's vigorous attention.

The great majority of shopping center leases also provide for payment of percentage rent on the tenant's gross sales volume, with quite a bit of variation in the method of computation. The two most common arrangements are (1) for the stipulated rate to be calculated on the entire volume with offsetting credit for the amount paid under the guarantee, or (2) for the percentage rate to be applied to all sales volume in excess of a specified dollar amount. The applicable percentage may be on either a descending or ascending scale at various levels of volume. Sometimes there is a differential in the rate as applied to various lines of merchandise, sometimes certain items are excluded, or there may be a ceiling above which no rent accrues. Occasionally, there is some kind of cumulation or averaging provision, whereby the excess of minimum over percentage in one or more years may be credited against future years in which the reverse occurs. Such an arrangement, however, is limited in most cases to the first two or three years of the lease term.

In the early days of the industry, it was the usual practice to call for payment of the percentage overage on an annual basis in accordance with a sales report certified by an outside auditor or a responsible officer of the tenant company. More recent leases have generally provided for overage payments on an uncertified basis quarterly, or sometimes even monthly, with an annual reconcilation on the basis of an audited statement by the tenant. Such an arrangement has the obvious benefit of leveling off the flow of income while, at the same time, keeping a tight rein on the less financially responsible tenants. A common provision in percentage leases gives a landlord the right to audit the tenant's books to the extent necessary to verify the annual statement, with the expense of the audit to be borne by the tenant should there prove to be an error of more than a nominal amount, typically 2 or 3 percent. Many managers avail themselves of that right by having a few such audits made every year, frequently on a random basis and usually employing an independent CPA for the purpose.

In addition to verifying the percentage calculations, the person who actually handles the rent receipts must be vigilant in checking them against the more obscure provisions of the lease, including any ancillary agreements that may be attached. For example, long-term, fixed-rent leases with certain kinds of tenants (such as financial institutions) frequently call for periodic increases of predetermined dollar amounts or in accordance with specific formulas. Another example is that of new tenants who may have stepped-up minimum guarantees during the early years. The most difficult ancillary agreements to keep track of, however, are probably those giving the tenant the right to offset other occupancy expense against the overage rent liability. These agreements can take many forms. Some of the more common are:

- Provision that if the tenant's share of the common area maintenance exceeds a stipulated amount, either in dollars or as a percentage of sales, he may deduct the excess, or a part of it, from overage.

- Similar provisions relating to the tenant's contribution toward real estate taxes, to a merchants' association, or other joint promotional activity.

- Agreement providing for recapture, in whole or in part, of the cost of a major leasehold improvement, such as a new storefront.

- Agreement covering a situation in which the landlord makes a capital improvement for the tenant's account and recovers his cost through a temporary increase in the percentage rent.

Where such agreements are in force, and they are quite common, there should be careful monitoring of all tenant payments with a view to immediate detection of any irregularity. If emphasis on counting every penny seems a little overdone, the manager should remember that an owner who may be reasonably tolerant of minor inefficiencies in other matters can be extremely intolerant of failure to collect every cent he is owed.

Following rent, the next most important collection job in most centers is the computation and billing of common area maintenance expense. Ideally, of course, the lease clause dealing with these charges is comprehensively written, identical in all leases, and with no ceilings or offsets, thereby providing for a 100 percent pass-through of all direct and indirect expense of operating and maintaining the common areas. However, this happy state of affairs is comparatively rare, and the overwhelming majority of shopping center managers must function under more difficult circumstances that call for greater attention to the individual billings and considerable tact in dealing with tenants when differences of opinion occur. As discussed in the part of Chapter 3 devoted to financial planning, budgeting, and control, every effort should be made to secure tenant payments either in advance of the actual outlay by the center or at least very soon thereafter, and to provide for smoothing out the annual expense in a series of fairly level monthly charges.

Recently, there has been a sharp increase in the number of centers that require tenants to assume a share of the real estate taxes. Such a provision is standard in the leases of almost all shopping centers developed since the mid-1960s and is, in most cases, being added in older centers as rapidly as tenant renewals and turnover permit. There is considerable variation in the methods employed, which will be touched on at greater length in Chapter 9. The objective is to stabilize the owner's expense, completely or partially, at a stipulated level, with additional levies to be prorated for reimbursement by the tenants. As with common area expense, the ideal condition is one in which all tenants are obligated without ceiling or offset but, again, this is a rare situation. Obviously, such a program would be implemented over a period of years in an older center. And even in quite recently built projects it is not always uniform; the developer's negotiations with certain tenants may have resulted in something less than full acceptance. Administration of the real estate tax portion of the lease calls for the same attention to detail by the manager as the common area charge.

In those large centers where the tenants are supplied from a central source with utilities such as water, gas, electricity, steam, or chilled water, there is ordinarily no problem with varying lease provisions, and it is simply a matter of calculating, by meter or otherwise, the correct charge, billing it, and ensuring prompt payment.

When, however, the manager must keep track of billing, receiving, and disbursing members' contributions to the merchants' association, or similar activities, it is good practice to keep that operation fully separate from those dealing with the owner's funds. Billing and follow-up notices should be on the association's stationery, and the funds should be held in a separate account at the bank. The larger aspects of a manager's relationship with a merchants' association are presented in Chapter 6.

There is a sharp difference of opinion among experienced managers, both fee and employee, on the subject of supplying service for a tenant's account within the leased space. The services in question are ordinarily minor but of an urgent nature, such as a stopped drain, electrical short-circuit or defective switch, broken door hinge—small matters for which an outside contractor would charge a stiff price. A fee manager would use one of his own handymen, if he maintains such a crew, or have the work done as an add-on to other work being performed for the owner's account by an independent contractor. An on-site manager in a large center can get the work done by personnel on the owner's payroll. In the first instance, the charge should be billed by the fee manager in his own name or directly by the outside contractor without passing through the owner's account; in the second situation, the billing must be in the landlord's name, with the item passing through the books as an expense and resulting income.

To the fee manager there are ordinarily no secondary complications, provided both owner and tenant clearly understand his role. However, if the owner's employees are involved, their services are customarily charged to the common area maintenance account and the diversion should be adequately accounted for, however trivial the amount. This will forestall the charge being picked up and blown out of proportion by a tenant unhappy with his share of the common area charge. And, in establishing the overhead loading to be added to the direct labor charge, care must be exercised either to avoid or to compensate for creating a taxable profit.

Those managers who favor providing such service claim it is almost essential for many small independent tenants, particularly for stores staffed by women; that it helps maintain good tenant relations; and that, to the extent it uses what might otherwise be idle time, it is modestly profitable. Managers holding contrary views believe that it encourages tenants to lean on the management for help in petty matters on which they should be self-reliant; that the amount of the service charge too often causes a dispute; and that there is too much potential for serious problems, such as a stepladder tipping over onto the wife of the town's leading negligence lawyer or, less dramatically, smashing an expensive glass showcase. However, practically all managers, fee or employee, actively discourage their employees from any form of moonlighting in the employ of a tenant.

Nonfinancial Aspects of the Lease

As administrator of the lease, the manager must also be concerned with the preservation of the property and its immediate environment. All shopping center leases obligate the tenant to maintain the leased premises in good order and repair, to properly contain rubbish and arrange for its disposal, to comply with all applicable laws, to carry adequate liability insurance, and to refrain from certain specified activities that might be detrimental to his neighbors. Most leases also contain provisions related to the integrated community aspect of a shopping center, such as store hours, limitations on the kind of merchandise carried, control of employee parking, and mandatory contributions to joint promotional activities. The first group of obligations has largely to do with the shopping center as real estate;

the second group deals with it as a going business.

In a well-written lease, the obligations having to do with preserving the property are precisely spelled out in terms that have been well tested in court, contain a minimum of ambiguity, and rarely provoke a dispute as to intent. Ensuring compliance is largely a matter of continual, or periodic, observation of the premises in order to detect small matters before they become large ones. A useful practice is to make sufficiently detailed notes at the time of observation to provide for a documented, specific statement of time, place, and exact nature of the infraction in a communication to the tenant. Unless the tenant is a chronic offender, such lapses are ordinarily oversights and should be dealt with by a friendly visit or phone call rather than a written complaint. It should be kept in mind that chain-store managers frequently operate under rules requiring that any written communication from a landlord must automatically be referred to headquarters for a reply. Thus, an inconsequential matter can put a store manager in a bad light with his superiors, to the detriment of his future relations with the center manager.

This is not to say that the manager should be lax or dilatory in enforcing tenant obligations—just the opposite is the better course. In most successful centers, the landlord-tenant relationship is marked by scrupulous observance of their commitments by both parties. Despite sporadic evidence to the contrary, retail merchants are also members of the human race, and if given fair, firm, and courteous treatment they will generally respond in kind. Conversely, the center manager who takes a martinet approach usually finds himself contending with nit-picking demands and carping criticism from the tenants. If a manager senses the development of a persistent adversary relationship with his tenants, it is time to pause for reflection—he is almost certainly doing something wrong.

In some specialized areas, a manager has ready allies in the outside community. As noted in Chapter 10, poor internal housekeeping observed by the local fire marshal is usually promptly corrected, at least temporarily, if the directive has been issued by a person wearing a blue uniform. Similarly, a persistent garbage-disposal problem can sometimes be ameliorated by a discreet phone call to the community health department and the resultant visit by an inspector. If it appears that a tenant's equipment is overloading a floor, wall, or column, the problem can often be solved by recourse to the municipal building inspector. In depending on such outside forces, a manager is in no sense evading his responsibilities or abdicating his authority, nor is he double-crossing the tenants. He is, instead, simply making intelligent use of the available resources to achieve a necessary result.

In the second category of nonfinancial tenant obligations—those related to the way tenants conduct their business—the manager's path is much less clearly marked, for a number of reasons. One reason is that, early in 1972, the Federal Trade Commission launched a wide-ranging study of the shopping center industry to determine the extent, if any, to which its practices might directly or indirectly result in restrictions on competition to the detriment of consumers as a class. Involved have been such things as restrictions on type and/or price of permitted merchandise, on kinds of advertising, on radius clauses, on store hours, and on various kinds of exclusive arrangements. A number of other limitations on the freedom of business activity by tenants were also investigated by the FTC. In general, such requirements and/or restrictions fall into two categories: (1) those uniformly applicable to all tenants, and (2) those specific to an individual tenant. It is the latter type that appears to be the main interest of the FTC. However, at the time of this writing (early 1977), the investigation had not been completed. The ultimate course of the agency's efforts is not predictable, and it remains an outside influence to be followed and considered by the shopping center manager as it continues to unfold.

Tenant obligations that are neither directly financial nor related to preservation of the property seem to fall into two categories. In one group are those obligations having to do with the operation of the center as a business unit, where it is clear that a violation by one tenant will adversely affect all tenants; in the other group are those having to do primarily with the internal conduct of a tenant's affairs, which have little or no impact on his business neighbors. As a general rule, the manager confronted with problems in the first group is well advised to insist on strict compliance with the letter of the lease in the same manner as for those matters related to money and property protection. In dealing with the second group, however, it is sometimes better management to apply the rule of reason rather than an overly rigid insistence on what it says in the fine print. A few examples illustrate the point.

Many centers provide in their leases that the tenant and his employees must park their personal cars in designated areas and that the tenant must provide the landlord with an up-to-date file of license numbers of his employees. Most tenant principals well understand the desirability of preserving parking spaces close to the stores for their customers and willingly comply, but their employees are sometimes more concerned with personal convenience than with the success of the business. There are various techniques for policing the situation, including encouraging the law-abiding tenants to report the cheaters. Employee parking illustrates the type of lease provisions that merits strict, literal enforcement because of its contagious nature. If Tenant A's employees get away with it, those of Tenant B are encouraged to do likewise; if they are followed by the personnel of Tenants C through Z, out the window goes the turnover value of the close-in parking spaces.

In the same category are practices such as the use of an exterior loudspeaker or the pushing of storefloor sweepings out the door onto the mall or sidewalk. The first of these can be an annoyance to shoppers that is detrimental to the whole center; the second shifts a part of the individual tenant's expense onto the common area maintenance, since it must be paid for by the other tenants or the landlord. Both practices tend to become habit, invite emulation, and are injurious to the tenant group as a whole and, through the tenants, to the owner. Such behavior is easily controlled if it is nipped in the bud, but if it is allowed to proliferate it can be difficult to stop and will downgrade the entire center.

On the other hand, tenants, particularly small ones, will occasionally be guilty of relatively minor lease infractions that do no real harm either to other tenants or to the landlord, and no useful purpose is served if the manager takes a hard-nosed approach. The small tenant may sometimes need to take a cross-sidewalk delivery of merchandise rather than receive it through his rear door, or he may occasionally have to close his store early because of a personal problem, or he may run a special on some item not included in the business description contained in his lease. It is a good idea for the manager to let the tenant know he is aware of what has taken place and does not want to see it become a habit, but making "a federal case" out of such events serves no useful purpose.

Store Hours: a Special Problem

This finally gets us to the matter of store hours; as previously noted, it represents a type of problem sometimes difficult to solve. The difficulty, peculiarly enough, is caused by the presence, rather than the absence, of some form of lease provision requiring the tenant to be open for business at times other than of his own unfettered choosing. If the agreement is silent on that point, a manager seeking to maintain uniformity of hours is wholly dependent on his powers of persuasion, a condition understood by all parties. It is the existence of an affirmative covenant, however, that sets the stage for either dispute over meaning or outright defiance.

In the early years of the industry, most shopping center leases were either silent on the subject or contained a tenant obligation to operate the store at "the hours usual and customary for that type of business," and that continues to be typical in effectively all neighborhood centers and probably a large majority of those classified as community size. During the first half of the 1960s, however, new regionals starting putting into their leases a clause calling on the tenant to abide by center-wide store hours as set variously by the landlord, the anchor stores, or the merchants' association, and this is where the rub comes.

The anchor stores, whether as tenants or co-owners, are rarely, if ever, parties to the general agreement and tend to go their own way, changing hours as they see fit—and where there is more than one anchor, they sometimes cannot agree among themselves. The strong major tenants frequently insist on the insertion of the word "reasonable" at the appropriate point in the lease, and thereafter take the position that they are the proper judge of what is reasonable. All of those conditions complicate a manager's life, but the real difficulty arises when a tenant, having no available loopholes, simply refuses to stay open at certain hours on the grounds of unbearable hardship.

In this situation the manager's alternatives are all poor. Theoretically, he can attempt an eviction for the breach of a substantial covenant in the lease or of a court-ordered compliance. However, if the tenant puts up a vigorous defense, such a proceeding would be expensive, of highly uncertain outcome, and would result in bad publicity for all concerned. If the term of the lease is near an end, the manager can threaten to refuse a renewal, but if the tenant is a strong rent-producer they will both know that is a bluff; if the tenant is weak he will not care anyway. If the manager tries making a special deal on the rental terms to subsidize the unproductive hours, he can count on the word spreading all over the center in short order. As a practical matter, about all he can do is put forth his best persuasive efforts to get the tenant to change his mind, to enlist the assistance of other tenants to apply peer pressure, and to keep the example from spreading.

Enforcing Lease Provisions

The greater the extent to which a lease restricts or dictates the manner in which the tenant conducts his business, the more often a center manager will be confronted with the problem of debatable interpretations or the dilemma of outright defiance. Typical examples of such clauses are:

■ A prohibition of change of ownership without the landlord's consent. What constitutes "ownership" of a corporation having several shareholders can be argued all night, and the same goes for the issue within a partnership.

■ Restrictions on the percentage of floor area that may be concessioned or sublet. The precise method of measurement can be debated all the next night.

■ A radius clause under which a tenant is prohibited from establishing another store within a specified distance. In the absence of an exact definition of how the distance is to be determined, that can become controversial where it is a close fit. Also controversial is the situation in which the tenant's brother opens a store across the street selling the same kind of merchandise but with a slightly different name over the door.

■ A lease provision requiring the tenant to spend a certain percentage of his gross sales for advertising can become an administrative nightmare if there is an attempt to secure other than approximate compliance.

All such matters are in the lease for valid reasons aimed at retaining maximum attractiveness of the center to the trade-area population, and the center as a functioning unit is in some degree damaged each time they are ignored. Therefore it becomes part of the manager's duty to try for full, literal compliance, but he is generally better off to do so with a sense of balance and proportion. It is possible to get bogged down in relatively inconsequential matters to the detriment of more important considerations. In the shopping center industry, as any other field of business, a manager's true effectiveness is not gauged by how many trivial arguments he wins against his associates.

In those shopping centers large enough to support some level of joint program for advertising and promotion (a subject discussed in some detail in Chapter 6), an important avenue for continuing contact between manager and tenants is a merchants' association. Without such an organization, the job of planning and implementing a promotional effort is difficult to the point of being impossible, and in the great majority of cases the vitality of the association is largely conditioned by the degree of leadership provided by the center manager. As previously noted, he will usually be responsible for collecting and disbursing the money, keeping the records, and generally providing for continuity of operation, but his involvement must go beyond that if it is to be really effective. He, or his representative, should sit in on all general membership and board of director meetings of the association, actively representing the owner's share of the budget. In addition to providing leadership when needed, his involvement also permits a manager to sense undercurrents that have not yet surfaced. Such meetings always cover a certain amount of business gossip in addition to the matters at hand.

Paradoxically, the manager of a large center having a great number of tenants is more likely to maintain a close relationship with all of them than the manager of a relatively small project. The obvious reason is proximity. However, despite their locational advantage, on-site managers frequently become too immersed in administrative detail. They fail to make those brief, informal visits to store owners or managers that can be so important in giving them the feel of how things are going. For the contract manager of a small center, the job of maintaining tenant contact, particularly if the center is distant from his office, is possible only by scheduling visits as rigidly as is done for inspection of the physical property. At weekly, monthly, or other appropriate intervals, the manager, or his representative, should see every tenant—even if he merely sticks his head in the door to say "Hello." As a matter of fact, that is about all that is needed in most cases.

The extent to which a shopping center manager should concern himself with the internal affairs of the tenants presents a question on which there are differing views within the industry. By "internal affairs" is meant those matters of store operation outside the scope of agreements embodied in the lease and any ancillary documents. Specifically, they include such matters as type of fixtures and store layout, choice of merchandise and manner of displaying it, extent and quality of advertising, level of housekeeping, store hours, employee relations,

76

and other such matters having to do with the conduct of a retail business.

Traditionally, to the extent that a business infant such as the shopping center industry can be said to have traditions, the generally accepted managerial posture has been one of laissez faire, with the manager figuratively saying to the tenant: "You don't try to tell me how to run the center, and I won't tell you how to run your store." In fairly recent times, however, a school of thought has developed that suggests that a manager's responsibilities should be enlarged to include counseling tenants of low productivity in the hope of improving their performance and, thereby, increasing the amount of rent they pay.

There has been some inconclusive experimenting with various techniques of tenant education, involving people recruited from colleges, newspapers, store architects, display companies, and similar sources of presumed expertise. This has generally taken the form of seminar-type meetings, frequently under the auspices of the merchants' association, although the expense is borne by the owner. The more ardent exponents of the tenant-counseling school, however, advocate efforts directed to the individual tenant.

There are no data on the extent to which such an approach—one that stresses the role of the center manager—has actually been put into practice and what the results have been. It will probably be several years before objective evaluations can be made of whether it is a sufficiently effective technique to warrant giving managers the specialized training necessary to its adoption. A large multicenter operator might be able to afford either having a specialist on its staff or employing a consultant to provide such guidance, but the typical employee or contract manager could hardly be expected to have the required level of all-around retail expertise. A manager is on safe ground in calling the tenant's attention to such things as sloppy window displays and rude personnel, but getting into merchandising practices is another matter.

The field of retailing in urban as distinguished from rural environments is highly competitive and, in some matters, quite specialized. The operations of a gift shop and a candy store have as many differences as they do similarities, and even within the same retail categories there are wide variations. A 1,200-square foot pharmacy and a 12,000-square foot self-service super-drug are both technically classified as drug stores, but that's about where the resemblance ends.

The operation of a high-volume, low-markup, minimum-service women's wear store is one thing, whereas the approach taken in a low-volume, high-markup, concealed-stock women's gown shop is something quite different.

Another consideration to which a center manager might address himself is the potential secondary effects of venturing into the role of retail adviser. Human nature being what it is, any increase in the rent receipts will constitute his sole reward should business improve. The tenants will almost certainly assume full credit for the higher sales volume. Conversely, if the tenant's position deteriorates, regardless of the reason, he will more than probably lay the blame on poor advice from the center manager, and this can result in a very sticky situation if it subsequently becomes necessary to terminate the lease.

In applying the preceding thoughts and comments on the manager-tenant relationship, it should be kept in mind here, as with other topics covered in this book, that there is no such thing as a standard shopping center environment in which a typical manager acts out his role. Centers exist in great variety of size, composition, and age, and the powers and responsibilities of their managers are also subject to much variation. It has been necessary, therefore, to stick to the broad-brush approach with the hope that readers interested in specific situations will be able to make their own extrapolations from the general to the particular.

QUESTIONS FOR DISCUSSION

1. *What is the legal relationship between the shopping center and its tenants?*

2. *How is the divergence of interest in store hours reconciled?*

3. *What are the two key roles of the center manager in his relations with the tenants?*

4. *Discuss the procedures used in computing and collecting rent.*

5. *Discuss the problems inherent to computing common area maintenance.*

6. *Explain the divergent views regarding the provision of services to tenants.*

7. *How does the center manager enforce the nonfinancial aspects of the lease?*

8. *Review the typical examples of the enforcement of debatable clauses in tenant lease provisions.*

9. *Describe the advantages of a merchants' association as a means of contact between tenants and center manager.*

10. *Discuss the views of the industry regarding the shopping center manager's concern with the "internal affairs" of the tenants.*

RECOMMENDED READING LIST

Evening Openings and Sales Volume. New York: International Council of Shopping Centers, 1973. 4 pp.

Gleason, Michael E. and Craig H. Edgecumbe. **What Shopping Center Managers Should Know about Chapter 11 and Bankruptcies.** New York: International Council of Shopping Centers, 1975. 4 pp.

Nyburg, Robert S. **Shopping Center Merchants Associations.** New York: International Council of Shopping Centers, 1970. 80 pp.

Smith, Roger S. **Auditing Shopping Center Tenants' Gross Sales.** New York: International Council of Shopping Centers, 1972. 12 pp.

Underberg, Neil. **Shopping Centers, 1976.** New York: Practising Law Institute, 1976. 510 pp.

Wingate, John. **Sunday Openings in Shopping Centers.** New York: International Council of Shopping Centers, 1971. 8 pp.

CHAPTER **5**

Community Relations and Security

Combining the topics of community relations and security may seem odd, but in many aspects of shopping center management they are closely interrelated, with the effectiveness of the former having much to do with the quality of the latter. Before examining the mutual relationship, let us look at them as separate concepts.

The Shopping Center as Part of a Community

No shopping center exists in a vacuum; each is a piece of the community, a part of its society. The choice is not between having relations with the community or not; the alternatives are only whether the relationship will be good, bad, or somewhere in between. The community is not a monolithic entity—rather, it is composed of many organisms leading separate lives but all bound together by the purpose of making the total society function.

To start with, there is government, which operates at four levels —municipal, county, state, and federal. Each level supplies services to the center or regulates its activities or both. There are the school system and the church, which have no direct impact on the center but exert a powerful influence within the community. The businessmen's service clubs, Boy and Girl Scouts, garden clubs, and a host of similar special-interest groups are all part of the community fabric. Finally, there are the individuals themselves, each of whom consciously or subconsciously has an opinion on what is pleasant or unpleasant about the environment. It is the sum total of those attitudes that makes up the climate in which the shopping center and its tenants conduct their business.

Security has somewhat different surface meanings to owner, tenant, and shoppers, but basically these individuals are bound by a common interest—they do not want the normal operation of the center disturbed or interrupted by unfriendly forces. To the owner, security connotes the preservation of the buildings representing his investment and the maintenance of peace and order, the absence of which will deter shoppers. To the tenant, security revolves around protection of his merchandise and employees, plus that same interest in a peaceful environment for his customers. In the mind of the shopper, security has to do with personal safety and the safety of property while in the center or traveling to and from it.

It is clearly evident that in providing protection for this diversity of interests, the center manager and the tenants are mainly dependent on the resources of the community. Even the largest centers are unprepared to cope directly with other than quite minor threats. A fire of greater than trash-can magnitude must be dealt with by the public fire department, and a disturbance more serious than a fight between two schoolboys calls for the intervention of the local police, as does the apprehension of a shoplifter inside a store. When traffic on the public road becomes so heavy that shopping center ingress and egress are hazardous, the solution is in the hands of the road commission, and if a restaurant's dishwashing procedures become suspect, the local health department will be looked to for corrective measures.

Internal Security Measures

With that background, we will first look at some of a center's security problems and what a manager might do about them, and then go on to some of the broader aspects of community relations. These comments and examples refer to a shopping center large enough to have an on-site manager, since on that scale the details become large enough for separate identification. In a small neighborhood-type center some of the conditions discussed are either not present or are of minor significance.

There is no agreed-on size at which a center should establish a full-time security patrol; the need is, to some extent, determined by characteristics of the shopper traffic and construction of the buildings. For unknown reasons, some locations more than others attract disorderly elements despite there being little difference in their socio-economic environments, and if the structures have a low fire rating a 24-hour patrol may be an insurance requirement. Observation indicates that a full-time security force seems to follow about the same pattern of incidence as full-time managers—rare in centers of less than 400,-000 square feet, usual with more than 600,000 feet, and varied in between. Below the 400,000-foot size the extent of security personnel specifically identified as such gradually diminishes—the neighborhood strip will probably use the services of one man during the busy hours of the week, largely for traffic-control purposes. At the other extreme, some very large regionals employ as many as 20 or 30 full-time security people in what amounts to a private police force.

Experienced managers disagree on whether security personnel should be armed and whether they should be direct employees or contracted for with a professional guard service. It is difficult to summarize the pros and cons of this debate for three reasons: the two matters are to some extent interrelated, there is a considerable variation in state or local regulatory laws, and the whole field has been changing rapidly in recent times. To a large extent, the differences revolve around the expense of the operation, however, and a few generalizations may help bring the matter into focus.

Proponents of the unarmed-guard position say that it enables them to employ on a part-time basis relatively low-skilled people whose essential duties consist of directing traffic, controlling disorderly children, and being alert to call the public police and fire departments when needed.

Those favoring the armed, higher-priced, special-police type contend that some elements in present-day society have no respect for authority unless it is backed up by visible evidence of force; that in some metropolitan areas it is effectively impossible to employ reliable men for after-hours patrol unless they are armed; and that response by the public police is sometimes too slow in critical situations.

Managers using contract guards point out that they can schedule the force exactly according to need, by the hour of the day and the season of the year. In addition, they are spared all the personnel-selection, bookkeeping, insuring, and other administrative burdens connected with payroll employees.

Managers who handle security with their own force believe that the added expense and trouble are warranted by being able to obtain more highly qualified men, whose stability of employment has advantages over the constantly changing personnel of contract guards. These managers emphasize that the regular employee can function as the eyes of management in reporting relatively obscure maintenance needs and other irregularities, and is likely to do a better public relations job than the individual having no vested interest in the overall operation of the center. In electing a modus operandi, the manager is not bound to go all one way or all the other. After a thorough cost-benefit analysis, he may determine that the optimum solution is a combination of salaried and contracted guards, some armed and some unarmed.

In entering into a contract, by either bidding or negotiation, it is important to specify the duties the men will be expected to perform and the base rate of their hourly pay. Without such stipulations the contractor will almost certainly fill the assignments with personnel receiving the minimum legal wages and skilled accordingly. The salaries and fringe benefits of direct employees are best set at a level that will attract and keep qualified people. A stable work force is desirable since these are sensitive jobs in terms of their continuous contacts with both tenants and the public.

One approach to the security problem sometimes successfully used is the employment of off-duty policemen from the community. Properly selected and supervised, such personnel can be quite effective at relatively low cost. However, there are sometimes latent political problems that can surface without warning and create unfavorable publicity. The availability of such personnel has decreased in recent years, possibly because of the national trend toward increased professionalism in police work, even in quite small municipalities, and the resulting official prohibition of moonlighting by individual officers. At one time, the managers of small centers often handled their security problem by an off-the-record arrangement calling for a little something under the table to the local police chief or precinct captain, but that practice also has waned as law enforcement has become increasingly sensitive politically.

A detailed presentation of the mechanics of setting up and supervising an interior guard system is pointless here. The great diversity of size and configuration in the shopping center industry dictates that this book remain very general. Moreover, electronic security and communication devices are improving so rapidly that today's innovation may be obsolete tomorrow. There is good literature available on the general subject of security procedures, and the individual manager has available, for the asking, expert professional advice from local law-enforcement agencies; they are only too happy to assist the private sector.

83

Among the more effective electronic devices being used in shopping center security systems are two-way radios of the walkie-talkie type and closed-circuit television. The former keeps the patrolman in direct contact with his back-up point should he need help, and makes him instantly available for reassignment by his supervisor. The latter, when installed in relatively confined areas, enables one person to maintain simultaneous surveillance of numerous locations remote from his station and from each other. In both instances, the result can be a saving of manpower that soon offsets the capital cost of the equipment.

A manager must keep abreast of changes in the criminal codes governing the actions of police-type personnel in the performance of their duties. Suits for false arrest, or the equivalent, are increasingly common and costly, and even if covered by insurance are bad publicity and a nuisance to deal with. The need to keep all personnel periodically refreshed and up to date along that line becomes an argument in favor of the salaried man versus the contract guard.

A center's security force is an extension of—and not a replacement for—the public agencies. All managers must keep this fact in mind, and must be sure that it is clearly understood by other members of their staffs. Specifically, the guard who detects a fire, or the evidence that there may be one, calls the local department first and only then makes his own effort to control it. The night patrolman who believes a burglar is on the premises sends for the city police and lets *them* win any medals for ferreting out the trespasser. If it appears that a gang of professional car thieves is working the parking lot, or a ring of shoplifters is operating in the stores, put the matter in the hands of the local police detectives and let them set the trap. A corollary to that concept is the requirement for an optimum level of communication, both by wire and/or radio and by personal contact, between the center's personnel and their opposite numbers in the municipal departments.

Direct lines into the nearest police station generally constitute a good security measure, and these "hot lines" can be used as a fail-safe device. For example, the night patrol can be instructed to call into the local station periodically. Should the call not arrive on time, the police can be directed to investigate in person. And since most police departments operate in-service training programs, it is possible for the center management to arrange for members of its staff to join the students in their classes—thus upgrading their skills while helping to maintain personal rapport with individual members of the local department.

84

If the center security men are special police or otherwise legally qualified for the purpose, they can endear themselves to the city department by assuming some of the routine paperwork that would otherwise take the time of the regular officers. Typical instances in which this is done are automobile accidents in the parking lot with no personal injury involved, thefts of and from vehicles, purse-snatchings and shoplifting when the thief is no longer in sight, and similar matters not requiring immediate law-enforcement action. Such matters take little time of the man on duty, they free the public police for more important work, and they constitute community relations in action.

The security force should be trained in writing up personal-accident reports. The proficiency with which this is done can have a significant effect on the center's insurance costs. Public liability insurance premiums are usually based on the physical characteristics of the property, with annual adjustments reflecting the carrier's experience; that is, the more claim dollars the carrier pays out this year, the higher the premium payments will be next year. For some time, there has been a steady broadening of the legal liability of property owners for personal injury or property damage suffered by visitors to the center's premises, accompanied by an equally steady increase in the size of damage awards. Such matters as a customer stepping into a pothole in the parking lot, or being hit in the face by a suddenly opened door, can grow from molehills to mountains if neglected. The surest way to control such inflation is to submit prompt, detailed reports to the insurer, complete with witnesses' names and statements—and useful photographs—where applicable. A center having its own security force can profitably schedule periodic training sessions with the insurance company's safety engineer, at which the center personnel are kept informed on what to look for in the way of hazards and on how to handle accidents when they occur.

Turning from the focus on outside agencies, the center's security force must of necessity have a close working relationship with the internal security people always present in department stores and most other large units. Theoretically, the center owner has no stake in his tenants' inventories, but from a practical standpoint he does. Inventory shrinkage, whatever the cause, is a cost of doing business and, in a roundabout but real sense, as shrinkage goes up the tenant's rent-paying capacity, or at least his willingness to pay it in that location, goes down. There is very little the center manager, either directly or through his security people, can do about the individual act of theft from a store, other than to ensure that center personnel stand ready to assist the in-store operatives within the limits of their legal power to do so. However, the manager can make some positive contributions to the overall problem in the form of organizing, through the merchants' association or otherwise, educational and mutual-assistance agreements.

In almost every community, police or department store sources can provide specialists in the detection and thwarting of shoplifters to speak before groups of retail store employees. If the center has a community hall, this can be done effectively in a series of short meetings immediately preceding or following the opening hour on the slow days of the week. Lacking a community room, an arrangement can usually be made with a department store or restaurant tenant to provide the space. If such a program receives strong tenant support, it is usually desirable to repeat it at regular intervals to compensate for the rather high rate of turnover typical of retail employment. The purpose of such programs is to acquaint retail personnel with the more common methods used by shoplifters, both amateur and professional, how to avoid establishing conditions favorable to their operations, and then what to do about shoplifters.

Supplementing the educational effort is organization by the tenants of what is commonly referred to as a round-robin arrangement. This is simply an internal alerting system designed to quickly spread the word if there appears to be an organized group of professional shoplifters in the center. In such a system, each store manager and his assistants have an assigned list of three or four stores to be alerted about the presence of a suspicious-looking individual or group. Each of those stores, in turn, is part of a similar cadre. A telephone network of that nature can be quite effective if properly structured and kept up to date, the latter aspect particularly being dependent on the center manager even though the activity is ostensibly a project of the merchants' association.

Sensitive Problems in Community Relations

Protecting the shopping center property and population against natural hazards and criminal activities falls within conventional watchman and police procedures, and a manager's responsibility is to see that the function is first properly planned and organized, and thereafter adequately supervised. There is another phase of security, however, that the manager can never completely delegate; since, to some extent, it is peculiar to shopping centers, he cannot follow precedents established elsewhere. The problem is controlling those elements of the community that, although not always welcome, have a right to be present and carry on their activities within certain limits. Usually, these elements are well-meaning people engaged in programs they believe to be socially desirable; therefore, dealing with them is a sensitive matter of community relations.

The activities generally fall into one of five categories—pickets in labor disputes, social demonstrators, political candidates, charitable solicitors, or obstreperous juveniles. Through trial-and-error over the past twenty-odd years, the industry has accumulated a certain amount of experience in handling such situations. But there are few firmly established practices and it remains an area of shopping center management in which there is continual experimentation. In fact, in some instances experienced managers cannot agree on the results to be sought. The subject is being treated here in the context of security because it concerns uses of the property that, if allowed to get out of control, can be disruptive of the center's business purpose.

Before offering some thoughts on each of the five categories, there is one comment applicable to them all: the first requirement in managing such matters is common sense. The manager who lets disputes over these issues degenerate into legalistic wrangles may win some battles in the security area, but he is often on the way to losing the war in the field of community relations. The second requirement is a general working knowledge of the various legal rights involved—and the manager should also know when his competence is inadequate and it is necessary to call for expert legal guidance.

Both the rights and the conduct of pickets in a labor dispute are well defined by statute and court decision, and the great majority of unions see to it that their pickets behave accordingly. With comparatively rare exceptions, if a picket line becomes unruly, a phone call to union headquarters will bring corrective action. If it does not, the problem should immediately be placed in the hands of the local police. Involving private guards, whether salaried or contract, with union pickets is rarely productive of anything but increased disorder. The objective is to confine the picketing activity to the immediate vicinity of the affected store with a minimum of interference with the normal business of the center. A little tact can usually accomplish this without incident.

Picketing or public meetings designed to express a social or political viewpoint are a very different matter and can be explosive if not carefully handled. The participants are ordinarily not under the tight discipline characteristic of labor union activities, the atmosphere is generally highly emotional, and there is frequently more than one faction present. In the very great majority of cases, the assemblage has nothing to do with the center per se—the site is simply being used as a public forum. The only ill effects to be expected are the temporary disruption of business and the incidental vandalism unfortunately so often present in the fringe of any public gathering. Both effects are, of course, related to the scale of the activity; when small, as is usually the case, such events are little more than a temporary nuisance.

Such demonstrations, or protests as they came to be called, were quite prevalent during the latter years of the Vietnam war but have at least temporarily gone out of style. The civil rights of the various parties—demonstrators, landlord, and tenants—have been the subject of considerable litigation and as of this writing are far from clarified. Such events are further complicated by the fact that the public police are reluctant to intervene in the absence of a clear-cut breach of the peace, and private guards are effective only as long as the crowd remains completely manageable in size and disposition. A manager's best tactic seems to be to meet in advance with the organizers to map out a program of mutual cooperation, and then to prevail on the local police to have some plainclothes observers on the scene. Bull-headed opposition to this use of center property is rarely successful in terms of the overall relationship with the community.

In shopping center management circles, there are three schools of thought on the treatment to be accorded candidates for public office: some centers welcome and actively seek them out as traffic-builders; others consider them as invaders of privacy to be threatened with prosecution for trespass if they mount a soapbox; and a third group views them as necessary evils—like a visit to the dentist—to be suffered through periodically as the price of good citizenship. All three factions strongly discourage candidates from distributing literature on a broadcast basis, particularly on the windshields of parked cars, because of the resulting litter problem. The decision to greet or spurn depends on the individual manager's evaluation of which course will make the most friends, or at least the fewest enemies. Either way, political candidates are unlikely to pose any security threat beyond a temporary crowd-handling problem induced by the presence of a political big fish, although there is always the outside possibility of violence.

88

Incidentally, the problem of handbills, either given to pedestrians on the center sidewalk or placed on parked cars, is by no means confined to office-seekers. In some communities it becomes a considerable nuisance, with ads for car washes and pizza parlors from miles around. The most effective means of control is to post at all entrances, both pedestrian and vehicular, small but legible signs to the effect that the center is private property and soliciting or distribution of advertising matter is prohibited. This can be followed with a letter to all violators notifying them that their distribution has created litter and that, if repeated, will cause them to be billed for the expense of cleanup. Should there be a repetition, send a bill for some reasonable amount. Experience indicates that few offenders will repeat their actions. If they do, turn the account over to a professional collection agency and let it keep what it can get.

A few managers take as hardnosed an attitude toward charitable solicitations as they do toward politicians, but rebuffing charities is not generally viewed as the way to make friends and influence people in the community. The more usual approach is to schedule and control those events so as to eliminate conflicts and reduce the likelihood of shoppers being pestered to the point of annoyance. A common procedure is to establish one or more permanent outdoor booths or indoor tables that can be manned by a solicitor or a pair of solicitors, with appropriate signs, and then to assign the stations to reputable organizations on a first-come basis.

To minimize the possibility of misunderstandings and to assure different groups that all are receiving the same treatment, a printed set of guidelines can be helpful. These guidelines should apply to any group carrying on an activity within the center, and should cover such matters as the use of loudspeakers, harassment of shoppers, interference with traffic, signs and display material, and the general conduct deemed likely to be offsensive to the public or disruptive of the center's business purpose.

Once the community understands that this is a uniformly applied policy, it becomes routine and can be safely handled at the clerical level. If the manager has a full-time promotion director on his staff, the supervision of arrangements is logically delegated to that person. It is sometimes possible to transform a community event into a center-wide promotion, thus serving a dual purpose. Irrespective of that possibility, however, dealing with outside groups helps the promotion director enlarge his community contacts. Furthermore, facilitating the philanthropic and community-betterment programs of local groups is an inherent part of an active public relations procedure aimed at giving the shopping center an identity in the community that supports it. The techniques involved are presented in detail in some of the reference material noted in the appendix of this book.

Disorderly children and teen-agers are a puzzle in the sense that, for reasons not well understood, they may constitute a serious problem in one shopping center and be all but unknown in another of similar characteristics. It is somewhat analogous to the familiar pattern in crowded urban areas: in every neighborhood, one particular street corner becomes "the" place to hang out.

In some cases, however, there is one important difference. Suburban shopping centers, especially the larger ones, have frequently become surrogate baby sitters for children below driving age who live beyond bicycling range. Almost every manager of a regional center is familiar with the early-Saturday-afternoon phenomenon—cars unloading Junior, aged 8 to 14, with parting instruction to "have fun with the other kids and be ready to be picked up at the usual place at five o'clock." In what seems to be an inverse order of justice, the practice is most prevalent at those centers with the best internal security programs, which is probably evidence of the parents' perspicacity—if a child is turned loose to play in a public place it might as well be the safest one available. Such a judgment multiplied by one thousand, however, can create a problem for those charged with keeping things running smoothly in an already crowded shopping center. Up to about age 14 the principal activity consists of running, jumping, screaming, bumping into their elders, and generally behaving like children; this is a problem with no known solution and, therefore, must be lived with. Experience has pretty thoroughly established that getting tough about it only worsens the behavior and makes the parents angry. The only workable approach is the presence of security people who can relate to children well enough to get their cooperation in maintaining a reasonable level of order.

A notch or two up the age ladder is the upper-teen group, who use the center as a gathering place for the age-old reason that that is where the girls are and vice versa. These groups generally remain aloof from the youngsters and, if well-behaved and not in oppressive numbers, are an economic asset since they represent substantial purchasing power. When they do get out of line, however, the older group is capable of creating a serious control problem—one that is best put into the hands of the public authorities as quickly as possible. Another security factor sometimes present in the high-school crowd is an above-average incidence of amateur shoplifting, which seems to run in cycles within a community. It is up to the tenants to detect the thieves and follow through with prosecution, but center management can sometimes assume leadership in bringing to bear community forces in the form of the police, courts, and news media. Vigorous prosecution, stern courts, and widespread publicity are undeniably hard on a few families in the community, but are the only effective methods thus far developed for curbing such an epidemic.

In the great majority of centers, the younger set is simply part of the scenery and presents no special security problem. Occasionally, however, a group exhibits a pattern of disorderly behavior that, if allowed to go unchecked, can deter some shoppers—especially the older ones. An alert management can generally detect such a development quite early and can bring it under control by prompt corrective measures. Some observation of such situations leads to the belief that, when a normally well-behaved group of teen-agers begins to act in an offensive or antisocial manner, there is nearly always a nucleus of individuals, maybe only two or three, who are emotionally disturbed, socially maladjusted, or just plain troublemakers. Children—in this instance those under age 18—are notably imitative. The example of a few of their peers breaking customary rules of social conduct, and getting away with it, can be quite contagious.

Identifying and eliminating the source of the trouble is not a job for amateurs and few, if any, shopping center managements are staffed to tackle it on their own. In almost every community large enough to support a center, a manager can seek help from various sources. Most police departments have youth officers on full-time assignment for such purposes, and most school systems have counselors familiar with those students who have personality problems. In addition there are social agencies, both public and private, that are specifically interested in keeping juveniles out of trouble and helping them when they do get into it. As is true of so many other aspects of shopping center management, no manager is expected to have the expertise personally to cope with this problem; his responsibility is to detect the problem, identify it, and know where to turn for help in dealing with it.

The great diversity of centers and the communities in which they are located, and the wide variations in management structure, make it difficult to prepare a manual to guide shopping center managers

91

in planning and implementing a program of community relations. For example, the circumstances attending a small center in a small city, managed by a successful local realtor, bear little resemblance to those of a large regional on the periphery of a major city with a full-time salaried manager in charge. In the first instance, the realtor's established position in the community was part of the package the owner bought when he hired him. If the realtor happened to be the mayor's brother-in-law and first cousin to the city assessor, those matters were doubtless given due weight in establishing the management fee. The salaried manager of the regional, on the other hand, needs to systematically budget a share of his time to being a good citizen of the community from which he derives his living, even though he may reside elsewhere. The manner in which the two people, realtor and manager, go about things will depend on their personal styles as well as the social and political structures of the respective communities, and each must chart his own route.

One safe generalization is that, while money helps, it alone will not do much to create rapport with the community. Paying one's taxes on time is not likely, alone, to get you on a first-name basis with the mayor, but a year of faithful service on one of his unpaid citizen commissions will generally result in your phone calls receiving a prompt and friendly response. A $500 company check to the annual United Fund campaign, plus some personal participation in the drive itself, is likely to pay greater dividends of good will than a $1,000 contribution minus the personal involvement. The conduct of such a program, of course, should not be the concern of the manager alone, but in a large center should include active participation by members of his staff, and in a center of any size he should endeavor to secure tenants' active participation as well.

In summary, a sound, ongoing program of constructive involvement in the affairs of the community can produce benefits of two kinds—it creates a favorable climate in which to present sales-promoting events, and it serves to lubricate the wheels of day-to-day operations.

QUESTIONS FOR DISCUSSION

1. *Discuss the different significances of security to the three primary entities involved in a shopping center.*

2. *Does the shopping center need the community, the community need the shopping center, or do they need each other? Why?*

3. *Conceptually, what approach would the shopping center manager take to security problems?*

4. *Discuss the relationship between shopping center security forces and the various regular public agencies.*

5. *What are the sensitive problem areas confronting the center manager's community relations?*

6. *Discuss procedures in handling a potential and actual strike of a tenant in your center.*

7. *Discuss an effective method of curbing amateur shoplifting in a center.*

8. *How can the shopping center manager effectively handle the problem of charitable contributions in his center?*

9. *Discuss means by which shopping centers can constructively become involved in community relations.*

10. *Explain the purpose of the center manager's continued involvement in community affairs.*

RECOMMENDED READING LIST

Shopping Center Security—Basic Principles for an Effective Security Program. New York: International Council of Shopping Centers, 1976. 32 pp.

Alexander, Laurence A. **Public Attitudes Toward Downtown Malls.** New York: Downtown Research and Development Center, 1975. 84 pp.

Bose, Keith W. **Video Security Systems.** Indianapolis: Howard W. Sams & Company, 1976. 160 pp.

Court Decisions Relating to Nonbusiness Use of Shopping Center Facilities. New York: International Council of Shopping Centers, 1972. 4 pp.

Kaufman, Arthur C. **Combating Shoplifting.** New York: National Retail Merchants Association, 1974. 72 pp.

The Lloyd Center Case: Implications for Management. New York: International Council of Shopping Centers, 1973. 4 pp.

Millison, Martin B. **Teenage Behavior in Shopping Centers.** New York: International Council of Shopping Centers. 24 pp.

More Security for Your Parking Facility. Washington: National Parking Association, 1976. 78 pp.

The Shopping Center as a Public Forum: The Supreme Court Reconsiders. New York: International Council of Shopping Centers, 1974. 8 pp.

CHAPTER **6**

Promotion and Publicity

as functions of shopping center management, promotion and publicity are in some ways closely related, but they have differences we should distinguish before discussing the approaches to handling them. The essential difference is that promotion is a completely controllable activity that, at least in theory, always benefits the center's business purpose, whereas publicity is frequently uncontrollable and can be either favorable or unfavorable. In terms of effect, promotion is intended to directly stimulate shopper traffic; publicity can improve or damage the general image of the center in the public consciousness. Publicity that is intentionally generated is an institutional form of promotion; when unpremeditated, its results are more often damaging than beneficial.

Promotion, and the planned publicity that is a part of it, is a specialized activity commonly delegated to an individual or outside agency. Uncontrolled publicity is better handled directly by the manager, especially if he holds any ownership interest. Since most publicity of the unsought variety stems from events of sudden occurrence and unpleasant connotation, such as fires, labor troubles, and criminal acts, the manager is best qualified to discuss them with the press, public officials, or other outsiders with whom it is necessary to communicate. Exceptions might be made if the individual in charge of promotion is a full-time employee of the center and is sufficiently familiar with the

94

management operation to understand the ramifications of the particular occurrence.

A thorough examination of shopping center promotion is not within the scope of this book, but there is now available a quantity of excellent published material presenting that activity in detail. However, before moving on to some thoughts regarding the relationship of the promotion function to the overall management operation, a few generalized comments about publicity may provide some helpful guidance for the inexperienced manager.

Publicity

To a large extent, the quality of publicity, both sought and unsought, is conditioned by the cumulative effect of the center's total public relations effort. The people who control the media commonly maintain a posture of complete objectivity in the selection of what is printed or put on the air in the form of news, and in most cases they do a good job of it. However, they too are human beings, and their level of respect for the manner in which a business enterprise is conducted sometimes becomes involved in what they choose either to publicize or to ignore. To first obtain and thereafter retain such respect at a high level has been described as a sustained program of living right and letting the world know it, and it is an integral part of a well-rounded management program. More than any other type of real estate, a shopping center needs community goodwill.

When an untoward event likely to draw attention from the press occurs, a temptation to be resisted is any attempt either to suppress or to distort the news. Efforts along that line are rarely successful and frequently result only in making worse an already bad situation, as is well illustrated by an actual case. A few years ago, a woman was brutally mugged in the parking lot of a large shopping center. In talking with a newspaper reporter, the manager tried so hard to play the matter down that he made a number of ill-considered statements. The next day, a lengthy article appeared in the local paper, giving all the ugly details—as provided by the local police—plus the interview in which the manager was portrayed as implying that brutal muggings were sufficiently frequent on his premises as not to be very newsworthy. Obviously, in his zeal to protect his center the manager had badly miscalculated.

On the positive side, obtaining favorable publicity is, first, a matter of doing interesting things and, second, getting the pertinent information into the hands of the press in a convenient manner. Preparing press releases is somewhere between a science and an art, but instructional material is available to the manager who, by necessity or choice, wishes to exercise his own talent rather than employ specialized help. A point to keep in mind is that newspaper and broadcast editors are human beings who can get fed up with too much of a good thing, especially if showered with an overdose of trivia.

A more subtle form of publicity is the essentially word-of-mouth kind that results from participation in an activity involving a particular segment of the community. For example, co-sponsoring a Mother-of-the Year selection with the local school PTA—an appropriate recognition ceremony at Mothers Day—will generate much person-to-person publicity in addition to any attention given it by the press. This is, of course, a part of community relations, which was discussed in Chapter 5. It is mentioned here to emphasize that relating a shopping center to the community, which is its reason for being, is more than a matter of keeping it looking nice and paying the taxes on time; it also includes reaching out actively to participate.

Promotion's Impact on Rate of Return

As was pointed out early in this book, the economics of the modern shopping center are such that the rate of return on the investment is extremely sensitive to fluctuations in the sales volumes of the tenants. The leveraging action of percentage leases, as related to the rigidity of operating expenses, makes a small increase in sales translate into a large increase in rate of return, a fact well understood by the industry's pioneers. However, considering their potential impact on profits, the evolution of organized promotional programs has proceeded at a rather slow pace during the past quarter-century.

Lease structures vary greatly in their treatment of joint promotional programs: the differences range from complete silence on the subject to firm financial obligations binding both landlord and tenants to stipulated contributions. Not universally, but to a considerable extent, there is a relationship between the age of the center and the scope of such lease provisions. To help those managers seeking to modernize that portion of their leases, some historical perspective may be useful.

The shopping center financial structure of today has resulted from a number of changes in the historical relationship between landlord and retail tenant. To a large extent, the changes were dictated by the nature of the evolving real estate form. They were essential to the attraction of capital, both equity and borrowed, and in the aggregate they acted to strengthen the position of the landlord vis-a-vis the tenant—a trend clearly perceived, but not welcomed, by most tenants. This process of change took place against the background of a period that stretched from about 1930 to the end of World War II during which there was a widely distributed surplus of commercial property, resulting in an unbalanced bargaining position as far as landlords were concerned. The advent of planned suburban shopping centers after the war, particularly those including department stores, tended to put the shoe on the other foot and gradually improved the bargaining position of the landlord.

The initial push by developers in the 1940s and early 1950s was to secure tenants' acceptance of *both* a percentage and a guaranteed minimum rent, a combination that had fallen into some disuse during the depression of the 1930s. Without the guarantees it was impossible to obtain mortgage money, and without the potential of percentage overages it made no sense to gamble the equity investment in such an untried and chancy type of real estate development. The "untried and chancy" view was also taken by many leading retailers, and getting enough of them to put their names to long-term leases on what they considered to be risky terms was usually not an easy task.

In the very early days of the big surge during the first part of the 1950s, it became painfully evident that in many cases the common area maintenance expense had been grossly underestimated, and that the indiscriminate granting of ceilings or tenant recaptures out of overage rent represented a serious drag on earnings. Mortgage lenders also became alert to this danger, and added their weight to the drive toward forcing tenants to accept a greater share of such expense.

The end of that decade saw a sharp upward trend in real estate taxes all over the country, coupled with a much less benign approach to shopping center valuation by local assessors. Up to that point, relatively few tenants were obligated to share payment of real estate taxes. Therefore, the often steep increases in that expense were borne entirely by the owner, presenting a serious threat to his profit and to the peace of mind of his mortgagee. During a good portion of the 1960s, developers of new centers and owners of existing ones accorded a high priority to building into their lease structures provisions of one sort or another obligating tenants to assume a part of the tax burden.

Needless to say, none of these moves to increase the scope of the

97

lessee's financial obligation was received passively by tenants, and the issue became a point of contention in practically all new and renewal lease negotiations. This may partially explain why it was not until the late 1960s that the industry began to direct serious attention to establishing a pattern of promotional programs based on compulsory participation by tenants. As in all such matters, there were a few front-runners who had built into their leases the groundwork for a strong promotional effort, but generally developers preferred to use their negotiating muscle to secure protection against the prospect of runaway expenses rather than direct it toward volume-building efforts. Quite rightly, in most cases, they saw the former as an immediate danger and the latter as desirable but of lesser urgency.

In addition to their preoccupation with getting control of the expense side of the operating statement, most early developers perceived the shopping center as being its own promotion, and in this they were also mostly right. It was not until the end of the 1950s that, with rare exceptions, shopping centers began to compete for the customer's dollar with other shopping centers. Prior to that time, and somewhat depending on size, they competed with downtown and/or an outlying business district, or they effectively had no competition at all. Essentially, the centers' competitive weapons were novelty, accessibility, and ample free parking, which in most circumstances made it a case of no contest. It is probable that, under such conditions, the expenditure of any substantial sums for promotional purposes would not have been economically justified by the incremental business thus obtained.

By the first half of the 1960s, however, this happy state of affairs was being replaced by a growing pattern of shopping centers with overlapping trade areas. Now, in the 1970s, few centers are not faced with present or impending vigorous competition. Of course, the advent of such a condition was clearly apparent for several years, and in recent times all segments of the industry have become more interested in the creation and improvement of joint promotional programs. This has, in turn, focused attention on the existing mechanisms for carrying out such programs and how well they work, and the remainder of this chapter is devoted to an examination of them.

Upgrading the Lease

The original leases in some older centers do not have strong clauses covering tenant contributions for advertising and promotions. As a result, a good deal of management attention in recent years has

98

been directed toward enlarging and making the leases more depend-able. As with most such matters, there is no one best way of going about it because of the great variety of circumstances, and a manager's approach will depend on his evaluation of that particular situation.

Older leases often either completely omit mention of funding for promotion or they provide for the formation of a merchants' associa-tion but fail to be explicit as to method and amount of funding. The manner in which the manager approaches either situation will be conditioned by the general climate. In a highly successful center where tenants obviously value their leaseholds highly a pretty firm attitude is indicated, but in a situation where a number of the stores are only marginally profitable the big stick approach is not likely to work. It becomes a matter of selling rather than telling, and a successful out-come is another one of those indicators that distinguishes good man-agement from the merely adequate.

Obviously, at any point in the life of a shopping center following its opening, the expiration dates of the existing leases will be spread out over a number of years in the future. Building into all of the leases a uniform provision dealing with merchants' association support will be a long-drawn-out proceeding, typically requiring eight or ten years. However, with good leadership the desired result can sometimes be achieved much quicker on a voluntary basis. Whatever the state of the existing lease language, and whether the approach is to be hard-sell or soft-sell, the manager's task will be simplified if he is backed by a cadre of influential tenants.

Such a program is not to be lightly undertaken. The first requisite is a firm resolution by the owner that revision of all future leases, new or renewal, is an absolute and will be carried forward even at the pos-sible cost of losing an otherwise desirable tenant. A manager must be in the position in all lease discussions to say, in effect, that the pro-posed clause will be uniformly incorporated in all future leases, that there will be no exceptions or modifications, and that it is not a negoti-able matter. And in taking that stance he must do so with the certainty that appeals over his head will be futile.

Depending on an evaluation of that particular situation, the de-cision to proceed might be either preceded or followed by a frank dis-cussion with a small group of those tenants considered most likely to favor and support a more vigorous promotional effort. It is inherent to the landlord-tenant relationship that there will be a certain amount of opposition to any change which increases a tenant's financial obligation. However, if peer pressure can be brought to bear, the manager's job will be made easier.

The lease form used in nearly all of the larger centers, and in many relatively small ones developed since the middle 1960s, has provided for formation of a merchants' association, required every tenant to become a member, and established the manner in which the association shall be governed. Typically, the lease article goes on to prescribe in detail a schedule of dues and/or assessments to be paid by tenants and specifies the financial contribution to be made by the owner, either as a fixed sum or as a percentage of the total supplied by the tenants. The individual tenant obligation is customarily expressed as a stipulated annual amount per square foot of GLA occupied, sometimes on a uniform basis but more commonly on a sliding scale in inverse order of size. Usually there is included some provision for escalation, either automatically by a link with the Consumer Price Index or by membership vote.

Such an arrangement does not serve its purpose unless it produces a significant amount of money, and phasing it into an existing shopping center at a meaningful level can be a real struggle if some form of compulsion is not already included in the leases. If he undertakes lease revision during an important internal event such as an enclosure or major addition, or external occurrence such as the advent of impressive new competition, a strong manager could expect to obtain a high degree of voluntary acceptance. Lacking such stimuli, however, there would inevitably be strong resistance on the part of those tenants who, because of lease expiration dates, were the first to be approached.

If the manager of an older center judges the time to be ripe to upgrade the leases, to finance a new program of promotion where there is none or expand an existing one, he must

- Realistically evaluate how far he can revise leases without encountering outright rejection or being obliged to trade-off points having higher priority during negotiations.

- Develop the precise wording to accomplish the purpose and secure the owner's blessing on both objective and words.

- Do the quiet groundwork necessary to ensure the concurrence and, if possible, active support of key tenants.

- Assemble a proposed program for presentation to the tenant group as a whole and seek their agreement to voluntarily fund it.

The funding would ultimately be implemented by the lease agreement.

The first and fourth steps involve matters of judgment and should be taken with great care. The new lease provision must strike a fine balance; it must be strong enough to warrant the effort without going beyond the point of acceptability by a comfortable majority of the tenants. Launching such a program with a great show of determination, and it would have to be done that way, only to back down later in the face of stiff resistance would seriously damage the whole fabric of landlord-tenant relationship. And it would certainly not endear the manager to the owner.

Less potentially damaging but still to be undertaken with due care is preparation of the proposed promotion program to be presented in conjunction with the initial approach to the tenants. It should be detailed enough to arouse interest and enthusiasm while still sensibly within the limits of the capabilities of that particular center. There is no universal formula for shopping centers of a given size. Unless a manager has direct experience in promotion, he should look around for some expert advice.

A New Concept

In recent years, and particularly since 1975, there has been some discussion about changing the merchants' association role in establishing a center's promotion program from decisive to advisory. The proposed alternative would be to place the entire responsibility for both planning and execution in the hands of a qualified professional employed by the center owner.

Advocates of the proposed plan contend that the typical board of directors, or promotion committee, representing the tenant group rarely includes individuals knowledgeable in the field of institutional advertising and promotion. Frequently, excessive dissension and bickering in the course of budgetary planning culminate in a succession of compromises that result in a disjointed annual program and inefficient use of the available funds. Even after a program has been laboriously agreed to under such conditions, a promotion director's problems are sometimes compounded by sporadic interference from tenants having second thoughts.

So far the idea has not progressed much beyond the discussion stage and its future is uncertain. In essence it calls for all lessees to contribute to a joint promotion fund that will be dispensed by the owner or his agent, the promotion director. Such an arrangement would put control of the available funds in the hands of a skilled professional rather than a frequently changing panel of store managers, which often represents disparate interests and tends to be dominated by the more assertive members.

Some recent experience has established that this type of lease provision has a high order of acceptance by prospective tenants when applied to a large center under development by a strong, experienced owner capable of making a persuasive presentation. Up to this time, however, the acceptance of this type of lease arrangement has been limited to those situations in which the developer has an established reputation as an aggressive, successful operator, and where the center is large enough to support a thoroughly competent individual or department to administer the promotion program. This limits its applicability and acceptance to but a limited number of new centers being built each year.

Still unknown is the extent to which such a method can be installed in the great majority of existing centers where the tenants now control the promotional fund through the standard vehicle of a merchants' association. Implementing such a change would involve obtaining unanimous consent of the tenants to rewriting that portion of the lease, an undertaking that in most instances is certain to be formidable. The procedure for accomplishing such a lease-change would generally follow that of any renegotiation, with particular care exercised to develop support among key tenants before broaching the matter on an across-the-board basis. It should go without saying that the manager must develop clearly and present forthrightly the benefits that will accrue from such a change. It appears that the next few years will see considerable activity in this direction, with as yet unpredictable results.

Irrespective of who controls the budget, there is no clear-cut opinion within the industry on the minimum center sizes at which various approaches become feasible, and size is not the only governing factor. Both geographic location and nature of the tenant group have something to do with the matter. The following examples illustrate the factors involved.

- A 200,000-square-foot center having a large complement of convenience goods (food, liquor, drugs, personal service), located in a major metropolitan area, would probably not be able to sustain a year-round program, but it should be able to mount a few seasonal promotions such as Easter, Back-to-School, and Christmas. Any smaller center with that composition and so located would have a hard time doing anything worthwhile, other than an occasional spot attraction of the kind that can be obtained at nominal cost and paid for on a pass-the-hat basis.

■ A counterpart center, located on the fringe of a city having a population of 150,000, free from the dominance of much larger shopping centers and competing with the downtown area and scattered suburban stores, could launch a year-round program of promotion. Both owner and tenants would almost certainly benefit from money thus spent.

■ If the 200,000-square-foot center in a major metropolitan area is of a specialized type—for example, dominated by home furnishings or higher-priced apparel stores—a sustained promotional program directed at that specific segment of the total area market would be more than desirable; it becomes essential.

■ As size increases from 200,000 square feet, opinion within the industry moves progressively nearer to unanimity that some form of joint owner-tenant effort is necessary, to the point at which there are few dissenters on joint programs at the 400,000-square-foot level and effectively none for centers of more than 600,000 square feet.

■ There is no general agreement on the minimum size at which a center can afford the services of a full-time salaried promotion director since that decision is related to the number of dollars in the budget rather than floor area. Observation indicates that full-timers are quite rare in centers of less than 400,000 square feet and quite common at 600,000 square feet.

What these generalizations boil down to is that few centers of less than 200,000 square feet conduct sustained promotional or joint advertising programs. Almost all those over 400,000 square feet do have an organized program, and in most of those larger than around 600,000 square feet it is handled by a salaried on-site director. From a management standpoint, therefore, it may be inferred that, among the great number of shopping centers in the 200,000- to 600,000-square-foot bracket, the percentage having a full-fledged promotional activity goes up with size, and in the great majority the work is handled on a fee or commission basis by an outside agency. In the much smaller number of centers of more than 600,000 square feet, such programs may be considered as universal, and they are rarely directed other than by a salaried employee of either the owner or the merchants' association.

The choice between employing the services of a salaried person or an outside agent is largely controlled by the total amount of money available for the promotion purpose. As a rule of thumb, experience suggests that the administrative expense (such as salaries, both direct and supportive, payroll fringe costs, and miscellaneous office expenses such as stationery, postage, and telephone) should not consume more than 20 percent of the total budget. Expressed in terms of a full-time director with a part-time secretary and the incidental other expenses, that translates (for large sections of the country) into a bare minimum of $12,000 a year at 1977 prices, which indicates that, unless the total annual budget, including the landlord's contribution in kind as well as cash, exceeds $60,000, it is better to go the route of the fee agent.

Subject to the usual variations of the marketplace, an owner or manager is going to get just about what he is willing to pay for in terms of promotional skill. The $12,000 administrative expense used in the above example provides room for only a quite junior person, and in this field, more than in some others, the lowest price does not necessarily indicate the best buy. Planning and executing a shopping center promotion program is far more of an art than a science, and the capabilities of the director, both creative and administrative, have much to do with the effectiveness of the dollars spent. The same principle, of course, applies as well to the employment of an outside agency—some buys are better than others, but in terms of value received for price paid there are no real bargains.

Who Should Employ the Promotion Director?

In those large regionals with a substantial promotion fund assured by obligatory contributions built into the lease structure, the promotion director is almost always employed by the center and functions as an integral part of the management team. A different arrangement, however, is fairly common in large community and small regional centers, particularly the older ones, that are largely dependent on what are essentially voluntary contributions on a yearly basis. Frequently, in such situations the promotion director is employed and paid by the merchants' association, sometimes operating completely autonomously but more often depending on the owner for supportive services such as office space and clerical assistance. In this case, the management of the center may be directly in the hands of the owner or he may be represented by either a salaried or fee manager.

Arrangements of that kind have been in effect for many years in some centers to the general satisfaction of all parties concerned. In others the various relationships have not always been harmonious, and in recent times that method of handling the job has met with increasing disfavor. Consider these factors:

- Because working for a membership organization usually means an uncertain tenure and an absence of fringe benefits, it is difficult to attract and keep good people. That condition is sometimes aggravated by a lack of internal discipline within the merchants' association, which results in the director spending as much time protecting his flanks as he does moving forward with his responsibilities.

- Rarely will an owner give *carte blanche* use of the center's facilities to an individual not under his full control, which means that the promotion director must secure prior approval from the manager before he can proceed with a special event or other public presentation on the mall or parking lot. This presents no problem if the two have a good working understanding, but if they are personally incompatible or otherwise at odds it can become difficult for all concerned.

- Underlying the arrangement is the basic condition, discussed at some length in Chapter 4, of the inherent adversary relationship between landlord and tenant in certain limited aspects of shopping center operation. When a situation of that kind crops up, the promotion director inevitably sides with the tenant as opposed to the manager representing the owner. In the larger scale of their dealings, owner and tenant obviously resolve such conflicts or they would not continue being in business together, but, human nature being what it is, at the manager/director level such differences can seriously impair the director's effectiveness. And to the extent that the promotional program is thereby damaged, the manager and the owner have also suffered a loss of value.

Employment of the promotion director by the owner as a part of the manager's staff not only eliminates most of the foregoing problems, but provides some pluses, such as an increased degree of control over the whole promotional program, increased efficiency of the total clerical operation and, probably most important, a back-up for the manager to assist him in some matters and be in charge during his absence. In centers operated by a contract management firm, there has been some experimenting with placing an employee, reimbursible from the owner's account, in the center with the dual assignment of running the promotional program and handling some of the more routine management details. Where this is done, an equitable portion of the individual's salary is treated as in lieu of a cash contribution by the owner to the promotion budget. Securing the right person for this kind of assignment is not easy, but if one can be found the arrangement is beneficial to both owner and tenants.

In those centers where it is not practical to have an on-site promotion director, the most common arrangement is the employment on a fee basis of an advertising agency, preferably one also experienced in special-event promotions and public relations. In most large cities there are agencies specializing in shopping centers. They are usually prepared to take on accounts anywhere within reasonable commuting distance, if the budgets are large enough to absorb the required travel expense. Here, as in any other type of enterprise, the quality of service rendered ranges from so-so to very good.

The Agency Contract

The usual business arrangement provides that the agency handle promotion for the center on the basis of a continuing agreement subject to 30-day cancellation by either party. In some cases firm contracts for a yearly term are employed, but many agencies experienced in this rather specialized field prefer the more flexible month-to-month arrangement. They maintain that what they are performing is essentially a creative function, that they cannot work with an unwilling client, and that if a loss of confidence develops it is in the interests of both parties to promptly terminate the relationship.

The services to be performed by an agency are customarily tailored to the specific situation, but the following functions are usually included.

■ Servicing the merchants' association by attending its meetings, doing the clerical work of keeping its records, and working with

106

the center management to provide guidance and leadership. Record-keeping might include bookkeeping but probably not the actual handling of receipts and disbursements, which is better left to the elected treasurer or, if he should so choose, the center manager.

■ Preparing an annual budget for the association's approval. The budget indicates anticipated income and contains a month-by-month projection of the cost of the advertising and promotion program and the events planned.

■ Implementing the approved program by contracting in the center's, or association's, name for the necessary media space and associated services and following through to ensure that things go as planned.

■ Working with the center management and merchants' association to coordinate and publicize community-related events.

The agency fee commonly ranges from 10 to 15 percent of the total budget, depending on size and complexity, plus reimbursement for specified out-of-pocket expenses. The larger agencies specializing in shopping centers also are scrupulous about crediting to the fee any advertising commissions received by them from newspapers, broadcasters, or other media, and it is a good idea to check this point in all agency contracts. If the agency can collect media commissions in addition to its service fee from the center, the objectivity with which it plans the program may be questioned.

The more experienced agencies prefer to make their contract with the owner rather than the merchants' association. Where that is done the usual arrangement, with the understanding of all parties, is for the owner, through his manager, to act as the fiscal agent of the association for the receipt and disbursement of its funds. Such a procedure allows the agency to contract with a financially responsible entity, and also grants the manager a reasonable degree of control over the uses to which the property is put and allows him to make certain that the center is properly insured where that is indicated.

In the case of a multicenter owner operating a number of dispersed properties, the usual practice is some form of combination, depending on size of the individual centers. In almost all such companies, the headquarters staff includes one or more persons of experience and proven ability in the field of publicity and promotion, represented at the center level by either a direct employee or a local agency. Not infrequently, the post at the local level is regarded as a training position for future center managers.

An Illustration

As an illustration of a range of the problems that may confront a shopping center manager in the field of promotion, and of some of the approaches he might take to solve them, the remainder of this chapter will be devoted to presenting and discussing a hypothetical case study. All dollar amounts, it should be understood, are illustrative only and are sometimes simplified and/or exaggerated for that purpose.

Assume that you have an established real estate management business in a medium-sized metropolitan area. You have secured a contract to manage a shopping center of about 300,000 square feet that opened for business in 1965 and has just come into the hands of its third owner, a successful local businessman. In placing the management with you, the owner has made it clear that he feels the previous management lacked aggressiveness and the property was not realizing its profit potential. The center is located in what is by now a solidly built up middle-income residential area; it is within the trade areas of two regionals, neither of them overpoweringly close, and it has a couple of medium-sized neighborhood strips within its own trade area. The center has good accessibility, ample parking, and an open mall, is of attractive appearance, and has been well maintained.

The center is anchored by a 100,000-square-foot branch of a local department store, which is strong on soft goods, and of the forty-odd other tenants, about half are units of either national or local chains. Examination of the financial records establishes that there has been little tenant turnover since the opening and that the shorter-term leases have had their financial terms moderately upgraded as they were renewed. The records also show that total sales volume has been essentially static for the past several years—increasing only at about the rate of inflation.

The standard lease form, prepared in 1963 during the center's early development phase, contains a rather vaguely worded article providing for the establishment of a merchants' association, a requirement that the tenant be a member, and an obligation to pay annual dues or assessments as levied by the association. Also included is an obligation by the landlord to make a $5,000 annual contribution, with the whole constituting an arrangement you recognize as having been common practice at that stage of the industry's development. Further scrutiny

108

establishes that a few of the larger tenants were given the right to partially recapture their contributions out of overage rent, and that none of these concessions has subsequently been eliminated in lease renewals.

The records of the association, which is a nonprofit corporation, have been well kept but tell the story of a steadily deteriorating operation. Dues income for the preceding year had been $17,000, including the $5,000 from the owner; some tenants were as much as three years delinquent; and the assessment schedule was erratic because a number of the tenants had cut-rate deals to which the association had agreed in past years. Tenant interest and participation in merchants' association affairs was clearly at a low ebb. The organization had been kept going for several years past by the largely unaided efforts of a half-dozen store managers, including the one from the department store, who had served as its perennial officers. One of the metropolitan dailies had helped them produce a zoned special section of cooperative advertising four times a year; a local weekly had handled the preparation of a pre-Christmas tabloid for door-to-door distribution; the association had staged a few minor special events such as a high school art show and back-to-school mini-circus; and the group had done a minimal job of Christmas decorating. The whole program had been maintained by the association officers, augmented by sporadic assistance from special committees of other members.

In reporting on your findings, you express to the owner the opinion that (1) he is not getting much for his annual $5,000 expense; (2) the center would benefit from an expanded promotional program; (3) to revitalize the merchants' association is going to require vigorous, and to some extent stern, action; and (4) if the effort is to be successful, it will almost certainly call for an increased financial commitment by him. He tells you to go ahead, see what you can do, and report back when you have a concrete plan for discussion. Thus fortified, you arrange to meet for lunch with the six association activists in a location where you can talk freely, and ask them to tell you what went wrong and what might be done to get it back on the track.

In substance, they tell you that the original developer exercised strong leadership, gave active support to the association's directors, occasionally kicked in with a few extra dollars for a particularly ambitious undertaking, and was a general participant in all association affairs. In 1972, however, he sold the center to a partnership of investors, located in another city, who put the property in the hands of a managing agent. The agent did not consider an active role in the

109

merchants' association to be part of his responsibilities, and he made only token efforts to force delinquent members to live up to their lease obligations. When the association officers asked him to really lower the boom on the chronic delinquents, his only response was a promise to take it up with the owners, which was the last heard of the matter. There followed a progressive breakdown of discipline, with some members withholding their shares when they thought specific activities would not benefit them; some tenants even demanded, and got, an overall dues concession on the grounds that there was something non-typical about their kind of business. A few escaped by pleading temporary hardship, and others by simply not paying. As this situation worsened, it became difficult to get the more aggressive tenants to accept positions on the association's board of directors, and the general apathy eroded tenant participation in all promotional efforts.

In a roundtable discussion of what to do next, there is unanimous agreement that the first step must be a visible restoration of active owner interest, which could best be signaled by a vigorous program of demanding that the delinquent dues-payers conform to their lease obligations, a move that the association itself is powerless to make. The group feels certain that, once convinced the owner means business, a safe majority of the tenants would endorse and support an enlarged promotional program. The program should be presented to them in a businesslike way and with the assurance that everyone who benefited was going to pay a fair share. Apropos of this last point, the department store manager expresses the opinion that the fixed $5,000 contribution was not in keeping with modern practice and warranted a fresh look by the owner.

In the course of discussing various ways of distributing the cost among the tenants, it becomes apparent that the fact that a few tenants have some sort of recapture clause in their leases is generally known and, while recognized as being strictly an individual tenant–landlord matter, it is a sore point with some other tenants. One of those present, the store manager for a national chain, is among the favored group. After a little cautious probing on your part, he admits that his recapture clause is an anachronism, that his company has not been able to obtain such concessions in other lease negotiations recently, and that he doubts they will make it much of an issue when the lease is up for renewal in a couple of years.

After a certain amount of beating around the bush by all of those present, the department store manager brings the matter to a head by stating that his most recent assessment has been at the rate of five cents per square foot, or $5,000 a year, which has been paid despite a conviction that it was a grossly unfair share of the total actually being collected. His firm's management, he asserts, is about to call a halt unless the center promotional program is drastically improved over what it has been for the past couple of years. Nevertheless, he goes on to say, if the association can be revitalized to something approaching the activity level of the earlier years, he feels confident of securing approval to increase the department store's commitment to seven cents a foot immediately, and possibly more later after some results have been demonstrated.

Thus given leadership, the group gets down to business and reaches a consensus that, if the annual dues were established on the basis of a no-exceptions formula scaled in reverse order of size (from seven cents per square foot for the department store to fifteen cents for the eight or ten smallest tenants) a majority of the membership would approve—bringing the total tenant contribution to about $30,000 annually.

At the same time, however, the group indicates that your presentation to the general membership meeting would have to include a reasonably detailed prospectus of what the money would be used for, a firm commitment from the owner that collection of the assessments would be enforced, and a further commitment of a reasonable increase in the owner's contribution. The meeting then breaks up with the general understanding that it was all off the record, with the next move up to you. (If, in real life, you actually accomplished all of that at one sitting, you would have a clear shot at being chosen manager-of-the-year in the shopping center industry.)

Following one such meeting or ten, however, your next move would be an invitation to two or, if available, three agencies to prepare for you a skeleton outline for a one-year promotional program using a $40,000 budget, including their fee and all other incidental charges. This was to be done with the express understanding that the matter is to be kept confidential and that, if there was a decision to proceed, the agencies would then be asked to prepare a detailed presentation as the basis for negotiating a contract. Thus equipped, and having done your own homework, you are ready to sit down with the owner. Having brought him up to date, you recommend that he authorize you to proceed along the following lines:

1. In future lease renewals, eliminate all provisions for recapture

111

or any other offset of tenant contributions to the merchants' association.

2. Institute a tough collection program on all delinquent dues, not overruling any special dispensation duly granted by the association but getting the message across that the language in the lease meant what it said.

3. Without tinkering with the leases themselves, give a firm commitment to the merchants' association that, until further notice, the owner will match the total dollar amount contributed by the tenants on a one-for-three ratio, in lieu of the fixed $5,000.

The owner's first question is whether you think either of the first two points might cause a vacancy; you reply in the negative. The practice of including recapture provisions in leases has been obsolete for years. Tenants no longer even try for it in new developments. Moreover, you point out, delinquent association dues are relatively small sums, and paying them will not work an actual hardship on any tenant although a few will make a lot of noise about it. His next question has to do with what he might be getting in for with the open-ended one-for-three matching commitment. You reply that there is little immediate possibility of the tenants going above a 15 cent-per-square-foot average, calling for a $15,000 contribution by him.

The owner then gets to the crux of the matter—your rationale for recommending that he increase expenses from $5,000 to $10,000 per year immediately, with an open door leading to a possible $15,000 in the near future. You divide your reply into two parts.

As part one, you point out that he bought the center because of the belief that it had a great potential that could be realized through better management, a belief shared by you. However, this was a two-way street—there was also a latent danger, which you thought was beginning to show itself in the fact that the recent years had produced no growth in sales volume other than that induced by price inflation, which meant no growth at all in terms of absolute volume. In the meantime, demographic data on the trade area indicated that, despite being fully built-up, total purchasing power had been increasing by the substantial amount that average family income had been rising *in excess* of the inflation rate. The center was getting a progressively smaller share of the market and this trend would almost certainly continue unless corrective action were taken.

Proceeding to part two, you state that it was the consensus of your tenant advisory group, all of them experienced merchants, that a $40,000 professionally directed program would increase absolute volume by, at the very least, 3 percent in the first full year of operation; it would probably add a minimum compounded 2 to 3 percent during the second year. For the purpose of getting a quantitative fix on what this would mean to the center's profit showing, you had made two detailed analyses, one based on an ultraconservative 2 percent increase in the first year and the other on a hoped-for 6 percent rise over the base for the second year (in constant dollars).

Starting with the previous year's sales volume of $25 million and an assumed 2 percent increase of $500,000, you had made the further assumption that the gain would be distributed among all the tenants exactly proportionately. Based on those assumptions, you had then computed the resulting increase in annual rent payment for each tenant, being careful to give effect to all descending percentage rate schedules and to all offset provisions. In abbreviated form, the 2 percent increase in sales volume would produce the result shown in *Table 1*.

Table 1

	Previous volume	Added 2%	Percentage rate	Increased rent
Dept. store	$ 9,000,000	$180,000	0.5	$ 900
Supermarket	2,000,000	40,000	1.0	$ 400
All others	14,000,000	280,000	4.0 av.	11,200
			Total	$12,500

Proceeding to a similar computation for a total of 6 percent increase during the second year of a revitalized promotion program, the result shown in *Table 2* was indicated:

Table 2

	Base year volume	Added 6%	Percentage rate	Increased rent
Dept. store	$ 9,000,000	$540,000	0.5	$ 2,700
Supermarket	2,000,000	120,000	1.0	1,200
All others	14,000,000	840,000	3.8 av.	31,920
			Total	$35,820

In completing the presentation, you point out that the potential income gain should not be measured against an expense item of

$10,000: that the true choice is between continuing to pay out $5,000 and effectively getting nothing in return, or putting in another $5,000 a year to act as the primer for the expenditure of a very much larger sum by the tenants. Not only would they be contributing $30,000 to the merchants' association, but the cooperative advertising programs—which would be an inherent part of the stepped-up promotional effort—would involve substantial outlays of direct advertising money.

In concluding this little success story, let us make one more assumption. After securing the owner's approval of the recommended programs, you point out that carrying the matter forward is going to call for devotion on your part that might be construed as being above and beyond the call of duty. Although you intend to put forth your very best efforts, something in the way of a small bonus might inspire you to do even better—say something like 10 percent of the annual increase in rental income from here on.

Naturally, the owner replies: "Why, of course."

A Glance Backward

Now that our protagonist has the ball in motion, and has gotten a small piece of the action for himself, let us take a look at the thought processes leading to his success.

His initial evaluation of the center's condition, of what needed to be done, and of the available means included these observations:

As constituted, the center was in all respects a viable entity. It was physically adequate, well positioned in a good trade area, not subject to any unusual competitive pressure, and had a good record of consumer acceptance. The anchoring department store was an aggressive, well-run business and, with minor exceptions, the other tenants were good merchandisers aggregating a mix appropriate to the market. The low tenant turnover and history of past activity indicate the existence of a latent sense of family feeling regarding joint activities which could be aroused with the proper stimulation.

On the negative side was the recent poor management performance which, taken in combination with the archaic lease clause, had demoralized the merchants' association.

It was obvious that the center was stagnating and any substantial improvement in profitability was dependent on an increase in tenant sales. Within a fully developed trade area the only way of improving volume would be to divert sales from other retail outlets. Building traffic to the center called for a sustained program of promotion and that would take money. The only sources of money were the owner and the tenants, and it was a certainty neither would loosen up easily. The problem, therefore, was to devise a strategy that would revitalize the merchants' association with sufficient funding to support a meaningful promotional effort.

The first move was to make sure the owner would lend his support since without it there would be no point in proceeding. Developing support among the tenants, however, was a more delicate matter. Experience warned that a mass meeting would bring out all the malcontents, particularly those delinquent in paying their assessments, and tend to be vocally dominated by the nay-sayers. The existing nucleus of promotion-minded managers suggested the place to start. These managers could develop the necessary majority support among the tenant group as a whole. It was a case of harnessing the available energy and putting it to work.

The next move, lining up professional assistance to block out and subsequently administer a program, recognizes that (1) even a quite modest effort cannot be sustained on voluntary time contributed by individual tenants, and (2) a contract real estate manager has neither the time nor the expertise to assume the direct responsibility. It will be his job to continue furnishing leadership and to supervise the agency, but the technical work is far better put in the hands of professionals.

In taking the final step of selling the program to the owner, the manager understood that he was dealing with an experienced businessman more likely to be swayed by cold figures than glowing rhetoric. Accordingly, he dispensed with platitudes about the virtues and rewards of advertising in general and presented his case in terms of dollars in the owner's pocket, supported by some believable arithmetic.

The methods employed in the illustration were specific to the hypothetical situation but the principle has general application. In today's competitive market, the shopping center dependent on more than neighborhood trade cannot thrive, or maybe even survive, without an ongoing cooperative promotional program. Seeing to it that such a program is in effect is an essential part of the management function.

QUESTIONS FOR DISCUSSION

1. *Distinguish between promotion and publicity as applied to shopping centers.*

2. *Give examples of favorable and unfavorable publicity applicable to a regional shopping center.*

3. *Briefly describe the history of shopping center promotion, indicating the reasons for changes in method and outlook.*

4. *Project the role of shopping center promotion when there is intense competition in the trade area. What is the role·of shopping center promotion when there is only one center in the trade area?*

5. *Based on size, under what conditions would you expect a salaried on-site promotion director on the center's management staff?*

6. *What percentage of the center's total promotional budget should promotional administration consume? Why?*

7. *What are the advantages of the center promotion director being an employee of the owner?*

8. *The illustrated promotion case in the chapter is characteristic of the professionalism of shopping center managers. Specifically what promotional assistance could you expect from an agency?*

9. *In the illustrated promotion case, why are the results presented as a financial evaluation?*

10. *Monitor a local newspaper for an adequate period for examples of shopping center publicity and promotion and critique your findings.*

RECOMMENDED READING LIST

Abrahams, Howard P. **Making TV Pay Off, A Retailer's Guide to Television Advertising.** New York: Fairchild Publications, Inc., 1975. 144 pp.

Callahan, William W. **Shopping Center Promotions: A Handbook For Promotion Directors.** New York: International Council of Shopping Centers, 1972. 380 pp.

Fulweiler, John H. **How to Promote Your Shopping Center.** New York: Chain Store Age Books, 1973. 165 pp.

Nyburg, Robert S. **Shopping Center Merchants Associations.** New York: International Council of Shopping Centers, 1970. 80 pp.

Sissors, Jack Z. and E. Reynold Petray. **Advertising Media Planning.** Chicago: Crain Books, 1976. 341 pp.

Wolf, Jess. **Public Relations/Publicity: Fundamentals for Shopping Center Professionals.** New York: International Council of Shopping Centers, 1977. 32 pp.

116

CHAPTER **7**

Maintenance

Physical maintenance of a shopping center can range from a rel-atively simple to a very complicated operation. The complexity is largely a function of the size of the center, but geographic location, structure of the leases, and the philosophy of the owner also have an influence. Location is significant because of climatic variations. The manner in which the maintenance obligation is distributed between landlord and tenant by the lease can vary considerably. And the qual-ity of maintenance desired by the owner also varies.

For a neighborhood strip center, the maintenance operation is essentially a matter of maintaining the structural integrity and outward appearance of buildings and parking lot. An enclosed regional center with a central utility system, however, requires much higher levels of both managerial skill and technical competence.

Managerial skill is necessary because the enclosed regional is, in effect, a single, multioccupancy building in which the maintenance obligation of the landlord, the co-owners, and the tenants are devi-ously intertwined. The manager must have a detailed understanding of both the REAs (reciprocal easement agreements) with the other owners, usually department stores, and the leases with the tenants, and must be able to relate those obligations to the physical realities of the center.

Technical competence is demanded by the presence of mechan-ically complex installations for heating, ventilating, and air-conditioning; for distribution of electricity, water, gas, and waste disposal; for public-address and electronic security systems; and the array of fixed and mobile equipment necessary to service such operations. It would be an extraordinary manager indeed who is expert enough to personally direct the maintenance of all of the foregoing in addition to handling the center's business affairs, and no sensible owner would expect to find such a paragon. However, any manager qualified to be in charge of that class of shopping center should have sufficient understanding of the workings of such systems to enable him to employ the right people and set up the right procedures to ensure that the job will be properly done under his overall direction.

Organizing to Cope with Housekeeping and Maintenance

In this book, the housekeeping and maintenance function is considered from a theoretical standpoint only. A detailed compilation of helpful hints for the "do-it-yourselfer" has been avoided for two reasons:

First, that once started on such a course there would be no place to stop. If an answer were provided in these pages for how to remove chewing gum from a cement sidewalk, the next question would deal with spilled paint on that same sidewalk, followed by coping with lipstick graffiti on a travertine wall, and then what to do about alligatoring in the parking lot, pigeons in the pylon, and mice in the planters.

Second, that it would lead to the naming of proprietary products —not a proper function for a book of this kind—and would inevitably result in supplying information that would become increasingly obsolete with the passage of time.

All of the housekeeping and maintenance problems of a shopping center are duplicated in other buildings, both private and public, and it is in the nature of the society in which we live that if a physical problem is at all prevalent there exists a product or a service to deal with it. It is still further in the nature of our society that most such products and services are continually undergoing technological improvement, and the efficient property manager must be constantly on the alert for new and better ways of getting things done. At least four methods of doing so are readily available.

First, every community large enough to support a shopping center is also serviced by at least one company selling janitor and maintenance supplies and equipment. Such firms ordinarily will supply free catalogs and manufacturers' literature, supplemented by informed advice from salesmen or other representatives.

Second, a number of building and grounds-maintenance handbooks or manuals, both comprehensive and specialized, have been published and are widely available in nonfiction bookstores and the larger public libraries.

Third, several monthly magazines are published devoted wholly or in large part to the day-to-day operation of publicly used commercial and institutional buildings. Both editorially and in advertising content, such publications emphasize new products and techniques. A center manager can make no better investment than a few dollars a year and a few hours a month on this source of information.

Finally, and probably most fruitful, the shopping center manager who wants to broaden and update his maintenance capability can participate in the wide-ranging educational activities of the International Council of Shopping Centers. The Council has published, and offers for sale at nominal prices, a number of Bulletins and Special Reports dealing with specialized maintenance problems, all available to members. The Council also conducts a variety of educational seminars and conferences at both the national and local levels which, with a few exceptions, are open to nonmembers.

Definition of Terms

Before proceeding with a discussion of organizing methodology, it may be useful to establish some definitions as they will be subsequently applied.

Housekeeping refers to keeping the premises clean and presentable; that is, sweeping the parking lot of litter and plowing the snow; scrubbing the mall floor and dusting the benches; cutting the grass and trimming the shrubbery; washing the windows and emptying the waste receptacles; and all the other endless little tasks implied by the word itself.

Maintenance involves the preservation of what is already there. For example, patching the parking lot and relamping the lights; painting wall surfaces and replacing deteriorated caulking; rodding the sewer line and changing the oil in the jeep; and in general doing those things that prolong the economic life of the property in its present form.

Replacement is a somewhat nebulous term. In a strict sense, it implies removing some portion of the property and restoring the missing part on a like-for-like basis. In practice, however, considerable ambiguity develops, as will be explained later.

Rehabilitation, as applied to real property, describes the process of catching up with an accumulation of deferred maintenance without thereby making any significant change in either function or form of what was already there.

Modernization is generally considered as having to do with style and appearance rather than utility, such as a new pylon entrance sign or a remodeled building façade.

Alteration implies a physical change in structure or appurtenances that will improve utility, such as subdividing a large store into small ones, reconstructing a parking lot entrance to provide smoother traffic flow, or enclosing an open mall.

Addition refers to enlargement of GLA and/or parking capacity by constructing new facilities in the form of buildings, paved surfaces, or a parking deck.

Renovation is an imprecise term sometimes used to describe a combination in varying degrees of rehabilitation, modernization, alteration, and addition.

The purposes of all the foregoing processes are to make a center attractive to the public, extend its economic life, increase its profitability, or a combination of all three. All of this costs money, and questions of how much, whose, and when are a major concern of the manager. In fact, in this phase of his stewardship a manager is most likely to incur the disfavor of the owner, in the event of misjudgments.

Clearly, the first concern is to obtain maximum value for every dollar spent, but the decisions on whose money to spend and when to spend it are sometimes complicated. In addition to the owner there are frequently two and sometimes three other parties whose interests must be taken into account. The two examples below illustrate the diversity of interests involved.

Assume that the common area maintenance clause in the leases includes parking lot repairs and that no expense ceilings or overage rent offsets are operative. Further assume that, for a major portion of the lot, patching is progressively less effective and that on a strictly economic basis the entire pavement should be torn up and replaced. In this situation, the immediate financial interests of owner and tenants are clearly opposed, since the capital cost of replacement must be borne by the owner whereas the continued expense of patching, though economically unsound, will be paid by tenants.

Consider next the same situation applied to a roof. Since the tenants have no interest in it unless it leaks, the diversity of interest is between the owner and tax collector. Patching is a tax-deductible operating expense, whereas a new roof becomes a capital cost recoverable only over a long period of time via the depreciation allowance. In addition, in some jurisdictions the local property tax assessor will treat the roof replacement as a capital addition and will add it to the ad-valorem tax bill.

Both of the above examples demonstrate why the word "nebulous" was used in defining replacement. There is no exact line at which an item leaves the scope of maintenance, which is a tax-deductible expense, and becomes a replacement requiring capitalization. In general accounting practice, the difference has something to do with relative size of expenditure and with the policy of the owner as to cash flow versus reportable earnings. All such situations, and they are numerous, require a manager to strike the optimum balance from the owner's standpoint of when it becomes timely to make the move from maintenance to replacement.

In this connection, it is important to observe that most owners, and all who are sophisticated investors, are keenly aware of the time-value of money. A successful shopping center manager needs to exhibit a similar perception. He should have a general understanding of the concept and a working knowledge of the mathematical technique of discounting future cash flows, as covered in Chapter 3.

As the background for all decisions involving expenditure of money on the physical property, with the possible exception of the housekeeping function, it is essential that owner and manager agree on an estimated future economic life of the center. This estimate should be realistically updated at least every three years. By "realistically" it is meant that this is no time for wearing rose-tinted glasses— it is usually better to underestimate than overestimate the future life.

By way of a somewhat oversimplified example, assume that the worn-out roof referred to above has reached the point at which patching will no longer keep out water. If the estimated future economic life of the project is 10 years, it would be wasteful to install a new 20-year bonded roof. Taking into account the time-value of money it would be better to buy a 10-year roof, and then stretch its life with patches if the end of the road turns out to be 15 years away instead of 10.

The shopping center as a real estate form is still much too young to have demonstrated a life-cycle pattern, but experience indicates that, in most cases, the economic life will be determined by outside forces rather than physical deterioration of the property itself. Admittedly, such forecasting is far from an exact science; until the end is clearly in sight these predictions should not greatly affect the scope of the maintenance program. However, in all matters calling for the investment of additional capital, especially of an optional kind such as modernization or alteration funds, it is essential that there be available a reasonable approximation of the duration of the future stream of income on which the return of the capital is going to depend.

Evaluating Future Income

In making such an evaluation, a center manager might want to ask himself certain specific questions and, having answered them to the best of his ability, examine their implications when taken as a whole. For example:

- In view of the purpose for which this shopping center exists, what is the trend in the immediate vicinity? Is it improving, deteriorating, or static? Are there new or impending land uses that will either enhance or lessen its attraction for retail shoppers?

- What is the trend in the entire trade area? How will demographic factors, such as changes in growth rate, income, family characteristics, and places of employment, affect the center?

- What is happening, or going to happen, to the road pattern immediately adjacent to the center, or elsewhere in the trade area, that will affect customer access for better or worse?

- What is new in the field of local taxation that might affect the desirability of this location as a retail business site?

- What, if anything, is planned for mass transit facilities that might over the long run strengthen or weaken this site for either shopping center use or potential other uses?

- What changes are imminent, or probable, in the competitive situation and what will be the severity of their impact?

- And a final, but very important, question. How do the anchor tenants read the future? Are they likely readily to extend their leases and operating agreements or do they appear restless and uncertain about the future? The manager's finger should be constantly on the pulse of this situation because of the obviously disastrous consequences of the loss of an anchor, be it supermarket or department store, unless an immediate replacement is available.

As emphasized earlier, the manager is responsible for seeking out such information, analyzing it, and transmitting to the owner both the findings and the manager's evaluation of their significance. Only thus can he be sure that both are seeing the same picture as they look at the future.

Preservative vs. Restorative Maintenance

In first organizing and thereafter supervising a housekeeping-maintenance-replacement program, the first rule is to leave nothing to chance and trust nobody's memory, especially your own. It is mostly a matter of attending to details, and in even the smallest center they are numerous; in the big centers the details multiply to the point at which no human mind can contain them. Some are daily tasks, such as sweeping the sidewalk; others are annual, such as draining the outside hose bibbs at the start of winter; and still others are regulated by usage, such as rotating the tires on automotive vehicles.

In setting up the frequency schedules, and thereafter monitoring them to ensure compliance, particular attention should be given to maintenance routines that are essentially preservative as distinguished from restorative. Oiling a door hinge is preservative; putting on a new hinge after the old one has broken because it was not oiled is restorative. Vigilant checking on the performance of preservative, or preventive, maintenance is made necessary by the fact that its neglect is seldom self-evident, as is the case with restorative maintenance.

Structural vs. Mechanical Maintenance

It is important to realize that a certain difference exists between structures and mechanical equipment. Buildings serve their essential purpose simply by existing, whereas the equipment must also function. Apropos to this point is the fictional Murphy's Law, which states that, "If in any mechanical system there is the possibility of anything going wrong, it eventually will, and when the breakdown occurs, it will be at the time of maximum inconvenience." To a large extent, breakdowns in mechanical systems and equipment do tend to be sudden and total, rather than gradual malfunctions. The maintenance program, therefore, should be so organized as to be capable of a fast response if the lights go out, if the fire loop ruptures, or if the elevator gets stuck between floors.

123

For the purpose of what follows, let us project a hypothetical situation based on a simple scenario. You operate a suburban real estate business that includes the management, in behalf of absentee clients, of several nearby commercial properties—too few to warrant the creation of a maintenance staff of salaried personnel. You secure from the owner, also an absentee, a contract to manage a nearby ten-year-old shopping center of (for the moment) indeterminate size. You learn that, for whatever reason, the past maintenance records are unavailable. In suggesting what you might do from this point on, the focus will be exclusively on taking care of the physical property, with no regard for the broader management aspects.

Clearly, the first move is a thorough examination and inventory of the property: what is there, what is its condition, and what, if any, are the immediate rehabilitative needs? In the case of a neighborhood strip center, and assuming a general understanding of construction practices and materials, a new manager can do the job by personal inspection and talking with the tenants. As size and complexity increase, however, you will be well advised to enlist the services of experts. In simpler cases a plumber, electrician, roofer, or paving contractor in whose objective judgment you have confidence can provide the necessary expertise at modest expense. However, if the center is a big one, and particularly if complex mechanical systems are involved, the initial inspection and preparation of written reports to the owner should be undertaken by professional engineers.

Continuing with our arbitrary and somewhat unrealistic assumption that you have no past records to fall back on, the next—or more likely concurrent—move will be to establish the nature and frequency of the on-going housekeeping and maintenance activities that will be required. From this information you can prepare written instructions and schedules to guide those who will actually perform the various tasks, and from these data you can set up the record-keeping system that is the heart of a good maintenance program. If your new charge is a simple, neighborhood strip, you can very likely formalize the program on the basis of your past experience. However, if you feel that the property is too complex for you to handle, you should not hesitate to call in expert help. Several sources can provide such assistance at nominal expense.

In addition to the International Council of Shopping Centers, there are several other business or industry organizations that publish checklists for a variety of property types and problems, keep them periodically updated, and make them available to all comers. By culling and combining from such established sources, you can develop a set of forms tailored to your particular needs. Another source of help is the same people who made the initial inspections. They can be enlisted, either in the hope of securing your future business or for a modest fee, to draft a maintenance program within their own field of expertise. As used in this context, the term "maintenance" should be understood as including what was earlier defined as "housekeeping," since there is much overlap of the two functions in day-to-day operations.

Complete Set of Plans Required

A complete, up-to-date set of building and mechanical plans is essential to the initial inspection and subsequent performance. In older centers, this is not always easy to find, particularly if ownership has passed through several hands. If an inventory of your new assignment's records fails to turn up a set of plans, or there is one with sheets missing, it is worthwhile making a considerable effort to replace the loss. Obvious sources are the original developer, architect, or contractor and, failing these, the building permit and inspection office of the municipality, the local insurance rating bureau, or possibly the fire department. In a large center having complex mechanical installations, it is important to distinguish between plans issued for construction purposes and final drawings that have been corrected to account for field changes made during construction. There is sometimes quite a difference.

As part of the take-over process you must establish the quality level of the housekeeping-maintenance operation, and this calls for a careful evaluation of the factors and forces involved. As mentioned in an earlier chapter, shopping centers serve different kinds of markets, are populated by different kinds of tenants, are used by different kinds of customers, and, very importantly, they are owned by landlords having different kinds of tastes and objectives. Your job as manager is to determine what might be called the norm for that particular center, check it against the owner's wishes, and then reconcile the difference if there appears to be a sizable spread between what you think is right and what the owner and tenants are prepared to pay for.

Since you are dealing with a ten-year-old center, it is rather unlikely that the entire common area maintenance expense is passed through to the tenants without offset. For the purpose of this example, the assumption is that the two parties share it in varying degrees. If your new client, the center owner, insists on an unrealistic budgeting for maintenance purposes, your best move might be to resign the account rather than attempt to live with the visible deterioration certain to follow. The resulting damage to your general business reputation in the community may outweigh the addition to your income.

It is in the nature of mankind for an individual to evaluate environmental quality in fairly direct proportion to two criteria—the extent to which he is exposed to it and the extent to which he bears the costs of it. In the case of the shopping center environment, the absentee owner has the least exposure and the shopper has the most, with the tenants somewhere in between. The shopper, bearing none of the expense, can be generally counted on to be most critical of the housekeeping level. Between landlord and tenant the acceptable level tends to be somewhat influenced by the division of expense, as spelled out in the individual leases, even though both may in principle subscribe to the belief that a well-run operation is to the benefit of all.

It is against this pattern of somewhat divergent interests that you, as manager, are employed to furnish the balanced judgment and managerial skill to establish the right program for that particular center, adjust it from time to time as circumstances require, and keep the other three parties reasonably satisfied with the results.

In other than a quite small center it is generally desirable for control purposes to separate the maintenance program into three main divisions—buildings, grounds, and equipment—since the obligation of the tenants to share in the expense is commonly differentiated along those lines. In a large enclosed regional, of course, each of the divisions will be subdivided according to the peculiarities of that specific property, or to establish areas of responsibility within the operating organization, or a combination of the two. There is no accepted formula or pattern of industry practice governing such a breakdown, but the *Standard Manual of Accounting for Shopping Center Operations,* referred to in an earlier chapter, provides some useful guidelines. In the main, however, it is a matter of your own common sense applied to that particular situation.

Correlative to setting up the maintenance schedules is establishing the record-keeping system. Such a system is always desirable, and it is absolutely essential if the mechanical installations are at all extensive. The scope of the system should be broad enough to cover every item that could be easily overlooked, and regular posting to the record should be rigidly mandatory. Emptying waste receptacles would be on the daily checklist, but it warrants no permanent record since it becomes a self-correcting oversight and does no permanent harm if occasionally skipped. Failure to check the valves on the fire line or to lubricate the sanitary wet-well pump, on the other hand, can go unnoticed for years with ultimately disastrous results. An important part of the managerial function is to monitor such records to ensure that all of these little hidden details are being taken care of.

When all of the take-over exercises have been completed and the parts stitched together into a pattern that can be viewed as a whole, you must then determine how to get the job done in the most efficient and least costly way. It is here that we must draw a line as to the previously indeterminate size of the center. The reason for so doing is that, except for a relatively few unusual cases, the manager's option to carry on the operation entirely with salaried personnel in the direct employ of the center is effectively limited to projects large enough to sustain a full-time on-site manager—generally centers of 600,000 or more square feet of GLA. This, in turn, usually implies a situation in which the manager is himself a salaried employee of the owner rather than a fee agent. Before considering the circumstances of that kind of operation, let us continue with the example of the newly appointed contract manager of a center below the critical size.

Three Basic Maintenance Methods

In setting up the program, you have three alternative methods from which to choose. Depending on the facts of the property and the circumstances of what is available in the community, you may elect to go all one way or devise some combination of the three. Your original decision is in no sense a forever-after choice, and you should be alert to changes of method that may be indicated by changes in the facts and circumstances. The alternatives are (1) to do everything with independent contractors, (2) to do a part of the work with one or more individuals assigned full time to the center with their total compensation charged to the client's account, or (3) to perform all or part of the work with a staff employed by you to work on *all* the properties in your management account on the basis of pro-rated expense. Let us now examine some of the characteristics of each of the three methods.

From the standpoint of both supervision and accounting, the use of independent contractors to supply all services is the simplest way

127

to do it, and, on balance, probably the best way unless there are significant cost savings from using one of the other methods. Under that method, supervision is focused on a few people having a clearly defined obligation to perform a certain task, with the knowledge that payment is contingent on their doing so in a satisfactory manner. Accounting consists of auditing a periodic invoice, usually monthly, and discharging the obligation with a single check and a simple bookkeeping entry. In most communities large enough to support a shopping center, you will find firms or individuals prepared and equipped to service every physical need of the property on a contract basis, and usually in numbers sufficient to permit competitive bidding.

The argument in favor of having at least one person assigned full time to the center is, to some extent, based on his performing a quasimanagerial function; he can maintain close liaison with the tenants and generally keep track of what is going on. Furthermore, from the strict maintenance standpoint, such a person is positioned to do two things that, in centers of greater than minimal size and complexity, can result in a worthwhile efficiency and economy. First, he can police the independent contractors to ensure that they are meeting their obligations; second, if he is the handyman type, he can attend to some petty maintenance items, such as a cracked sidewalk, a minor roof leak or a stopped drain, that can be relatively expensive if you must call in an outside contractor.

Such an arrangement may produce measurable benefits to the owner while concurrently being disadvantageous to you as manager, a point to be considered in setting your fee. Such people are hard to find and, if they are any good, hard to keep. Since the charge-over to the owner must include all the fringes and incidentals as well as the actual salary, the bookkeeping becomes more complicated. Consider, too, that an individual working 40 hours a week, 50 weeks a year, cannot fully cover a center probably open for business more than 70 hours a week for 52 weeks. In short, the benefits to the owner may be realized at the expense of your general overhead and personal convenience.

Perhaps, with the addition of the shopping center, your total property-management portfolio has become quite large. Therefore, the third alternative you can explore is the possibility of creating a crew of your own to perform the routine housekeeping and preventive maintenance. This is, of course, predicated on the assumption that economies of scale will result and that the total cost will be equitably apportioned among the benefited owners. Where the properties are reasonably close to each other and the tendency to include too many skilled tradesmen is resisted, such an in-house capability can be an efficient and economical method of operation. It does, however, have three built-in pitfalls that are difficult, and sometimes impossible, to avoid.

First is the ethical problem presented by your dual role as guardian of the owner's investment and, simultaneously, being a vendor from whom, as his manager, you are buying services to be charged to his account. You are automatically in the position of working both sides of the street and must avoid even the appearance of making a profit on the maintenance by overallocation of general overhead, unless you are entitled to do so by explicit agreement with the owner.

Next is the opportunity provided a disgruntled tenant, unhappy with his common area maintenance charge, to pick a fight with you and/or the owner over the apportioning of services between the center and the other properties. This can get really vicious if you happen to hold a personal interest in one of the other properties.

Third is the lurking danger that the captive nature of the business and absence of a competitive spur will result in creeping inefficiency. This can, in time, erode the economic advantage present in the beginning.

The independent contractor approach is the method by which the overwhelming majority of all shopping center housekeeping and maintenance is accomplished. Its optimum application is one of the basics of good management. Even the largest and most self-contained centers go outside for such specialized services as pest control and elevator maintenance, and generally there is little room for negotiation in such matters. The available vendors do business with a standard-form contract that is quite rigid as to extent of service and schedule of charges. In the more generalized areas of service, however, the contracting process is more amenable to the application of managerial ability.

The Service Contract and Checklist

As in most other matters calling for intellectual skill, there is no ready-made package of standard forms having universal applicability, although some worthwhile guidance is available from the sources referred to above in connection with checklists. In making use of such forms from outside sources, it must be kept in mind that in most cases they were formulated in one of two ways: either as a catch-all form planned to cover every conceivable circumstance, or as a special form designed to fit a specific situation. Rarely will they serve your purpose until carefully tailored to suit your own facts and circumstances. The service contract and the appropriate checklists are obviously complementary documents to be developed together and thereafter amended together. It is sometimes useful to make the list an integral part of the contract. A comforting thought while going through all this toil and trouble is that, once done and done reasonably thoroughly, the main body of the system is good for the remaining life of the center, subject only to periodic updating as may be indicated by the combination of experience and technological innovations.

The three elements of an efficient contracting system are: (1) a comprehensive, precise definition of the service to be furnished; (2) the best obtainable price, which may be by either bidding or negotiation; and (3) an effective field checking procedure. Of the three parts, the first is the most difficult and underlines the preceding statement that you cannot rely on a published form or on copying from a friend on the other side of town, although inputs from both sources can be helpful. The physical variations among shopping centers are infinite and the quality desires of owners significantly differ; both must be taken into account in preparing service contracts. Writing up the specifications for a major repair or replacement, which involves few subtleties or opportunities for misinterpretation, is best put in the hand of an architect or other professional who can be depended on to prepare a package ready for competitive bidding on a firm-price basis. However, defining the scope, detail, and timing of a continual service contract, and taking into account the unpredictables involved, is a very different matter and one that does not readily accommodate to lump-sum bidding.

In the early period of the industry's development, the housekeeping and preventive-maintenance services were often bought by the month or year on the basis of a broad description. A fixed base price, subject to periodic adjustment to take into account extraneous influences such as labor rates, was established for these services. This method gained wide acceptance by both parties for somewhat different reasons. The manager liked it because it was easy to administer and enabled him to project precisely his expenses for budget purposes. The contractor liked it because it gave him some leeway when faced with unanticipated variations in extent of service or in his cost of supplying it. As both the complexity of shopping centers and the sophistication of their owners and managers have increased, the trend has been to contractual agreements designed to more accurately relate the contractor's compensation to those services actually furnished. At the same time, this gives the manager greater flexibility to employ the service as and when needed. This has led to a greater use of unit prices and probably to more reliance on negotiated contracts than on competitive bidding.

Snow Removal: an Example of Flexibility in Service Contracts

Even though snow removal has no direct application in some parts of the country, it provides a good example of the principles involved in establishing service contracts with the flexibility to meet conditions of unpredictable variation from the norm.

Generally, only very large shopping centers attempt to handle snow with in-house personnel and equipment, and then only in areas of high annual fall. In no case do they gear up to cope with extraordinary conditions. At such times, the centers depend on stand-by agreements with contractors to augment the centers' internal capability with additional, and usually heavier, equipment. Contracting the work, fully or partially, is the universal practice, even where the falls are light and infrequent, and by this time a good deal of experience has accumulated within the industry.

When centers were relatively small and had parking areas of uncomplicated configuration, the usual arrangement was a quite simple agreement with a local construction contractor: he kept the lot clear of snow for the entire winter either at a flat price or on the basis of equipment-hours required. An alternative often employed was for the center to have first call on the contractor's equipment and personnel at a stipulated hourly rate on an as-needed basis. A refinement, probably originating in Canada, was to take preseason bids on a fixed price per inch of snowfall; that practice is still often used in smaller centers. However, as shopping centers increased in size and the parking areas grew in complexity, the disadvantages of the simpler arrangements became more obvious. Fixed-price, flat-sum, or per-inch contracts often involved moving more snow than was seasonally necessary at the time, and such agreements became increasingly difficult to obtain.

131

In the case of as-needed agreements, it all too often turned out in severe conditions that the contractor had signed up with more than one first-call customer.

Over the years, innovative managers have experimented with different approaches designed to achieve optimum results on a cost-benefit basis for their particular center. A variety of arrangements have evolved that are linked to the facts of size, shape, and climate, and to the circumstances of what is available in that community.

Assume that you, as the newly appointed manager, must either develop a snow-removal program of your own or critically evaluate the one you have inherited. The following are some of the factors to take into consideration, always keeping in mind that the expense, as well as the benefits, will be shared in some manner between owner and tenants.

The climate of your area is a factor in ways other than establishing the average annual snowfall. It also has a bearing on the extent to which snow is likely to accumulate and its effect on the community. A six-inch fall in Washington, D.C., will have a temporarily paralyzing effect, but it will be fairly certain to melt away before the next fall occurs; it will also keep your shoppers at home until the streets are readily passable. Yet a similar fall in Minneapolis will have little effect on customer traffic, and every inch of it will likely still be unthawed a month later.

Timing is very important. A heavy blizzard in February can be less of an emergency than a half-inch fall in the early morning hours of a day in December. In the former instance, you will have little traffic to be concerned with until the shoppers have shoveled themselves out of their homes. In the latter case, obliteration of the parking-space striping can cause chaos in the parking lot, with early-arriving Christmas shoppers unable to get out and the later ones unable to get in.

A related aspect of timing is that most shopping centers have a surplus of parking during the off-seasons, and if you are not in an area having sustained low temperatures there can be an important saving in leaving part of the space uncleared after January 1—being sure, of course, that all ingress-egress paths are kept passable and that plowed snow does not create pockets from which a shopper may have trouble extricating herself. If snow can be expected to accumulate at your center, due thought must be given to the plowing pattern to be followed, starting with the first snowfall, to avoid

132

painting yourself into a corner as the season progresses. A common practice is to establish snow-storage areas at predetermined points throughout the parking area and start using them after Christmas, when some loss of capacity is not important. In doing so, keep in mind that the distance snow can be moved with a plow is quite limited and trucking it is so expensive as to be warranted only in extreme cases.

If you have no experience in these matters, a conference with the responsible official of your local public works department can be useful. If you are considering establishing some degree of in-house capacity, he will probably point out that a plow-equipped vehicle that functions well in eight inches of powder snow will be helpless or will seriously damage its power-train when confronted with four inches of sugar snow. If you have icy slopes to contend with, he will tell you that rock salt is largely ineffective at temperatures below eight degrees and that sand is not affected by temperature but is also not soluble; eventually, it will clog the drains. And if you have not already thought of it yourself, he may note that trying to keep a large open area cleared of snow while a stiff wind is blowing is wasted effort—you might as well relax until the wind dies down.

Having sorted out mentally all the variable factors bearing on the situation at that particular center, a suggested procedure is to locate a competent construction or road contractor who is interested in your business. Be certain he fully understands the problem and then negotiate an agreement that is tailored accordingly. Typically, this will provide for a stand-by fee plus an hourly rate on each piece of equipment with its operator; the contract will also call for an automatic response with a minimum level of equipment under specified conditions and with additional equipment as you may direct. If the center is large enough to make it practical to do so, the contract might provide for some equipment being stored on the site during the winter months, which will tend to shorten the response time when snow begins to fall. The same kind of contractual arrangement is common in very large centers, except that initial response is by salaried personnel with the contractor going into action only as called.

The foregoing is of no interest, of course, if you are doing business in an area of the country that never has snow. It has been presented in some detail, however, as an example of the process of establishing a service contract shaped to the exact needs of a specific situation. It also shows why a manager must, to a considerable extent, do his own thinking rather than shop around for ready-made solutions or off-the-shelf schedules and contract forms. Those things are useful as frames within which to assemble the picture, but there really is no substitute for doing your own homework. Fortunately, as was emphasized at the start of this chapter, the community, both immediate and at-large, abounds in sources of specialized information and, in this day of increasing specialization, knowing how to identify and tap such sources is better management practice than trying to cram your own head with a lot of seldom-used minutiae.

These suggestions have largely related to the role of a fee manager. The on-site employee-manager of a large center goes through the same general process with one important distinction. He must constantly reevaluate the relative cost-benefit advantage of performing each separable function with his own staff versus contracting it out. As noted above, even the largest centers do not attempt to maintain in-house capability to cope with major snow storms, but the cut-off point at which reliance is shifted from center-owned equipment to the outside contractor is determinable only by experience and does not necessarily remain the same over the life of the property. This is true sometimes of even quite minor operations, such as changing the air-conditioning filters, in which a contractor may be able to handle the job at a price that will enable the center to operate with one less body on the payroll. Such matters should be subject to periodic study and review to avoid the inertia of doing things in a certain way for no other reason than that is how they always have been done. This is one of the reasons it was so strongly emphasized in an earlier chapter that the larger the center, the greater the need for well-detailed expense accounting.

Choices of the kinds mentioned can be made only in the light of analysis, based on accurate and complete cost figures over an adequate period of time. They also require a thorough understanding of the whole fabric of the operation to ensure that the function being examined truly is separable, and will not leave too many loose ends if pulled out for separate treatment. A new manager is well advised to avoid precipitate changes on the basis of preconceived ideas. He should take time to trace out the secondary and possibly tertiary results of changing a maintenance activity from in-house to contracted, or vice-versa.

In concluding the presentation on maintenance, let us look at the significance of even quite minor differences in the efficiency with which the maintenance function is performed. In Chapter 2, attention was directed to the peculiar economics of shopping centers—minor changes in either gross income or expense can have a major effect on return on investment. Later, the point was made that in relatively few centers now in operation does the lease structure permit a complete distribution of the common area maintenance expense among the tenants. Ordinarily, the annual expense beyond a certain dollar level must be absorbed by the landlord. Consider, then, a situation in which the collective tenant contribution is sufficient only to cover 75 percent of the annual expense with the owner left with the remaining 25 percent. If, by running a tight ship, the manager can reduce the total by 5 percent, the result is a 20 percent cut in the owner's expense; and conversely, of course, if the total annual expense goes up 5 percent the effect on the owner is a 20 percent increase in that portion of the expense budget.

As noted before, it is factors like this that, from an owner's standpoint, warrant paying for the difference between good and poor management.

QUESTIONS FOR DISCUSSION

1. *How much specific maintenance knowledge should a shopping center manager be expected to possess?*

2. *To what extent is the center manager's tenure dependent upon the effectiveness of his maintenance program?*

3. *In what way is the maintenance program affected by the owner's realistic evaluation of the future economic life of the center?*

4. *Why is it important to identify maintenance as an expense and not as a capital improvement? Give an example.*

5. *Define and distinguish between preservative and restorative maintenance.*

6. *What is the correlation of Murphy's Law to shopping center maintenance?*

7. *Explain how housekeeping and maintenance programs are financed.*

8. *Discuss each of the three basic methods of shopping center maintenance.*

9. *Explain the elements of an efficient service contracting system.*

10. *Analyze the relative merits and cost of service and maintenance as performed by an in-house staff and an outside contractor.*

RECOMMENDED READING LIST

Feldman, Edwin B. **Building Design For Maintainability.** New York: McGraw-Hill Book Company, 1975. 232 pp.

Grothus, Horst. **Total Preventive Maintenance for Building Utilities.** New York: Executive Enterprises Publications Co., Inc., 1976. 180 pp.

Maintenance and Repair of Asphalt Paved Parking Lots. New York: International Council of Shopping Centers, 1975. 8 pp.

Sack, Thomas F. **A Complete Guide to Building and Plant Maintenance.** 2nd ed. Englewood Cliffs, New Jersey: Prentice-Hall Publishing Company, 1971. 677 pp.

Shopping Centers and the Energy Crisis. New York: International Council of Shopping Centers, 1977. 12 pp.

The Worry-Free Roof. New York: International Council of Shopping Centers, 1975. 8 pp.

CHAPTER **8**

Renewal and Replacement Leasing

---

the care and skill with which the re-leasing of a shopping center is
conducted can make the difference between good management
and superior management. The result is rarely dramatically visible, is
not achieved by spur-of-the-moment intuition, and sometimes requires making unpleasant decisions. The difficulty of the task and the
amount of forward planning called for tend to vary in direct proportion to the size of the center and the resulting complexity of the tenant
population.

The typical neighborhood strip is anchored by a supermarket and
drug store, with the remainder tenanted by shops dealing mainly in
convenience goods or services. The initial lease term for the anchors
has typically been 10 to 15 years, with the others grading down to as
short as one year. If, at the end of the first term, the future of the
center contains any uncertainties, the anchors will be likely to prefer five-year renewals and the satellites will want to shorten their
terms sufficiently to avoid the possibility of being left stranded if the
anchor vacates.

Regional centers anchored by department stores usually have
leases or firm operating agreements running from 20 to 30 years,
with 25 years being probably the most common term. The major
satellite tenants, those having 10,000 square feet or more, usually have
initial terms of 10 to 20 years with a concentration at around 15
years, and the relatively smaller space users scale down to two or three
years. Here again, the satellites will be cautious about the future and,

137

if the anchors are on 20-year terms and have not extended, the 15-year tenants will not renew for more than five years.

As noted in Chapter 7, there is no hard evidence at this time on which to predicate a theoretical life cycle for shopping centers. However, observation, supported by some tentative data, indicates that neighborhood centers tend to achieve peak production within two or three years after opening, maintain a strong position for about ten years, and thereafter suffer accelerating economic obsolescence. Regional centers, on average, tend to maintain a steady growth pattern for five or six years to a plateau level, which is then maintained for an as-yet-indeterminate period. There is some indication that, again on average, a decline begins to occur at about age 15 in the absence of substantial addition or renovation. Community-size centers appear to follow an intermediate course, but one more nearly approximating the regionals than the neighborhoods.

However, these estimates have no present statistical support and must be treated as opinion rather than established fact. They are set forth here only as background for some suggested approaches to renewal and replacement leasing. It should also be duly noted that the estimates refer to averages; the probable life-cycle of any specific center may be shorter or longer, depending on its environment and the quality of its management.

In Chapter 7 we stressed the importance of being constantly aware of the probable future economic life of the center. That same awareness must attend a manager's approach to the re-leasing program. For some period of time following the opening, assuming the project was soundly conceived, he will be figuratively negotiating in a rising market, but after some number of years have passed he will almost certainly experience a turn of the tide and find himself leasing space in a buyer's market. It is an axiom of military science that the tactical problems connected with managing a retreat are more difficult than those involved in an advance, and it may well be that the highest test of a shopping center manager's skill is his ability to maintain the economic viability of a center that is over the hill.

To continue briefly with the military analogy, the re-leasing program for the early years should be in the nature of an active offensive aimed at constantly improving the tenant mix, the efficiency of space utilization, and the financial terms of the individual leases. This implies a boldness of approach and a certain amount of risk-taking, often in the form of a temporary loss of income incidental to deliberately creating short-term vacancies in an aggressive rent-renewal policy. However, when the far edge of the plateau comes into sight, the strategy switches from offensive to defensive and the overall objective becomes keeping the space occupied with least possible retrogression in quality of tenants and their financial obligations. In other words, the goal changes from improvement to preservation.

In the early years of the industry, shopping center developers paid much less attention to the selection of a balanced tenancy compatible with the needs of the trade area than they do now. In many centers built during the 1950s, once the anchors had been nailed down, as much additional space as seemed feasible for the market was built and thereafter leased pretty much to whoever would pay the rent. By the 1960s the industry had acquired a fairly general understanding of the benefits to be derived from the proper tenant mix— one that would result in the synergism of complementary store types and provide maximum attraction to prospective customers in the trade area. This more scientific approach has done much to reduce the incidence of inefficient occupancy patterns, but it has by no means eliminated them.

It is safe to say that no center has yet been built about which the developer could truthfully claim, one year later, that if he had to do it all over again the pattern of occupancy would be unchanged. Even where a developer's negotiating position is so strong that he has effectively absolute control of tenant selection, store size, and location —a rare state of affairs—there will still be errors of judgment.

Demographic Changes

Over any ten-year period there are changes in the demographics of a shopping center's trade area that can be drastic in the case of the relatively small area tributary to a neighborhood strip. Such changes, whether for better or worse, can act to weaken the market position of a specialty store that is locked into its merchandise presentation. An extreme example might be a store selling Catholic religious goods in an area where a predominantly Catholic population was being replaced by residents having other religious beliefs.

Another factor always present over a period of time is the deterioration of managerial ability or market appeal among a certain number of tenants, and this is a condition that afflicts large chains as well as individual proprietorships. It would be interesting to call the roll of national and regional chains that were considered prime tenants

139

twenty years ago and note how many are either missing or have become marginally desirable. However, the decline in merchandising vigor is more common among essentially one-man businesses. The combination of age and a comfortable degree of prosperity sometimes results in a complacency that leads to stagnation, or the original entrepreneur may retire and turn the business over to a successor having less ability to cope with changing public needs and tastes.

The Challenge to the Manager

Taken in combination, the preceding factors lead to the generalization that, at any time prior to the start of its final decline, a shopping center is never producing rental income at 100 percent of its potential. Here lies the challenge to the manager. He must sell the use of the gross leasable area at the highest price the market will bear. In doing so, however, he must be thinking at all times of the area as a whole as well as of the individual piece with which he may be dealing at the moment. Too myopic a view may result in a rental agreement that represents the best use of a free-standing store building, but is detrimental to the shopping center as a whole. The first test in evaluating a prospective tenant is whether he has the greatest rent-paying potential of the available prospects (and the operative word here is "available"), but other factors must be considered and given due weight. Consider some simplified examples:

- If there is a candy store doing well and a vacancy of the same size, will a second candy store also do well—or will they simply divide up the previous volume?

- Will a store catering to the high school set bring net new business into the center—or will it drive away enough older shoppers to result in a net decrease in traffic?

- If the center already has three outlets for children's clothing, will a fourth have the synergistic effect of making it increasingly dominant as the place to shop for that type of merchandise—or will it simply split up the business?

- In some large centers, a well-known local better women's wear store, a low rent-payer, acts as a subanchor for a group of small specialty shops producing much higher rent per square foot. If, after the center is well established, there occurs the opportunity to cut the major tenant into an additional collection of shops, will the enlarged group then survive or collapse?

In every shopping center more than two or three years old the renewal of leases becomes a continual activity and, as such, should be organized on a systematic basis by the manager. To do so, he needs accurate records, a long-range plan, and a realistic understanding of his negotiating position in each instance. It is a good idea to have a plan for the future within which to set the direction and establish the priorities for each renewal as it comes along. The first decision, of course, is whether to renew or replace, but for the sake of this discussion assume the tenant is doing a good job and no change in either size or location of space is indicated. Also assume that the outlook for the center as a whole is such that the tenant will wish to continue occupancy but is certainly not going to shut his eyes and sign anything put before him.

The first step is to identify all of the variables within the scope of the present lease, or those that might be added to it, which are subject to change for the benefit of the owner; next to evaluate their relative importance; and then to assign them a priority number. Putting this all down on paper may be unnecessarily laborious in the case of a barbershop, where the renewal agreement is going to be reached in one short meeting, but it can be extremely useful in negotiations involving several sessions and covering a wide range of topics. It helps keep the discussions directed toward the primary objectives, instead of straying into matters of relatively little importance. In identifying herein some of the points for consideration, it should be clearly understood that the order in which they are presented has no bearing on the priorities that might be assigned in a specific case.

The Variables at Issue

1. *Minimum rent guarantees* become important under two circumstances—if a refinancing is contemplated within the term of the renewal or if the center faces a declining future. In both cases, the higher the guarantee the better.

2. *Percentage rent* is always important. The first renewal in a successful center presents a good opportunity to retrieve concessions found necessary in the original lease negotiation.

3. *Contributions to common area maintenance*, if less than open-ended or with offset against overage rent, are also important items to be renegotiated, since maintenance is an uncontrollable expense that is highly dangerous in an inflationary period when not passed through to the tenant.

141

4. *Participation in real estate taxes* is in the same category, and if it was not in the original leases becomes increasingly difficult to secure as a center ages. When it is in the existing lease, there may also be provision for tenant offset against overage—which becomes a subject for renegotiation.

5. *The tenant's increasing obligation* to support the merchants' association is sometimes, contrary to all other financial considerations, easier to obtain as a center grows older and the pressure of external competition becomes more evident. It is also different from other monetary items in that this demand is likely to stimulate a counter demand that a like obligation be imposed on all other tenants and the landlord, too.

6. *Length of the lease term* can be influenced by several factors, some of which may be conflicting at the time when the choice must be made. A rosy general outlook, the possibility of expanding an adjoining store, a coming major remodeling, or skepticism on the tenant's own future prospects all point toward the renewal term being kept short from the center's point of view. On the other hand, a gloomy view of the center's future, an impending refinancing and/or sale, or a sense of restlessness in the tenant's behavior all lend weight to seeking a lengthy term. The more contradictory the factors may be in the individual case, the more important it becomes to think them through before starting the negotiation.

As a Center Matures

Getting now to the desirability of a longe-range plan, it is clear that introducing new subject matter into the leases and making it broadly applicable is a slow process with the lead time measured in years. As a center matures, part of the management responsibility is to look ahead to major physical changes that may be necessary or desirable in the future and to start preparing the way when they are in rough outline form. Such changes most commonly are additions, but can include improvement of receiving facilities, correction of traffic problems, enclosures, or anything else that changes the physical characteristics of a tenant's leased space or environment.

Waiting until such a change is ready to be executed before seeking the necessary lease modifications from the affected tenants can create serious problems. Most of those problems can be avoided by starting to pave the way via lease renewals as far in advance as the general plan is known. In a situation of this kind it is neither possible nor necessary to spell out in the renewal lease precisely what physical changes will be made affecting the leased premises and what the compensating financial changes will be. It ordinarily suffices to outline the probable scope of the physical changes and establish the principles that will govern the financial changes. This will indicate the general intent of the parties and eliminate any element of surprise. Even if the lead time is too short for all involved tenants to be covered, the word gets around, the program becomes a matter of common knowledge, and a pattern is established that simplifies things with those remaining.

The bargaining strength with which the landlord's representative enters a lease negotiation is not entirely a matter of personal skill, although that helps. Rather, the ability to gauge accurately the intensity with which each of the two parties feels compelled to reach an agreement is one of those managerial skills developed by experience. The manager's position in that respect can vary drastically according to the overall strength of the center as a retail location and, within narrower limits, according to the bargaining power of the tenant. The manager of a successful large center securing a renewal of the barbershop lease, for instance, has an overpowering position vis-a-vis the barber. His position is much weaker when he tackles a strong local chain of women's sportswear that has other outlets in or near the trade area. If the chain's owners consider that the terms commit them to higher-than-normal store-occupancy costs, they can simply close shop on the assumption that they will pick up 30 percent of the lost volume in their other units, with that much less total store expense. In both cases, and particularly the latter, the expertise of the manager in evaluating his negotiating position lessens the likelihood of his either under- or overreaching.

Replacement Leasing

Renewal leasing is usually a routine procedure with less call for creativity than replacement leasing. Replacement leasing is called for by one of two events—a tenant decision to vacate voluntarily or a landlord decision not to renew an existing lease. In the first event the landlord has no control over the decision. He may try to persuade the tenant to change his mind by offering a renewal on lesser terms—in effect a replacement lease.

The second event represents a considered judgment by the landlord that there is available a qualified replacement tenant capable of making more productive use of the space. When the present occupant

143

is either having chronic difficulty meeting his financial obligations or is conducting an obviously deteriorating operation, the decision to replace becomes automatic. Unless, of course, when the whole center is in such bad shape that almost anything is better than a probably unrentable vacancy. The critical decisions are those involving tenants who cause no problems but consistently produce income at or below the center's square-foot average despite a fair rent-rate schedule.

A different sort of situation, which occurs infrequently, sometimes inspires a program of deliberate replacement. That is when some change in either the demographics of the trade area or the competition within it indicates the desirability of changing the overall nature of the shopping center's customer appeal, ordinarily by way of merchandise price levels. If the proposed price change is downward, it is not a particularly difficult transition since the tenants dealing in higher-priced goods will either adapt or eliminate themselves. An attempt to move in the other direction, however, and upgrade the merchandise quality of the tenant mix by means of a systematic replacement program, is an extremely risky undertaking and one that is rarely successful. Before committing itself to such a course, prudent management would call for testing the market in sufficient depth to permit specific identification of the probable replacements; in this instance, the controlling word is "probable," not "possible."

Returning to the more typical replacement program, the usual objective is either to replace like with like—i.e., one men's clothing store with another handling the same kind of merchandise but with more aggressive management—or to balance the mix where there seem to be too many card shops and not enough candy stores, for example. In the case of a thriving shopping center with a reasonably secure future and what amounts to a waiting list of prospective tenants, changes of that sort call for no managerial attention beyond taking care that the replacement is the best available and the lease terms are negotiated to the best advantage of the owner, with the whole exercise representing about the same level of skill as shooting fish in a barrel. Where conditions are less favorable from the landlord's standpoint, which is more often the case, a less peremptory approach to the problem is indicated.

An Example

Let us first create a hypothetical situation and describe how a manager might approach it. For this purpose, assume you are the

144

contract manager of a medium-sized community-type center that, while not setting the world afire, is doing a good business and has a stable long-term outlook.

It is the end of the fourth year since opening and you are studying the records of those tenants having five-year leases, among them a 2,000-square-foot paint and wallpaper store operated by a successful local chain. The tenant is paying rent on a minimum guarantee that met the leasing objective in the planning stage, has had much less than the average growth rate, is not paying percentage overage, and, based on the past trend of sales volume, is not likely to get into overage for at least another three years, and then minimally. Both the common area maintenance and tax participation clauses in his lease provide for a 50 percent recapture out of overage above specified dollar amounts, which have not yet been reached but probably will be within a very few years. The tenant pays all charges promptly, adequately supports the merchants' association, is a consistent advertiser, causes no housekeeping problems, and is in general a good citizen. The junior department store that anchors one end of the center carries a small line of similar merchandise, but it does not put enough emphasis on the department to represent serious competition.

In reviewing the other retail classifications represented in the center, it is evident that women's shoes have had the best increase in volume, with the three stores in that group having shown a composite annual growth rate more than double that of the center as a whole. Among the group, the two stores selling popular-priced shoes have done a little better than the one handling medium-priced merchandise, but none of the three has yet shown any signs of leveling off. A telephone contact with the leasing agent who had represented the developer establishes that there had been other interested shoe retailers, but the three were decided on as giving proper balance to the total occupancy package. Examination of the existing leases with the two anchors and the three shoe stores reveals that one of the latter leases contains a restriction on the landlord against a fourth competitive store. However, it is only a seven-year lease without options and you feel confident that, if the matter is presented in the right way, a waiver can be obtained with little difficulty. The "right way" in this case concludes with the words ". . . or else". . . delivered with a smile, of course.

Your next move is a meeting with the general manager of the paint and wallpaper chain, at which a number of viewpoints are expressed and suggestions offered. He points out that, on a city-wide

145

basis, the store is in a highly competitive business, with margins pretty much externally controlled, and that selling and advertising expenses leave little room for flexibility in the area of occupancy costs if they are to show a profit. He proposes that, without waiting for the end of the five years, there be an immediate extension of four or five years on the same terms except for increasing the percentage rate by 1 percent, which would have the effect of putting them modestly into an overage position at once.

You point out this would not do very much for you unless the common area and tax offsets were eliminated. He replies that to do so would expose the store to an unpredictable occupancy cost—one that is unrelated to sales volume—a risk it could not accept. You suggest doing away with the minimum-against-percentage concept in favor of a flexible fixed rent, adjustable from year to year according to an average of the amount being paid by all other stores of similar size in the center, and he vetoes that idea for the same reason—it is unrelated to volume and therefore is unpredictable. Your next offer is to include, with an appropriate upward adjustment in the minimum, a revision of the use clause, which would permit the store to sell certain high-margin items such as decorative gifts, hobby supplies, or similar articles having some relationship to the main business. His answer to that one is that he had experimented along those and similar lines a few years back and found that, although it produced some quick profit, on balance it was harmful to the main purpose.

Having reached this impasse, you state your intention of seeking a replacement and ask his cooperation in making the transition as smooth as possible for all concerned, which he agrees to do. You then note that his lease expires on March 1 of the next year, an awkward date for him since the Christmas and midwinter seasons are low-volume months while March is the start of his best selling season. He is well aware of this, and indicates he will be grateful if you can arrange an early termination that will allow the store to vacate up to six months earlier without any financial penalty. In the course of these exchanges of goodwill, he also mentions his appreciation of the considerate manner in which you are handling the situation and indicates the store owner's probable willingness to sign a short-term renewal on the same terms if your further plans have not fully matured when the lease expires.

Being thus fortified with what amounts to an option situation, you proceed to the next step, selection of the most logical prospect to

146

fill the intended vacancy. Based on your own knowledge, conversations with business friends, some inquiries to your banker, and a scanning of listings in the local telephone book, you know that other than your present tenants there are three other popular-priced women's shoe chains with substantial representation in the metropolitan area, all financially acceptable and with good records as volume producers. You also have ascertained which one has the least coverage in or near your center's trade area. You then invite the real estate director of that chain to stop in for a visit the next time he is in the vicinity.

When he does, you show him the store that, without going into the details of why, will be available on March 1, and show him the sales records of the present three shoe stores, after receiving his promise to keep them absolutely to himself—a promise you are aware will probably be forgotten by the time he is on the plane out of town. After a few weeks he is back with the word that his company is interested, provided the price is right. You settle down to a discussion of terms, with things going reasonably smoothly except for two matters on which your prospect obviously has strong feelings.

He claims March 1 is the worst possible date to take possession, since one month is needed to remodel and to fixture the store, and they will thus completely miss out on the Easter business. Thus, he will not accept that date unless you will give him three months' free rent. His other sticking point is that the present storefront is fine for the paint and wallpaper business but impossible for the display of shoes. It must be extensively remodeled, he says, and that is up to the landlord. After the usual amount of haggling, agreement is reached: you will assume any expense incidental to obtaining possession on October 1, giving him a good shot at the Christmas business, with the rent to start November 1; he will remodel the storefront at his expense; and during the course of the lease he may withhold 50 percent of the overage due from time to time until he has recaptured 50 percent of the remodeling cost plus 6 percent interest on the outstanding balance. While shaking hands on the way out, he expresses appreciation to you for being completely truthful about the sales records of the present tenants, since the figures you gave exactly coincided with those he had obtained from other sources.

You next confirm the deal with the owner and then inform the mortgagee because, even though it involves only the loss of one month's rent and the substitution of one good credit for another, the mortgage agreement prohibits lessening any tenant's financial obligation without consent. Having attended to those details, you are free to tell the present tenant's general manager that, after great difficulties, you have arranged for them to vacate at the end of September, and offer your services as his friendly neighborhood broker in finding a new location.

Glance Backward

As we have done before, let us pause at this point for an examination of the manager's thinking as he went about the replacement. To begin with, this was a borderline decision, calling first for a careful weighing of the pros and cons and then caution in not getting caught out on a limb that might be sawed off behind him.

The paint and wallpaper store had been included in the initial leasing program because it was felt that it offered a service appropriate to the market area and because its credit rating helped the financing. The impairment of the tenant mix if the store left was not thought to be serious since the department store would probably expand its presentation to fill the void. However, if the tenant involuntarily vacated without being promptly replaced with another good credit risk, the mortgagee would be unhappy, and that would be bad for the owner's future relations.

Since the present tenant is a first-class operator, probably the best in town, there is obviously no point in seeking a like-for-like replacement. The problem, then, becomes one of finding either a store type that will bring something new to the center, or a replacement that will enlarge an existing merchandise category. If the latter course is chosen, care must be exercised to minimize the possibility that an addition will simply divide up the available volume and act to dilute the future flow of overage rent. Also to be taken into account in this particular case is that while the center is reasonably successful it is not a situation where prospective tenants are battering at the manager's door.

Taking all of the foregoing into account, the decision was to proceed cautiously and attempt to either improve the present lease to an acceptable level or, failing that, get into a position of being able to look around. In accordance with that approach, the manager initiated his discussion with the tenant in a manner designed to avoid acrimony and maintain a friendly, businesslike attitude in resolving a common problem in a cooperative way. The objective was an understanding that would allow him to openly seek a replacement while preserving a fallback position in case something better could not be obtained.

148

The little by-play between the manager and the shoe chain real estate director regarding the volumes of the present tenants is just a gentle spoof of one of the shopping center industry's durable myths: to wit, that an individual store's sales volume is a deep secret, shared only by the tenant, the owner, and the tax collector. The fact of life is that in the situation here portrayed the shoe man would either already have the figures when he arrived or would subsequently verify them through the channels of his own industry. Any misrepresentation by the manager would have only damaged his own credibility. On the serious side, however, it should be recognized that some retailers are highly sensitive about their business figures, and a manager should be most discreet in making any use of them.

The procedure followed in identifying a logical replacement prospect and then working out an agreement was simply routine leasing practice; the thought processes involved need not be amplified.

Another Example

A second example may serve to illustrate a more complicated situation frequently present in shopping centers of all sizes and ages. In this case, you are the full-time manager of a ten-year-old regional center with a successful past and a promising future. Your problem is one of those developer mistakes that sometimes occur, although possibly less frequently in recent times than formerly.

Occupying 20,000 square feet in a choice location on a twenty-year lease is a large, financially strong chain tenant whose merchandise line, for some reason, never caught on in that particular market. The minimum guarantee is low, there is a cap, long since reached, on the common area contribution, no tax participation, and the operation has never resulted in overage rent. After ten years, the situation has reached disaster proportions from the landlord's standpoint; every time the common area maintenance expense or the real estate taxes went up, which was often, the effective rental income diminished by a like amount. The tenant, however, is undergoing no hardship and is quite prepared to sit out the remaining ten years of the lease.

The nature of the business, largely self-service, is such that about the same number of people can staff a 20,000-square-foot store as one half that size. There is no problem with stale merchandise, since the inventory is effectively in a pool with the tenant's other area stores. Cleaning expense, heat, light, and power are somewhat out of line in relation to sales volume, but these are not major expense items, so

149

rent becomes the controlling factor. The rent—and rent equivalents such as the common area charge—is so low and so stabilized for the future that the store is profitable and can be expected to remain so. After much maneuvering, you, the center manager, have finally secured the tenant's agreement to relinquish half the space, provided this is accomplished at no expense to him and the rent thereafter never exceeds, as a percentage of sales, the average of the two preceding years. Your responsibility includes not only the structural and mechanical alterations but also the rearranging and, where necessary, refinishing of his fixtures, complete interior redecorating, and modernization of the storefront, including a new sign.

Working with an architect, you develop a plan to convert the liberated 10,000 square feet into four shops, providing a total of 9,500 feet of rentable floor area for which you anticipate no difficulty in securing tenants at top-dollar rents. Your next step is to cost out the total job with particular attention to the estimates covering the work within the present tenant's reduced space, which is of a highly specialized nature involving contingencies difficult to foresee. When you then sit down to discuss the cost with the owner, who has traveled this route before, his initial move is to increase your estimates by 20 percent, the overrun to be expected on the basis of industry experience. The final cost estimate is a sizable figure, more than can be provided out of current funds, and therefore will have to be borrowed.

The owner instructs you to come up with a recommendation on whether to proceed or forget the whole thing and suffer through the next ten years at status quo.

As a starter, you prepare two ten-year projections. The first one is designed to establish the financial consequences of continuing the present tenancy for the next ten years, and it is accomplished with sufficient accuracy by a linear projection of the record from the past ten years. The second projection, however, calls for assuming income levels of rent and rent equivalents from the entire 19,500 square feet of rentable area for each of the next ten years and matching them with the assumed expenses that will follow remodeling. For such a purpose, prudent management indicates a conservative treatment: equal care must be taken not either to overestimate future income or to underestimate probable future expenses. In relatively long-term projections of this kind, the really hard income consists of the minimum guarantees, with the anticipated overage getting softer the farther into the future the assumptions are made. Similarly, on the expense side the only firmly predictable items are interest and depreciation. All else is on a best-judgment basis.

As part of the second projection, you have scouted the financing possibilities and concluded the most feasible plan is a bank loan for the entire cost, with the principal repayable in quarterly installments over three years. With this input, you have available for comparison what might be called "before" and "after" operating statements, both divided into annual time frames running from Year One to Year Ten. Incidentally, the alteration is obviously not going to happen by waving a wand, and the first year will include a phasing-in period of several months' duration.

Assuming that a comparison of the two projections throws a favorable light on the project, the next order of business is your analysis of the effects on the owner's pocketbook, a matter you are pretty sure will be much on his mind, and you do so on the basis of both net taxable income and cash flow. In the former instance, the results are quite favorable even in Year One: his interest payments will be minimized since he is not drawing upon the bulk of the loan until after the new tenants start paying rent, and the depreciation, on an average fifteen-year-life basis, will not start accruing until even a little later in the year. The cash flow projection is another matter, however, and the principal payments to the bank, particularly in Years Two and Three, are going to have a severe impact. Your report to the owner on this aspect of the matter, therefore, is to the effect that the proposed alteration will benefit taxable earnings a little in Year One, considerably more in Year Two, and thereafter at an accelerating rate; and that it will depress cash flow considerably in Year One, severely in Years Two and Three, again more moderately in Year Four, and then improve it substantially over the present level in Year Five and thereafter.

The final step before preparing your report to the owner is a thorough scrutiny of the entire center to see if you can identify any alternative condition under which, by improvement, alteration, or addition, the amount of capital involved might be invested to better advantage. Not finding any, you proceed with organizing the exhibits to go with the report. These include appropriate outline drawings of the work to be done and reasonably detailed cost estimates; the financial record of the present tenant, including the deficiencies in common area maintenance payments resulting from the ceiling in the lease, and a ten-year projection based on that record; identification of the types of tenants proposed for the subdivided space, with the anticipated rental terms and ten-year projection for each; and a composite ten-year projection for the as-altered 19,500 square feet, setting forth all income and all expense allocable to that area, including the capital charges, shown on both a taxable-income and a cash-flow basis.

In the body of the report you would include your opinion concerning those factors too intangible to be quantifiable but that should be given weight. One of these might be your estimate of the rentability of the 20,000-square-foot space ten years hence if it is left undisturbed; another is your opinion on the extent to which the added stores will either take business away from present tenants or improve the business of all by attracting more shoppers. In conclusion, of course, you make a recommendation to go or no-go, based on your evaluation of whether the long-term benefits are sufficient to outweigh the near-term drop in cash flow.

Some General Rules

One of the lessons implied in the first of the preceding examples is the desirability of having plenty of lead time in which to work out details of a tenant replacement, and this is equally true of renewals. In the case of a small space-user in a prosperous regional, where the renewal is a matter of minor adjustments in the lease terms, a manager can afford to delay until shortly before the expiration date, but this is never a safe course in dealing with important intermediate or long-term lessees whose terminations could create a problem. Unless there is a valid reason for delay, renewal negotiations with such tenants should be started at least one year in advance, or even longer if there is any suspicion that there are to be complicating factors. This is particularly important if the principals, or decision makers, are remote and the negotiation must be through a representative—a condition that always causes delays and one that is particularly dangerous in the case of a tenant having difficulty in deciding whether to stay after getting word of the proposed renewal terms.

In the event of failure to reach agreement, the farther in advance this is established the better the manager's position in securing a replacement by the time of the actual vacancy. As noted earlier, the owner's stock in trade consists of use of his space, which is, by its nature, sold within a frame of time—and time is, by *its* nature, a perishable commodity. That takes the long way around to say that a day's rent, once lost, is not recoverable and is gone forever. Another bad feature of a vacancy, particularly in a prominent location, is the depressing effect it has on the subconscious of the passing shopper and its measurably depressing effect on the sales of its neighbors. Finally, there is the fact that a retail store, if not in a prime location, is generally harder to rent when vacant than when occupied. When a vacancy does occur, the first order of business—which is, surprisingly, often neglected—is to make the premises as presentable as possible, both to passersby and to prospective tenants. Dirty windows and an abandoned store sign are visible from well out into the parking lot, and if the view of the interior from the sidewalk includes assorted rubbish, an already bad situation is made that much worse.

There can be no single prescription for how to go about finding prospective tenants. In the case of a vacant store, certainly an obvious way is a sign in the window, and equally obvious is a canvass of the present tenants to see what ideas they might have. A frequently productive course is a form letter or printed flyer to all commercial real estate brokers in the general area, or to a trade list if the search is for a specific retail classification. In some localities, a modest display advertisement in a newspaper will draw inquiry. It should be kept in mind that for even a quite small center, the geographic field for potential tenants is as large as the whole metropolitan area, or even the nation, for certain specialized retailers. Depending on the nature of the community and the manager's personal familiarity with it, a few well-placed phone calls or visits can be helpful, but any attempt at personal canvassing beyond the limits of the center itself is unlikely to warrant the investment in time required. That is better left to the brokers active in the field of commercial leasing, who generally have up-to-date files on retailers interested in new locations.

A shopping center manager's ability to appraise the relative desirability of prospective tenants will depend in considerable measure on the level of his understanding of retail operations. This is a useful skill to the manager in a position to be selective among prospects to fill an impending vacancy, but obviously its value diminishes in direct proportion to the shrinkage in the number of prospects available for evaluation. There is also some correlation between the amount of scrutiny the prospect should be given, the size of the center involved, and the size and nature of the tenancy being considered. For example, in a large regional with a high level of internal competition, where the desired tenancy is in the apparel field, a good going-over is in order to ensure that the prospect will be compatible with the overall tenant

153

mix and has what it takes to survive in fast company; and the larger the store in question the more important this becomes. If there is more than one apparently qualified prospect in sight and the space is sizable, a manager is well advised to employ a consultant to do a detailed comparative evaluation if he feels the job is beyond his own level of expertise, which it probably is in most cases.

At the other end of the scale would be the manager of a strip center concerned with replacing the dry cleaner who moved out three months ago, leaving a gap in both the monthly rent roll and the tenant mix. In that situation, an appraisal of the prospective tenant is likely to be confined to the bare essentials—has he capital enough to equip the store; is he good for at least the first few months' rent; is he likely to provide reasonably good service; and how soon will he move in?

There are a number of differences between leasing a new shopping center in the process of development and re-leasing that same center at a later time, two of which are pertinent to this presentation. They are the allocation of space and the establishment of rental terms. Some thoughts on the former may be helpful before proceeding to the latter.

The developer's leasing plan starts off with a blank sheet of paper on which is entered a hypothetical occupancy pattern listing each desired type and size of store tenancy. The whole represents a theoretically ideal tenant mix for that particular trade area. As leasing progresses, the plan is usually somewhat modified to accommodate the needs of particular tenants, but it ends up representing the best judgment of all concerned, developer and tenants, as to the amount of space in each store. Five years later, or sometimes much sooner, it becomes evident that some tenants are overspaced while others could profitably use more. It is the manager's responsibility to maintain a continuing analysis of such developments with a view to altering individual store sizes as lease expirations or interim negotiations permit. In making such changes, he should be constantly on guard against overdoing an expansion, whether by building additional space or annexing from another tenant, to the point at which efficiency of use is impaired and income per square foot is lessened. Retailers are much more likely to overestimate their space needs than the reverse, and no expansion should be undertaken without a detailed projection of probable income and expense for several years ahead. If a tenant is pressing for enlargement, a good determinant of his confidence in the results is the extent to which he is prepared to assume a share of the

154

capital cost, or his willingness to accept a rental guarantee that will assure the landlord of at least the same total rent per square foot.

When it comes to setting rents and related occupancy costs, a developer is guided by two considerations: what the market will bear, and what is needed to support the financing without which he cannot proceed. The former is controlling on the up side and the latter on the down side, with usually a very thin margin between, a condition well understood by most prospective lessees. It is a recognized phenomenon of the industry that the level of guaranteed rent obtainable in a well-conceived new shopping center is above that prevailing for equivalent accommodations in older facilities, a differential generally confined to the guarantee and infrequently extending to the percentage rate. Prospective tenants are prepared to pay such a premium—it might be called "franchise rent"—in order to ensure their position in a location they anticipate will show sustained growth for some years to come. As a center ages, that advantage dwindles rapidly, except among centers that for some reason enjoy an unusually favorable outlook for the future in their present condition, or are preparing for a major addition. In most cases, however, once the gloss of newness has worn off, the rental terms, in both renewal and replacement leases, are largely controlled by the alternatives available elsewhere in the community. An essential part of the management function is to maintain channels of communication adequate to keep abreast of the going market.

In a center having many tenants, the re-leasing activity tends to be brisk enough for the manager to have an ongoing feel of the market. Even so, it is worth his while periodically to do some systematic scouting on what is happening down the street and on the other side of town. Whether a fresh negotiation starts twice a week or twice a year, however, the essential requirement is to have a clear idea of the objectives and their relative importance in order to finish with the best possible agreement from the owner's standpoint. Theoretically, the negotiation should be concluded on terms such that, if there were three equally qualified prospects, one—and only one—would pay the price. Such a bullseye of perfection is unlikely in practice but it illustrates the principle.

QUESTIONS FOR DISCUSSION

1. *Discuss the economic characteristics in each of the four stages of a regional shopping center's life cycle.*

2. *What is the shopping center manager's re-leasing strategy during each stage of a regional shopping center's life cycle?*

3. *Explain the synergistic approach to the development of a center's tenant mix.*

4. *How do the demographic and managerial factors affect lease renewal?*

5. *Explain the factors of allocation of space and lease terms, as they apply to leasing in a new shopping center.*

6. *Discuss the variables to be considered by the center manager before starting lease renewal negotiations.*

7. *What are the likely problems in changing the merchandise image of a shoping center through replacement leasing?*

8. *What tests can you as a shopping center manager undertake to evaluate a prospective tenant in replacement leasing?*

9. *Discuss the two primary considerations a developer establishes in setting rents and related occupancy costs in a new shopping center.*

10. *Explain the importance to a center manager of having a finger on the pulse of the overall area rental market.*

RECOMMENDED READING LIST

Lebhar, Ruth, Dr. Frank A. Borsenick and Landis Eby. **Appraising Prospective Tenants.** New York: International Council of Shopping Centers, 1972. 12 pp.

156

CHAPTER **9**

Real Estate Taxes

t he taxes with which the shopping center manager is concerned are
of two general types: those related to the capital value of the property, and those having to do with the business activity carried on there.
The former consist principally of the ad valorem real estate tax; of the
latter, by far the most significant are the income taxes imposed by the
federal government, by most states, and by some cities.

In practically all shopping centers, real estate taxes are the largest
non-capital-related cash operating expense. Their impact on the owner's cash flow and profit is determined by the extent to which they are
passed on to the tenants.

There is not much the manager can do to influence the amount
of income tax to be paid, although he can to some extent control the
time when it becomes payable. The real estate tax burden, on the other
hand, can sometimes be significantly affected by properly directed
efforts on the manager's part. To do so, it is necessary to understand
first the underlying principles involved and then to determine the manner in which they are applied in a particular jurisdiction.

Assessment

The procedures for determining and levying real estate taxes are established by the states, and the methods vary somewhat from state to state. In general, the amount of the annual bill is the product of two factors—the tax rate, which is uniform for all properties within the district, and the assessed valuation, which is individual to each parcel. The rate is set by the budgetary requirements of the governmental unit to be financed by the levy, and there is ordinarily little the individual can do about that. The valuation is a different matter, however, since there can be considerable difference of opinion concerning the approaches used to determine value, the weight placed on various elements that comprise value, and the application of local practices to the specific problem. The personalities of assessing officials should also be taken into account.

Viewed nationally, real estate assessing in the United States is extremely fragmented, with a total of nearly 15,000 separate primary assessment districts and no semblance of a national pattern. Hawaii, where assessing is a state function, consists of a single assessment district; California, the most populous state, makes assessing a county function and has 50 districts; New York, the second most populous, is divided into 990; and Texas is broken down into almost 4,500.

The exact number of individual assessors is unknown, but informed estimates run to about 90,000 persons engaged in administrative or technical capacities related to tax assessment. Some are elected by popular vote and some are appointed in various manners; some are under civil service but most are not; some are skilled technicians with a broad grasp of real estate economics and a few are barely literate. Personal venality among assessors has become fairly uncommon, but political considerations are unquestionably a factor in many districts. Since homeowners tend to be quite sensitive about real estate taxes, collectively they cut a lot more ice on election day than shopping center, store, and factory owners.

Most, if not all, states have constitutional or legislative requirements providing for fair and equitable assessment of property, within certain specified guidelines. They also provide that tax rolls must be open to public inspection and that there be a relatively simple appeal procedure by which a taxpayer may protest his assessment before a local review board. Failing relief at that level, the taxpayer usually has recourse to either a state court or a tax commission for judicial consideration of his claim of unfair treatment. Because this last step is expensive and time-consuming, it is usually warranted only when large sums are at issue.

In most tax jurisdictions, the assessment roll—the basis for computation of taxes to be levied during the ensuing year—is established as of December 31 and is opened for public inspection soon after that date. Dissatisfied taxpayers thereafter have a limited time in which to file an appeal and present their cases to the review board for adjustment, if any, prior to final certification of the roll, which is usually done by early April. Following that step no change is possible until the following year.

Manager Should Examine Assessment Roll Annually

It is an important responsibility of the shopping center manager to examine the assessment roll every year. If there has been a change from the year before, he should decide whether an appeal is warranted and he should inform the owner of his decision. When an appeal is decided on, the case must be prepared promptly because, as noted above, time is short and extensions by the review board are usually unobtainable.

In preparing an appeal it should be kept clearly in mind that, unless there is a background of political consideration, review boards are not much impressed by hardship pleas. The case for lowering an assessed value must be based on evidence of a demonstrable inequity, and a comparative sample of other similar properties should be provided. This can get to be a pretty technical matter. Unless the manager has some experience as a real estate appraiser, he would be well advised to call in some expert help at this point, the nature of it depending on the size and complexity of the property and the amount of tax money at stake.

In most communities there are appraisers and lawyers who specialize in handling real estate tax appeals, and the reputable ones, who are a large majority, are well worth their fees. Where there are substantial sums involved, lawyers will sometimes handle the matter on a contingency basis, i.e., a percentage of the first year's saving, and, if it is a tough case, that can be a good buy even if the lawyers get the lion's share.

Legal advice and valuation advice fall into different categories and should not be confused. Since everything that is revealed concerning the property may have both a short-range and a long-range effect on the assessment, it is vital to obtain competent professional advice in every situation that involves substantial sums.

The dates and procedural details will vary in the different states, but the process as a whole will be similar to that outlined, and the message is twofold. First, the burden of determining if there is a change in the assessed value is on the manager; in only rare cases do the tax authorities provide notice. Second, if a protest is indicated, it must be factually supported and promptly filed; after the tax bill has arrived is too late.

In addition to his annual examination of the roll, the skillful manager endeavors to lessen the chance of an unpleasant surprise by establishing an informal line of communication with the assessor. A sociable luncheon three or four times a year, with a little shop-talk mixed in, sometimes provides the opportunity for an exchange of information that is mutually helpful. If nothing else, such contacts frequently indicate how the wind is blowing and what advance planning would be in order.

However, property valuation is not a matter of public relations. In fact, a manager who is friendly with tax officials may well be misled into believing that all will be well. He may lose valuable time that might have been spent gathering facts and figures and consulting with professionals who can help him. Assessment problems tend to be best settled among professionals, rather than in the courts, on the basis of cold appraisal and informed interpretation.

Three Approaches to Estimating Market Value

Although the manager who is untrained in technical appraisal matters should not attempt to bypass the professional, he should try to grasp some of the essentials of appraisal so that he can deal intelligently with his professional advisors and his owner. He should be familiar with the broad outlines of the three approaches to estimating market value on which the assessment of property is based.

1. *The cost approach.* The value of the property is obtained by estimating the replacement cost of the improvements, deducting the estimated depreciation, and adding the value of the land, as estimated by the use of the market-data approach described below. Although this approach has been under fire in recent years as applied to shopping centers, a high percentage of appraisals include the cost approach in the analysis, and in some states it is obligatory for the assessor to include it in his considerations.

2. *The market-data approach.* This appraisal technique, using actual market transactions, is based on the theory that the prices of equal, substitute properties establish value. It, too, has been criticized when applied to shopping centers because of the difficulty of finding properties that are genuinely "equal and substitute."

3. *The income approach.* This technique takes the historical net income as a basis on which to calculate the capital value of the investment producing that net income. According to this method, the value of income-producing property, such as a shopping center, tends to be set by the amount of future income that can reasonably be expected, and the present value of the property is the present value of future income. Although there is room for argument concerning the rate at which income should be capitalized to determine value, and although determination of net income can become a highly technical problem, on balance this approach appears to be favored by many authorities.

In practice, many appraisers try to blend all three approaches, checking the results of each method against the results of the others.

As noted at the beginning of this chapter, the impact of tax increases on the center's profit depends on the extent to which they are passed on to the tenants, a condition that has extreme variation within the industry. At one end of the spectrum are centers in which the landlord pays the whole bill; at the other are ones in which the tenants bear almost the whole burden. To a considerable extent, the existing condition is a product of two factors—the time when the center was built, and the negotiating strength of the developer, both then and since. To understand the significance of age it is necessary to take another one of those perspective looks at the evolution of the industry.

Until about the mid-1950s, almost all shopping center leases provided that all real estate taxes were the sole obligation of the landlord; the only exceptions were single-occupancy buildings that were essentially free-standing, such as department stores, restaurants, banks, and service stations, which were traditionally net-leased. In those early days the developers' first priority was to get unlimited percentage clauses and unlimited common area maintenance contributions. Few foresaw the tremendous increases in property taxes they were to experience a few years later, and most believed that rises in taxes would be more than offset by the percentage rent generated by higher sales volumes. About the only exceptions were a few centers in which the share of taxes attributable to the parking area was made part of the common area charge.

During the second half of the 1950s, both developers and mortgage lenders became increasingly concerned with the trend toward increased assessments of shopping centers. Owners began to write into leases a provision for the tenant paying all or a share of the increases above a stipulated base year, and this was not easily accomplished. Some of the national chains, particularly the variety stores, were either completely opposed or accepted the obligation only with the further provision that they could fully recapture such contributions out of future overage rent payments. The latter position tended to satisfy prospective mortgagees, but obviously did not do much for the owners. It was not until the mid-1960s that developers in a strong negotiating position were able to write all of their leases with some form of effective tax contribution by the tenants.

The other variable in the overall industry position has been the relative bargaining strength of the initial developer and of the subsequent managers who have negotiated the lease renewals and replacements. Even today, not all new shopping center developments are economically strong enough to insist on across-the-board tenant participation in the tax burden, and the rate of conversion in the older centers is, of course, dependent on the strength of the landlord at renewal time. In this connection, it is likely that a good many managers of centers more than ten years old underestimate their ability to secure tax clauses in renewal leases. Retail chains, both national and local, which a dozen years ago were adamant on the subject, have come to accept the tax-sharing principle and offer only perfunctory objection when renewing their leases. If the store is a profitable one, the tax clause simply becomes another recognizable item in the package of lease changes accompanying the renewal negotiation.

The rationale for requiring the tenant to absorb, or at least share, the increased tax burden rests on two assumptions: first, that increases in the assessed valuation are indicative of the improving value of the store location for retail purposes; and second, that increases in the tax rate are largely the result of inflationary pressures against which the landlord is inadequately protected by the percentage lease. As noted at the beginning of this chapter, real estate taxes and the manner in which they are distributed have a major effect on the owner's cash flow and profit and should have a high priority in the manager's consideration of ways to improve the quality of his leases.

Obtaining Tax Sharing by Tenants

There have been many different approaches to obtaining tax sharing by tenants; here are some of the more common ones. It should be clearly understood that the numbering is solely for reference identification and has absolutely no bearing on the preferability of one over another.

1. As mentioned previously, an early approach was to include in the common area maintenance charge all real estate taxes attributable to that portion of the land used for parking. At first, this practice was largely confined to developments built on unusually high-priced land, but it was in many cases an unsatisfactory solution for two reasons. First, assessors established the practice of dividing the shopping center land into one category for parking and another for buildings—with the latter being assigned a much higher square-foot value than the former. Second, in the early days of the industry it was quite common for stronger tenants to have either a ceiling on their common area contribution or the right to recapture all or part of it from overage rents. Taken in combination, these circumstances can seriously erode the owner's position over a period of time.

2. By the late 1950s, a good many of the more active mortgage lenders became seriously alarmed, as noted above, and joined with developers in applying pressure on prospective tenants to accept the so-called "tax stop" or "tax escalator." Incidentally, it should be kept in mind that the first lien of the mortgagee loses its primacy and drops to second place behind the lien automatically established by unpaid taxes. The most common form of tax clause in the lease at that time provided for proration among the tenants of increased taxes above those levied in the base year, usually defined as the first year of operation. Sometimes the proration is short of 100 percent, with an agreed share being taken by the landlord; particularly during the early years of this phase it was quite common for the stronger tenants to bargain for, and get, either a ceiling or some form of recapture out of overage rent.

3. Another approach is a sort of hybrid of the preceding two: the lease calls for adding to the common area maintenance charge the increases over the base year of the taxes attributable to all of the land within the center, regardless of use. The theory here is that over a period of time the increases in assessed valuation are going to be largely on the land, since the buildings are subject to depreciation as an offset to the increased cost of replacement.

4. A fairly recent innovation has been the practice of inserting in the original leases a provision limiting the landlord's contribution in the total real estate burden to a fixed amount—usually expressed as so many cents per square foot of GLA—with all taxes over that figure to be spread among the tenants pro rata to their share of the total GLA. In the main, the sum to be paid by the landlord is pegged at approximately the total amount anticipated for the first year, but this is not necessarily the case. Depending on the developer's evaluation of the strength of his negotiating position, he may set the figure above or below the first-year estimate.

5. There has been some experimenting in which real estate taxes in their entirety are assumed by the tenants right from the start, and this may be the wave of the future. It makes sense in the same way that gradually persuading tenants to accept full responsibility for common area maintenance made sense 15 to 20 years ago. As of this writing, however, the movement has had only limited success; tenant resistance is such that it could be accomplished only at the expense of uneconomic tradeoffs in the percentage rent terms. Some tenants make the point that the owner should have some tax obligation as an incentive to contest unfair valuations. They contend that the owner is the only one who can do so in sustained fashion for the shopping center as a whole.

In addition to the five approaches outlined here, there are some others representing variations or combinations. As a result, the managers of centers more than five years old are confronted with a bewildering variety of existing conditions. The skill with which existing agreements are upgraded or new tax clauses introduced is an important measure of the manager's effectiveness. It requires constant reevaluation of the strength of his bargaining position vis-a-vis each individual tenant as well as the whole pool of prospective tenants. Over a period of years it can have a significant bearing on the profitability of the operation.

There are a number of other levies related to the business activity of the center that have minor effect on profitability, and the manager cannot directly influence them. Included are the taxes, both federal and state, applying to payrolls, sales, rents, franchises, intangibles, utilities, inventories, signs, vehicles, etc., which are mainly borne by tenants or consumers. A shopping center manager should acquire a general understanding of their nature and application, particularly as they affect retailers, as a part of his background in dealing intelligently with his tenants.

The federal and state income taxes, however, are a different matter. The manager needs to know enough about their complexities to enable him efficiently to manipulate his income and expenses within legal boundaries. Since most states take their cue from the federal laws, a working knowledge of Internal Revenue Service regulations will generally suffice. Let it be emphasized, however, that the income tax laws and their derivative regulations are complex and highly technical, full of pitfalls for the unwary. It is a field in which a little knowledge can be a dangerous thing and an area in which all but the most obvious answers should be left to the experts.

There are a few applications, however, in which a general understanding of the principles involved will be helpful to the manager in his day-to-day decisions. He should understand the difference between costs that must be expensed and those that must be capitalized, and be able to identify those on which the accounting treatment is optional. A fairly good grasp of the rules governing depreciation is almost essential, as is some understanding of the limitations on the accrual and deferment of income and expense. It is in these relatively simple matters that the manager can implement the owner's planning for the financial results he seeks. As discussed in an earlier chapter, an owner's objectives can vary from time to time and it may suit his purpose to minimize earnings one year in order to maximize them another; this purpose can be aided by shifting the incidence of the income tax from year to year.

One last word on the subject of taxes. There should be clearly in mind at all times the difference between the *avoidance* of taxes and the *evasion* of taxes. It is an essential part of the managerial responsibility so to operate the business as to minimize the tax burden, and to that end every legal procedure should be followed to avoid incurring the obligation to pay unnecessary taxes. But an attempt to *evade* payment of taxes, whether by direct or indirect means, is a quite different matter—and the manager who adopts that course has set foot on a foolish and dangerous road.

QUESTIONS FOR DISCUSSION

1. *Investigate and explain the procedure for determining and levying real estate taxes in your community.*

2. *What is the assessment appeal procedure in your community?*

3. *Why should the shopping center manager examine his community assessment roll annually?*

4. *What are the two general types of taxes with which the center manager is concerned?*

5. *Discuss the cost approach to estimating the market value of a shopping center for assessment.*

6. *To what extent does the recapture of tenant tax contribution from overage rent payments affect the center's profitability?*

7. *Explain the rationale for requiring tenants to absorb or at least share the increased tax burden with the landlord.*

8. *Discuss the various approaches used by management to obtain tenant tax sharing.*

9. *Explain the difference between the avoidance of taxes and the evasion of taxes.*

10. *Visit or write to your nearest Internal Revenue Service (I.R.S.) office. Obtain and become familiar with the forms, schedules, and instructional material relating to commercial real estate. Be prepared to discuss them as they relate to shopping centers.*

RECOMMENDED READING LIST

Assessing and the Appraisal Process. 4th ed. Chicago: International Association of Assessing Officers, 1971. 199 pp.

Depreciable Lives of Shopping Centers. New York: International Council of Shopping Centers, 1973. 32 pp.

Gettel, Ronald E. **You Can Get Your Real Estate Taxes Reduced.** New York: McGraw-Hill Book Company, 1977. 275 pp.

Gladstone Associates. **Shopping Center Useful Lives: An Economic Analysis.** New York: National Retail Merchants Association, 1976. 80 pp.

CHAPTER 10

Insurance

---

the aspects of insurance pertinent to the management of a shopping center include types of coverage, methods of purchasing, and administration of a program.

The field of insurance is a broad one. It is a specialized business, full of complexities and technicalities. A few generalities:

■ The purpose of insurance is to prevent, or limit, financial loss as a result of unforeseen and uncontrollable occurrences. It should not be thought of as a substitute for managerial diligence and prudence.

■ The premiums paid are, at least in theory, commensurate with the risk assumed by the insurer. They are influenced both by the physical characteristics of the center and by the manner in which it is operated.

■ The insurance coverage falls into two broad categories: that related to physical damage to the insured's property, including any resultant loss of income, and that related to damage to the persons or property of others incidental to the activities carried on at the center.

■ The burden of determining the amount of insurance to be carried is on the insured. In the absence of a precise determination

167

it is better to risk being overinsured than underinsured.

■ There is an important distinction between an insurance *agent* and an insurance *broker* that a manager should keep in mind. The agent is a representative of an insurance company, authorized to issue policies in the company's name and receiving a commission from the company for so doing. Of course, the company's interest must be paramount in his thinking. A broker, on the other hand, solicits business from buyers of insurance on the premise that, after studying their needs, he will apply his expertise to negotiating the best available package from the standpoint of the insured, and is compensated by a share of the agent's commission. To obtain and retain business, the broker depends on the confidence of the buyer that he is being ably represented.

■ Insurance is for the most part a highly competitive business. To some extent, premium rates are regulated by the states, but as a practical matter the shrewd, knowledgeable buyer can effect substantial savings at no sacrifice of quality.

Planning Coverage

Probably the best starting point in establishing and maintaining a sound, economical insurance program is a clear understanding of exactly where in the owner-manager structure the responsibility lies. "But I thought *you* were taking care of it" can be sad words when spoken over hot ashes on the morning after, but that does happen now and then. The point not to be overlooked is that insurance coverage is not a static condition to be thought of once every year or so when the policies come up for renewal. Both the physical and occupancy conditions of the property are subject to constant change, and the insurance industry makes frequent changes in the types of coverage available and in underwriting practices having a bearing on rates.

Administering the insurance program takes various forms, depending on the type of management in effect. Irrespective of the administrative channels, however, records should be maintained to provide the individual directly responsible for managing the center with immediate access to the information needed in an emergency.

The owner or manager with a minimum of organizational backup and without a safe level of personal expertise is well advised to select a competent broker and turn the matter over to him. Multicenter operations, or those affiliated with large companies, generally have an insurance department at the central-office level staffed by specialists.

Contract managers who handle a substantial volume of real estate almost always have skilled people on their staffs. If such a manager also operates as an insurance broker, it would be quite in order for him to negotiate the purchase of insurance on behalf of his management client. However, if he functions as an insurance agent, directly or via an affiliated company, there is clearly the possibility of a conflict of interest in the two relationships. It is not innately impossible for the contract manager to function impartially and fairly as representative of both insurer and insured, but when this is done it should be with the full knowledge and consent of all parties concerned.

In planning and negotiating the coverage on loss or damage to the physical plant, consideration should be given to certain financial characteristics existing in greater or lesser degree in all shopping centers.

- At any time the center's true value is determined by its potential for producing future income; the original cost of construction is meaningless for this purpose.

- Book value is an accounting abstraction, with any relationship to true value being coincidental.

- Shopping centers typically have a high debt/equity ratio, with the result that the spread between in and out cash flow tends to be narrow.

- The costs of operation are extremely rigid and, in most instances, almost completely unaffected by loss of income.

- The net cash flow is ordinarily immediately drawn off by the owner and put to other uses—the center itself rarely accumulates surplus cash.

- Although functionally a single entity, the land and buildings may have two or more owners, which is often true where department stores are included. A loss in one ownership segment may impair the function of another segment even though there has been no communicated physical damage.

- Roadways, sidewalks, and parking areas may have more than one owner, or may be within the leased area of a tenant, but they are ordinarily made available to the shopper as a whole with no signs of demarcation. As a result, it is sometimes impossible to pinpoint the liability for a personal injury claim originating in a public area.

169

In sum, the economic well-being of the enterprise is highly vulnerable to any event resulting in an unindemnified loss of capital and/or income. If the dollar extent of the protection cannot be exactly matched to the potential dollar loss, the prudent manager will risk some possibility of over- rather than underinsuring. The penalty for overinsurance is premium payment for a level of loss payment that can never be realized; underinsurance, by contrast, creates the possibility that the difference between an actual loss and the insurance recovery will come out of the owner's pocket.

Fire and Extended Coverage

The basic insurance on the property is embodied in the Fire and Extended Coverage policy that routinely includes, in addition to fire, numerous other perils such as windstorm, hail, explosion, riot, and smoke. The same policy customarily also includes the vitally important coverage against what is variously known as consequential loss, use and occupancy, or rental value—the income lost during the restoration period.

In contrast, the so-called standard fire policy customarily provides quite limited coverage. The standard fire policy varies from state to state but is generally uniform for all companies operating within a given state. It covers little more than fire itself and identifies a long list of excluded perils. It also quite usually provides for payment, up to the agreed maximum, of loss on the basis of actual cash value, which is defined as replacement cost less depreciation.

In buying insurance, as with most other commodities, you get about what you are willing to pay for—any program presented as being a great bargain is pretty sure to have a catch in it somewhere. As has been said, however, insurance is a very competitive business and a skilled, knowledgeable purchaser will negotiate benefits not realized by the uninitiated who, so to speak, buy what is displayed on the counter. The benefits are less likely to be in the ostensible price tag than in the real extent of the coverage, as spelled out in the fine print of the contract.

A qualified expert can also isolate and evaluate the marginal coverages on which a cost-benefit decision must be made. Since there is a price tag on every form of coverage written into the policy, an owner may elect to save the premium and carry the risk himself on some of the more remote perils. The most important of these cost-benefit decisions, however, have to do with the deductibles, and this calls for some careful weighing of the trade-offs involved.

In the case of most risks, it is uneconomical to insure the first dollar of loss because of the disproportionate administrative expense to the insurer and, in a lesser degree, to the insured as well. Reporting, investigating, settling, and cleaning up the paperwork on a $50 loss could cost the two parties combined five times that sum, and the insurance company's share is sooner or later going to find its way into the premium rate. The usual practice, therefore, is to include in the policy a deductible feature—i.e., the insured assumes small losses without reimbursement. Obviously, the higher the deductible the lower the rate since there are many more small losses than large ones, thus benefiting the insurer in both administrative expense and claims paid. However, an abnormal string of losses just below the deductible limit can be ruinous to the insured. To protect against that contingency, there is commonly some sort of cumulative ceiling. Again obviously, that kind of carefully tailored coverage is not acquired by a purchaser simply walking into the insurance agency and saying, "I'll take that policy with the big gold seal and the pretty blue border."

Suggestions for Coverage

Having made the point that the detailed negotiation is a job for an expert, the following suggestions are presented as particularly interesting to the manager who must thereafter live with the coverage as finally written.

The basis for loss payment can, by endorsement (specifying changes in or additions to the policy) and additional premium, be changed from actual cash value (replacement cost less depreciation) to replacement value, which is the full cost of replacement as of that date. This change adds to the annual expense of insurance, but can be well worth it on two counts. First, it eliminates the gap between the out-of-pocket cost of restoring the loss and the insurance recovery, which can be a substantial difference in an older center. Second, it largely does away with the lengthy bickering and uncertainty often attending the determination of actual cash value at the time of loss.

The coverage for consequential loss should include all income derived from tenants, not just guaranteed rent—a factor that is particularly significant in older centers with low minimums. Loss of overage rent, when it occurs, is readily computed on the basis of past performance if adequate records of monthly sales volume have been maintained. It is important that the loss be computed on an actual monthly

171

basis rather than treated as one-twelfth of the annual total; Christmas comes but once a year and a shut-down during December is different from one in February. Coverage should also include loss of common area maintenance payments and any other tenant charges subject to abatement by lease terms. Particular attention should be given to the consequential loss resulting from a business interruption suffered by another owner, such as a department store; a protracted closing of the only department store in a center can have a disastrous effect on the volumes of the satellite stores.

The usual practice is to base the rental value premiums on the total amount of income considered probable for the covered period, but it is sometimes possible to obtain a premium adjustment when the actual collection is below the estimate. In the light of societal developments during the past few years, particular care should be accorded the endorsements and the exclusionary clauses relating to vandalism, civil commotion, and riot.

Ordinarily, an insurance company that pays its insured for a loss has the right of action against a third party who may have been responsible for the loss. This right of action is called the right of subrogation. There has been a trend in recent years to mutual waivers of that right of subrogation as between landlord and tenant, and insurance companies will usually agree provided the waiver is reciprocal. Since the insurance company waives potential reimbursement from a third party, the premium over a long term may be increased in the absence of reciprocity. As between landlord and tenant, a good way to handle the matter is to incorporate such an agreement in the lease.

The basic Fire and Extended Coverage policy, with rare exceptions, does not cover boilers and certain other kinds of machinery on which the insurance is written separately with companies specializing in that field. Also excluded are trucks, sweepers, and similar mobile equipment, the coverage of which is customarily made part of the casualty insurance. Losses sustained from theft, burglary, and embezzlement are also included in casualty, and all of these things will be spelled out in the excepted-property clause of the fire policy.

A lease provision not directly affecting the insurance contract but related to it—which can prove useful under certain conditions—is one limiting the landlord's obligation to rebuild in the event of a major loss. This takes the form of an option available to the landlord in the event of a loss rendering untenantable more than 50 percent, or a similar figure, of the floor area of the building occupied by the tenant, in which event the landlord may elect to terminate all of the leases within that building. In that circumstance, the owner may choose to rebuild in a different form, put the land to some other use, or simply pocket the insurance proceeds, subject to settlement with the mortgagee. Such an election, of course, depends on the identical provision being in all the leases, which can take some time to accomplish. However, the older a center becomes, the greater the potential value of such an arrangement.

Casualty Coverage

Two trends in recent times have served to emphasize the importance of casualty insurance. Court decisions have steadily enlarged the rights of users of property to receive compensation from the owner, or lessee, for injury or other damage; and court awards as the result of litigation have soared dramatically. The details of such coverage are too numerous and technical to warrant detailing here, and the negotiation for the insurance should be put in the hands of an expert. Yet a few matters somewhat peculiar to shopping centers bear mention and should be checked for inclusion by the manager.

- The named insureds, in addition to the owner, should include the contract manager and the merchants' association.

- Tenants should include the center owner's name as an additional insured in the stores' liability policies; this can minimize the owner's own liability insurance premiums.

- Certificates of insurance should be submitted to the landlord, through the operation of a lease provision, prior to occupancy, and the center manager should keep his file of certificates of insurance up to date.

- Sometimes, particularly in older centers, the landlord is liable for damage to the tenant's fixtures and stock in the event of roof or water-pipe leakage. This can be a serious matter and should be covered.

- If the center employs security personnel, false-arrest coverage is indicated.

- If there is any possibility of an employee using his own automobile on the center's business, on or off the premises, that should be covered.

- When the cost of the insurance is to be divided between the owner and the common area maintenance expense, an appro-

173

priate separation of the premium charges will minimize possible disputes with tenants.

■ It is essential that the merchants' association carry liability insurance, both in its interest and that of the owner. If a merchants' association contracts for outside events to be held on the parking lot or in the mall, there immediately arises the need to require the operators to carry liability insurance protecting the merchants' association, the owners, and the operators against claims that may arise because of the event. Such special events include fireworks, kiddie rides, circuses.

■ Service contractors should supply evidence of current insurance coverage in proper form, and the shopping center manager should keep that evidence in his files. Current expiration dates should be recorded so that the manager may request evidence of renewal coverage prior to the expiration of current coverage. All such policies should name the owner of the center as an additional insured.

Conditions Affecting Cost

In establishing the rate for the basic policy, by far the dominant consideration that fire and insurance companies take into account is a long list of factors in evaluating the degree of risk. Broadly speaking, the criteria fall into three categories, all of which are to some extent susceptible to improvement by the manager and thereby, over a period of time, to a lowering of the rate. The insurer looks at (1) the conditions bearing on the likelihood of fire occurring, (2) the conditions controlling the rapidity with which it can spread, and (3) the conditions having to do with the speed and effectiveness of the response. The first two categories are largely controlled by type of construction, quality of maintenance, nature of occupancy, and housekeeping practices of both landlord and tenants.

All insurance companies make periodic inspection of their insured properties, either with their own personnel or through the services of a local rating bureau. Part of the inspector's job is to point out existing flaws and make suggestions for their correction. Obviously, the manager cannot tear down and replace the original buildings in response to an inspector's criticisms, but sometimes the relatively inexpensive installation of a built-in fire-stop at a critical point, or a new door, will result in an offsetting saving of premium expense, either existing or contemplated. The really large difference in this respect is usually connected with the installation of sprinklers, which will be treated in a separate discussion, but the little alterations can be treated as expense items rather than capital additions, which can be worthwhile if done judiciously.

Quality of maintenance and housekeeping are concerns of the tenants as well as the landlord—far more the former than the latter since practically all shopping center fires start in a store. All leases contain a provision requiring the tenant to keep his premises in good order and repair and free from accumulations of rubbish and litter. Enforcement of the agreement, however, is a never-ending task that must be treated by the manager in an organized way. His most effective ally is customarily the local fire marshal, who will make periodic inspections anyway and can be encouraged to do so frequently and vigorously. In most communities, the fire marshal possesses considerable authority to take peremptory action in any situation that, in his judgment, poses a threat to human safety.

Certain types of business are considered by insurance companies as special hazards, and their presence will affect the rate not only on their own space but on the entire building of which they occupy a part. The two such types most commonly found in shopping centers are restaurants and supermarkets, and the insurance side effects of such tenants should be taken into account in evaluating rental terms. Where they were part of the original tenant package at the time the center was built, provisions would almost certainly have been made during construction to minimize the overall risk, but in re-leasing space as time goes on such prospective new tenants should be checked for the possibility of abnormal hazard.

The insurer's rating of the fire-protection system is generally centered on two matters: the quality of the local fire department and the availability and dependability of the water supply. Both factors are beyond the direct control of the manager, but over a period of time he can have some influence toward improving them if they are seriously substandard. If the center is being penalized for poor public facilities, so are all of the other properties within the affected district, and a manager with good ties to the community can sometimes serve as the catalyst of action toward correcting the deficiencies.

Of more immediate effect is the manager's effort to develop an internal capability for coping with fires pending the arrival of the professionals. Both insurance requirements and state law call for the installation and maintenance of extinguishers at convenient points

175

throughout the buildings, but more often than not store employes have absolutely no idea of how to use them. Some form of periodic instruction in the use of extinguishers, and other emergency procedures, can be provided by the local fire department. Such programs pay dividends in those vital few minutes after a fire is detected. If the center's policy has a $500 deductible feature, the difference between, say, $100 and $400 in damage per fire can add up during the course of a year. An active merchants' association can serve as the vehicle for conducting such a program.

During recent years, insurers have been looking with increasing disfavor on centers without sprinklers, particularly where they found an inadequate level of public protection, either in supply of water, capability of the department, or both. The result has been that, for some older properties, the installation of sprinklers has become more important than merely a question of rate—it has become the price of obtaining insurance at all. The insurance companies' attitude continued to harden throughout the 1960s and early 1970s, and it seems probable that in the near future the managers of all unsprinklered shopping centers are going to be faced with the problem. In the meantime, the differential in rates has become great enough to warrant a close look at installing sprinklers, even without the pressure of an ultimatum. A number of variables enter into the equation.

The starting point is the amount of premium saving versus the capital cost of a sprinkler installation, and viewed solely as a landlord matter the balance will rarely tip in the favor of sprinklers. Such a comparison is clearly unrealistic, however, in that it ignores the substantial benefit to the tenants insuring their stores' contents, which may in the aggregate be worth more than the center to the owner. From a practical standpoint the question boils down to two variables —how much will the tenants contribute and on what terms, and what financing is available to the owner on his share. Working out the agreements on a center-wide basis is a time-consuming matter; it involves patient negotiation coupled with careful cost-benefit analysis on the part of both landlord and tenant. As in all such situations, the composite result is going to depend partly on the negotiating skill of the manager and partly on the relative bargaining positions of the two parties. If the center is prospering and the future appears bright, collective agreement on a mutually equitable basis can usually be found.

A crash program to install sprinklers should never be undertaken unless the insurer is actually pointing the gun with a finger on the

176

trigger. If the idea is launched several years in advance of the planned installation, time is provided for tieing it in with some lease renewals and ensures that a leisurely pace can be taken with chain tenants, for such expensive decisions involve the chains' central offices in customarily slow bureaucratic processes. In this connection, care should be taken that all cost estimates are based on the installation being performed at a specified time in the future, that it be done on a relatively piecemeal basis, and that it be done without interrupting the center's daily business. If the center is prospering and the economics work out reasonably well, there is a good chance the tenants will accept their shares without much fuss. If conditions are less favorable, it becomes a matter of negotiating the contributions on a contingent basis until all the pieces are in place and the final decision can be made to proceed or put it aside and suffer the consequences.

Sometimes, smaller independent tenants may be willing to accept their share of a sprinklering program but have a problem coming up with the money. If the center owner has credit, a simple method of financing fair to both parties can generally be set up. The owner can pay the cost and take a three- to five-year installment note from the tenant at an interest rate slightly above the bank rate charged the owner for an equivalent borrowing. Larger tenants may find it advantageous to expense the cost of the installation as additional rent over a term of years rather than treat it as a capitalized leasehold investment. In short, putting together a center-wide sprinkler program is a good test of a manager's ingenuity and negotiating ability, but is well worth the effort if the alternative is that the owner himself pays for the installation with a massive infusion of purely preservative capital.

Personal Injury Claims

In those parts of the casualty insurance that apply to personal injury suffered by shoppers and other invitees, it is desirable to have coverage for very high dollar amounts to protect against the one-in-a-million possibility of a disaster affecting a large number of people. The excess coverage is relatively inexpensive whereas its absence has the potential for being ruinous. This has significance for the contract manager as well as the owner, since both will ordinarily be named in any litigation. Concomitantly, the same precaution should be built into leases by requiring high dollar limits in the tenants' insurance to protect against a possible spill-over onto the owner and/or manager from a deficiency in the tenants' coverage.

177

Other than for those specialized items such as boilers and automotive equipment, the basic premium for casualty insurance is calculated on the floor area of buildings, adjusted for the type of occupancy, and the land area of the parking and pedestrian facilities. It is then adjusted at intervals, usually annually, for the loss experience, which means that over a period of time the cost of insurance becomes closely related to the sums paid out by the insurer, plus his cost of processing the claims. Some centers have adopted the practice of handling minor claims directly on an agreed, or tacit, deductible basis, similar to that employed with fire insurance. But that approach tends to have four drawbacks:

- Dealing with persistent claimants who refuse to take "no" for an answer can be burdensome.

- The public relations aspect can get sticky; for example, when the mayor's wife comes in to talk about her car receiving a dented fender in the parking lot.

- What seems a minor claim sometimes turns into a major one, at which time the insurance company complains that its position has been damaged by inept handling before it got into the act.

- The effort generally ends up not saving much money anyway.

An alternative, particularly for a large center, is a negotiated arrangement whereby all claims, no matter how frivolous or insignificant, go to the insurer for handling. In cases for which no settlement is made, the insured's experience record is debited with a processing fee; if a pay-out results, it is split among insurer and insured up to an agreed ceiling on the latter's share. An approach of this sort has several possible variations in helping hold down the steadily increasing expense of casualty coverage, but in the final analysis the surest cost-cutting system is to run a safer center. A manager must be constantly alert to detect and correct hazardous conditions, and in this he can ordinarily count on willing assistance from the insurer. All major companies active in the casualty field have traveling safety engineers on tap to provide their customers with expert advice on a gratis basis.

No attempt will be made here to cover the various forms of insurance having to do with the employer-employee relationship, such as fidelity, workman's compensation, and hospitalization. It is assumed that a developer or management firm having payroll employees has the in-house capability of administering the related tax and insurance procedures.

Two final recommendations may be helpful in administering the insurance program. If all policies of every kind are timed to expire on the same date, it lessens the chance of oversight and tends to force an annual review of the program in its entirety. The total coverage should be concentrated among the lowest possible number of insurers; needless division can cause serious administrative problems in the event of a major loss.

Safely and economically insuring a shopping center is a complex and technical matter, one that managers are equipped to handle personally only if they have made a serious study of the field, which is rarely the case. A good rule might be: don't try it if you only think you know; unless you *know* you know, call in an expert.

QUESTIONS FOR DISCUSSION

1. *Why is insurance a matter of concern to the shopping center manager?*

2. *What is the distinction between an insurance agent and insurance broker?*

3. *Who is responsible for establishing and maintaining the center's insurance program?*

4. *Explain the deductible feature of an insurance policy.*

5. *In general, discuss a basic Fire and Extended Coverage insurance policy.*

6. *Explain how the "right of subrogation" affects your insurance policy.*

7. *Discuss items of importance that should be considered by the shopping center manager in evaluating casualty insurance.*

8. *Explain the conditions considered by insurance companies affecting the cost of a center's basic Fire and Extended policy.*

9. *Discuss the cost calculation of the basic premium of casualty insurance for shopping centers.*

10. *Give a complete exposition of the reasons for and the methods of tying in tenants' insurance with that of the shopping center.*

RECOMMENDED READING LIST

Magee, John H. and Oscar H. Serbein. **Property and Liability Insurance.** 4th ed. Homewood, Illinois: Richard D. Irwin, Inc., 1967. 944 pp.

Matwes, George J. and Helen Matwes. **Loss Control: A Safety Guidebook For Trades and Services.** New York: Van Nostrand Reinhold Company, 1975. 341 pp.

Schoening, Edwin D. **Basics of Shopping Center Insurance.** New York: International Council of Shopping Centers, 1973. 8 pp.

CHAPTER **11**

Enclosing the Open Center

Very few enclosed shopping centers were built before the early 1960s, and when the trend did start enclosure was at first confined to the larger regional-type developments. By the end of the decade, the form was so well established that new regionals of open mall design had become a rarity. During the 1970s the enclosed mall concept was extended to include smaller centers. Today a major share of the larger community-type centers, particularly those in areas of climate extremes, and a number of small convenience shopping centers are enclosed.

Because it provides protection from the weather and a climate-controlled environment, the enclosed mall design is well liked by the shopping public. Shoppers also appear to be favorably impressed by the usually more compact arrangement of the enclosed center as contrasted with the open one. In large projects, the enclosed concept has fostered the design of two-level malls which contributes to the proximity factor while also effecting some saving in land use, an important consideration in developing on high-cost land.

Initially, the swing toward enclosed malls was viewed with something less than enthusiasm in retail circles. The dissidents based their reluctance on three contentions: (1) they feared (needlessly) that without a prominent entrance directly from the parking lot they would lose visual identity to the approaching shopper; (2) they felt (correctly) that the greater capital costs would exert a strong upward pres-

180

sure on minimum rent guarantees, and (3) they foresaw (also correctly) a substantial rise in the levies for common area maintenance. The corollary development of bilevel malls also troubled some retailers who felt that whichever level they chose, or were assigned to by the developer, would inevitably turn out to be the one with the lesser traffic.

Such reservations on the part of prospective tenants were shortlived, soon swept away by the demonstrated acceptance of the new form by their customers. As things now stand, it is becoming increasingly more difficult to attract and hold high-performance retailers in open mall centers. The difficulties of the owners, particularly among the larger open centers, are exacerbated by the rapidly increasing competition in all of the major metropolitan markets and most of the secondary ones.

For nearly all of the 25-year period following World War II, the metropolitan areas of the United States and Canada expanded steadily, both in population and geographic dispersion. About 1970, in all except a few areas, both kinds of growth began to slow, and the demographic outlook is for a continuance of that trend. In a sense, the shopping center industry has pretty well run out of frontier and, to an increasing extent, new developments are largely overlapping the trade areas of existing centers.

At least partially offsetting that condition, however, is the strong probability that present and impending governmental constraints will limit the construction of new shopping centers. Various antipollution laws, land-use controls, and a generally more critical attitude of local regulatory bodies are already having a dampening effect on construction and the outlook is for more of the same. Predicting the outcome of these new societal forces on the dynamics of retailing is an uncertain business, but one result that appears likely is the heightened locational value of existing shopping centers, particularly those capable of expanding.

Today, a considerable number of owners of open shopping centers ten or more years old, including some small ones, are faced with a complex problem in real estate economics. On the one hand they see the competitive threat from enclosed centers, present or potential, that offer the shopper, in that respect, a superior facility; on the other they perceive an emerging pattern of social concerns that may limit the expansion of retail store space. The one trend accelerates the functional obsolescence of their property, the other prolongs its economic life.

181

Such is the background against which the individual owner must ponder the wisdom of making a new, major capital investment.

This chapter examines the management activities related to the enclosure of an existing open center, and the additions to revenue-producing area that almost invariably accompany it. As in the rest of the book, the focus will be on the management function. There is no attempt to cover architectural design and engineering, construction materials and methods, leasing and financing details, or any of the other aspects that are, by their nature, peculiar to the individual project and have no general application.

Before proceeding, we should warn the reader that this topic necessitates a new use of terms. Throughout this book the term "manager" has connoted an individual employed by the owner, on a salaried or fee basis, to be in active charge of supervising the operation of a shopping center, and the material has been presented from the perspective of such a person. When discussing the internal procedures connected with an enclosure, however, we cannot use this definition. The scope of the enterprise, both as to the amount of money involved and the long-term effect of the actions, mandates a high level of ownership involvement. The appropriate designation in this chapter, therefore, would be "the management" rather than "the manager" and wherever the latter term is used it should be understood as referring to the individual in direct charge of that particular phase of the operation. Unavoidably there will be some confusion in differentiating and the reader needs make his own determination within the context of use.

The process of enclosing a previously open center does not lend itself to a diffusion of authority. Once the project moves from the exploratory to the operational stage there occurs a rapid proliferation of interrelated activities that can become chaotic if not tightly controlled. Obviously, in the case of a large center the work will have to be distributed among several people having various capabilities, but it is important that their efforts be coordinated by one person having an overall grasp of the undertaking sufficient to understand how each part fits into the whole. The performance of that individual and his principal on-the-job assistants will have much to do with the quality of the end result. It is no time to hire cheap help.

The Importance of Added Leasable Area

Based on industry experience to date, there does not appear to be any minimum size below which enclosure becomes impractical.

There is, however, some evidence indicating that feasibility is related to the ratio of GLA added by enclosure to existing GLA, regardless of size. If the market demand and physical characteristics permit, building a substantial addition as well as enclosing the center is much more economical than a straight enclosure. Typically, the new space will result in a greater share of the overall cost being borne by the tenants as a whole compared to that assumed by the owner, and that will in turn act to improve the financing ratio.

If a significant expansion is not possible, and particularly if the lack is the result of market conditions, the owner is faced with a hard decision, one that does not reduce to mathematically orderly terms. If the center is experiencing increasing competitive pressure from more modern facilities, the management dilemma serves to dramatize the nature of the basic question confronting every owner, to be resolved in the light of his reading of the future. Reduced to the simplest terms, there are three choices: enclose, sell, or sit tight and hope for the best.

Part of the difficulty in arriving at a decision in the borderline cases stems from the lack of industry experience on which to base judgments. The pioneering days of the shopping center as such have been over for 20 years, but the life-prolonging or rejuvenating effect of an enclosure still is largely unknown. At this time only a scant handful of previously open centers with completed enclosures have been operative in that condition for as long as five years. Certainly all of them are proclaimed to be successful, and in terms of acceptance by the shopping public that appears to be so. However, there is as yet no conclusive evidence that the substantial reinvestment frequently required represented the optimum use of the capital. It will take several more years to accumulate sufficient experience on which to base a useful set of guidelines.

If the competitive threat is such that an owner feels he cannot sit still, the choice is between withdrawing the accumulated equity for other uses or plowing a large part of it back into the property. Almost by definition, a shopping center being considered for enclosure is at least ten years old and successful enough to have built up a substantial equity. In this instance, the true equity is not what the books show; it is the market value of the property less the obligations that would have to be discharged out of the proceeds if it were sold.

In making the choice, an owner must weigh, among other things, the time-value of money in the context of his overall business interests. If the capital is withdrawn, either by sale or refinancing, it immediately becomes available for use in other ventures; if it is reinvested in an enclosure the probable result will be a sacrifice of nearterm income in favor of greater future earnings. Since the trade-off between cash in hand and future income introduces the element of risk, an evaluation of the future economic life of the center becomes central to the owner's decision. Determination of future economic life should be based on a study of the socioeconomic trends of the trade area rather than on the physical life expectancy of the regenerated center itself. Typically, the magnitude of the added investment will be such as to call for amortization over a period as long as 15 years, and stability of income for at least that long is an imperative. Some of the elements going into a future economic life study are set forth in Chapter 7 in the section "Evaluating Future Income."

The Go or No-Go Decision

When management confronts the issue of enclosing an open center, the go or no-go decision can depend on circumstances so simple and clear that the answer is obvious or so complicated and obscure that it requires a blind, gut decision. Enclosure of a prosperous two-department store open regional with ample land and a third department store knocking at the door obviously does not call for much head scratching. The manager not so fortunately situated, however, is likely to follow a more plodding course.

The initial move is to ascertain whether there are any virtually insurmountable obstacles that make enclosure unworkable. An example might be a marginal water supply that can be enlarged only at prohibitive cost, coupled with an inability to secure insurance on the greater risk of an enclosed center unless the water situation is improved. Another example would be a negative attitude exhibited by the anchor or key tenants as regards extending their leases or operating agreements. It might possibly be economically sound to proceed without financial participation by the anchors. However, in the absence of assurance that the anchors' presence will continue for an adequate period, general tenant participation and long-term financing will almost certainly be unobtainable.

It is a good idea to be discreet while determining whether enclosure is indeed feasible. If it becomes necessary to let the matter drop, the less talk about it the better. Taken out of context, a decision not to proceed could be interpreted by tenants as a vote of no confidence in the future by management, and that could be harmful to any

184

alternative plans for improving the operation.

Once the decision to undertake a full-blown study has been made, however, the reverse becomes true and maximum exposure to the tenants is desirable. Since they all will be affected to some degree, and their cooperation is an essential factor in obtaining the optimum result, every effort should be made to involve them in the planning process early in the game. The more they feed on facts rather than rumors, the healthier it will be for all concerned.

Scope of Management Involvement

When the proposal to enclose has passed the initial critical screening and has become an ongoing activity, the management must begin working in close harmony with five elements:

1. The tenants, both present and prospective.
2. The architectural and engineering team.
3. The construction contractors, including those doing tenant work.
4. The source of financing.
5. The general public.

Enclosing an open shopping center, particularly if it includes a substantial addition with the concomitant rearrangement of tenancies and parking facilities, is an extremely complicated process. Individuals having experience with both describe it as a more difficult management task than developing a new center of comparable size. The difficulties stem from two characteristics not common to a new development. One is the necessity of accommodating all construction activity, from start to finish, with minimum interference with the existing businesses; the other is related to problems inherent in conducting major negotiations with tenants who already have established contractual rights.

An enclosure differs from a new development in another important way. An experienced developer can prepare a financial pro forma for a proposed shopping center with a fairly good degree of accuracy as to both capital cost and anticipated income. However, the figures for an enclosure are harder to project, particularly on the cost side, because of the much greater incidence of unforeseen contingencies. A fairly precise projection of income to be derived from added leasable area can be made, but the increase to be obtained from the existing space will depend on some not readily predictable negotiations. It is

185

this dual uncertainty as to cost and income that makes the final decision—to either go ahead or drop it—in marginal cases so difficult. It also helps to explain why a high ratio of new to existing space improves feasibility since it results in a greater proportion of both cost and income being more firmly predictable. In those marginal cases where the probable financial outcome is unacceptable it is sometimes possible to resolve the dilemma by finding a buyer having either a higher level of optimism or a lower level of investment expectation.

The remainder of the chapter is devoted to some observations about a manager's activities as they relate to the five elements with which he will be dealing if the project goes forward. A shopping center enclosure can, of course, be as simple as walling in the sidewalk fronting a strip of stores. For the purpose of this exposition, however, the comments will be in the context of a regional center where the program includes adding a significant amount of new space.

Types of Space to Be Leased

It is appropriate to consider first the role of a manager in his dealings with the tenants. This is the phase of the operation in which he is likely to be most actively engaged personally, and it is by all odds the most sensitive in terms of long-run effects. Architectural and construction mistakes are usually quickly apparent and either they can be remedied or do not significantly impair the future functioning of the property. Inept handling of the public during construction may ruffle some feathers, both tenant and customer, but such irritations tend to be short-lived. In conducting the leasing program, however, the results of mistakes made, or opportunities missed, can be felt for many years to come. For the long term, that is where the money is made, or not made, as the case may be.

The first step in this part of the program, taken hand-in-hand with the architectural-engineering team, is a determination of the amount of additional leasable space it will be economically sound to create. For study purposes, the space to be added may be divided into three categories, with each having distinctive economic characteristics.

- Type One consists of kiosks, either free-standing or of the window-box variety attached to the face of what would otherwise be a blank wall.

- Type Two is represented by the enlargement of existing stores as happens when a new storefront line is established at what had

186

been the edge of the sidewalk canopy and the store interiors are extended out to the new line, or when existing stores are subdivided.

■ Type Three is space provided in what are essentially new structures, the addition of which is completely optional.

From the owner's viewpoint the economics of Type One space are just about perfect. In a successful center such space is in strong demand, produces high per-square-foot rent, and the entire capital cost of the installation is customarily borne by the lessee. The amount of such space to be incorporated into the new leasing plan is ordinarily limited only by aesthetic consideration and the necessity of maintaining an orderly flow of shopper traffic through the courts and mall. Major tenants may provide a further restraining influence by insisting that the areas near their entrances not be overly cluttered. The kiosk income is quite predictable and highly profitable, but it is rarely so lucrative that it becomes a major factor in the pro forma projection. The estimated total income should be included, but exact size and placement of structures and determination of occupants is best left until enclosure is completed and the pedestrian traffic pattern is evident.

The additional income to be derived from the Type Two areas, on the other hand, cannot be predicted with certainty, and the degree of profitability can vary widely within the same center. This area can produce substantial added income, and this is the arena in which the manager proves his skill. The actual net amount of added leasable floor area will be largely dictated by design considerations, but its productivity, when coupled with that of the existing space, will be a result of the imagination and ingenuity brought to bear.

The extent to which design considerations will influence the amount of Type Two space to be added will depend on the configuration of the individual center. The controlling factor is the ratio of finished common area within the enclosure to leasable area of the completed project. A generally accepted design standard for recently built enclosed centers is to hold the square footage of finished common area to around 25 percent of that portion of the leasable area expected to pay for its operation and maintenance. To enclose an open center that has spacious courts and malls without changing existing interior building lines can result in an excessive ratio of common area. This can yield two undesirable results. To avoid a barnlike

187

appearance requires the introduction of either costly amenities such as planters and pools, or an unaesthetic and potentially uneconomic proliferation of kiosks. Worse, however, is likely to be the extravagant burden on the tenants to cover the expense of lighting, heating, cooling, cleaning, and maintaining the area, which can place the center at a competitive disadvantage within its trade area. The management cannot forget that, in the long run, the primary level of competition between shopping centers is not for shoppers; it is for those desirable tenants who will power the drive for the consumer's dollar. There are substantial costs involved in producing Type Two space and the manner in which they are distributed between landlord and tenant obviously has much to do with the feasibility of the project as a whole. More on this later.

In the discussion of replacement leasing in Chapter 8 it was noted that at no time is a shopping center populated by the ideal mix of tenants. External forces in the trade area are in a constant state of flux, as are the collective internal affairs of the tenants. It was stressed that the manager should constantly study individual performance so that at the appropriate time he can make changes calculated to optimize productivity of the leasable area in his charge. An impending enclosure presents opportunity for a major acceleration toward that objective.

Establishing a Game Plan

The first step in that direction is a systematic analysis designed to categorize the entire tenant body into four groups, with the understanding that in some individual cases the dividing line will be blurred.

1. Those tenants whose past performance, trend, and potential indicate they could profitably use additional space.

2. Those who appear to be adequately sized for the future in their present area.

3. Tenants who would probably operate more profitably for both themselves and the landlord in a smaller space.

4. The tenants who, for one reason or another, the center would be better off without.

Obviously, the rearrangement finally achieved is not going to exactly match the guidelines as suggested by the study. The tenants will have something to say about that, and the final product will reflect the outcome of many separate negotiations. However, such an exercise is the essential prelude to preparing a leasing plan for the Type Three space, and thus establishing an overall game plan before working plans are drawn. Sketches and schematics are quickly and cheaply altered, changes in working drawings are time-consuming and expensive, and once construction has started changes can become prohibitively costly. The greater the extent to which the principal elements can be discussed in advance with important tenants, both present and prospective, the more valid the plan will prove to be as the project proceeds.

Ideally, all of the new agreements with both present tenants and those to be added should have been worked out and put on paper before the working drawings are begun, but this is rarely possible in other than relatively small, simple projects. In the case of large centers the costs, and to some extent physical details, cannot be determined with sufficient accuracy until construction is actually underway. The usual practice is to obtain a letter of intent stating the nature of the agreement and setting forth in general terms the principal understandings that will be spelled out in detail as the required information becomes available. The final decision to proceed is generally based on the number of such letters in hand.

There are pitfalls, however, in using letters of intent for such a purpose. Industry experience establishes that the ease and certainty with which they are subsequently translated into a formal instrument is dependent on the comprehensiveness and clarity with which they express the understanding between the parties. Occasionally a tenant will renege because of his changed circumstances, but trouble more often stems from a tenant's contention that a pertinent fact was either withheld or misrepresented in the discussions leading up to the letter. It is essential that the manager, or other management representative, charged with obtaining letters of intent has a thorough grasp of what is planned and then exercises extreme care in seeing that the tenant is fully and accurately informed.

Type Three space is the category that presents the real problem of how much to add, assuming that an upper limit is not arbitrarily imposed by the amount of land available to meet the enlarged parking requirement. The economics of Type Three are relatively clear-cut—cost estimates will be fairly reliable and rental terms can be forecast with some assurance. The relationship of cost to income will be approximately constant providing the amount of space added is not so great as to exhaust the market. And herein lies the crux of the problem.

Certainly in the great majority of situations it becomes a case of more is better, and the added leasable floor space will act to increase sales volume of the existing tenants because the enlarged group will attract more shoppers. Such a result is particularly to be anticipated when the addition includes a major store that will bring shoppers who would not otherwise be likely to visit that center. However, as with most other good things in life, it can be overdone, and the trick lies in stopping just short of that point.

It must be assumed that benefit from the increased traffic will not automatically be evenly distributed among all of the original tenants; some will benefit, some will feel no effect, and some may be harmed, temporarily or permanently. The maximum return on investment from an addition is realized by constructing the optimum amount of space the market will readily absorb at a profitable rent level, and then populating it with tenants who will individually and collectively best complement the stores already there. The preceding statement offers two separate objectives that are actually inseparable parts of the ultimate goal—to have the finished product also represent the maximum return on the total capital then invested.

In searching for that optimum point, the equation is to some extent simplified by the rigidities of two characteristics of shopping center economics: the absence of significant economies of scale in production, and the almost total lack of price elasticity in selling. The unit cost of producing and maintaining a square foot of additional GLA, with its supporting parking, is nearly constant regardless of quantity. In addition, the available supply of desirable tenants will not be significantly increased by reducing the price as expressed in rental terms. In taking aim at how much Type Three space to add, the management is not bedeviled with the problem of trying to hit a moving target. Rather, it is a matter of measuring the size and nature of the trade-area market for goods and services in excess of that already being attracted to the center, and then determining the most efficient way of housing those tenants likely to bring in that trade.

If the proposed addition is proportionately minor, the danger of going economically astray by fouling up the tenant mix is correspondingly small. A major addition, however, warrants spending some time and money on a reasonably thorough market analysis that will pinpoint the potential uses of the new space which will best complement what is already there. The same study will, of course, serve as a guide in the process of rearranging the existing occupancies and selecting the kiosk tenants.

Even if there has been no previous market study to provide a starting point, an investigation of potential uses of added space will generally be accomplished quicker and cheaper than one of comparable scope involving a proposed new center. The sales records of the established tenants indicate trends, the trade area is well delineated, and the competition is identifiable. Working with that kind of information, plus the original study (if available and not too old), a relatively modest effort can take most of the guesswork out of how much new space to build and what to put in it. Keep in mind that the expression "more is better" is not exemplified by simply pouring water into the soup.

The Pro Forma

When a hypothetical rearrangement of the existing space has been put on paper and a tentative decision made on the amount and location of the leasable area to be added, it is time to prepare the pro forma on which to base the final decision. The financial projections included in the pro forma should identify all items of capital cost, with their timing; all future income, with its timing; and the future operating expense to be deducted from the gross in order to arrive at the net income applicable to justifying the capital investment. The three elements, including carrying charges on the capital cost, need to be projected far enough ahead to permit meaningful comparison with a similar projection based on maintaining status quo. (The format of such studies is discussed briefly in the section on "Long-Range Projections" in the final chapter of this book.) In this case, the projection should cover a period of at least ten years following completion of the proposed enclosure.

The process of assembling the components of the pro forma for an enclosure is generally similar to that employed for a new development. Of the differences that do exist, only one is helpful. Estimates of income and expenses can be based on figures from previous years. All of the other differences, however, have the effect of impairing accuracy—a weakness the management must recognize and make allowance for. The sections that follow will examine those differences and the manner in which they complicate financial planning.

191

Sharing of Capital Costs

In new development, standards have been developed for computing and distributing the capital cost of buildings, as distinguished from site work. The developer provides at his cost the basic shell and gives the tenant a negotiated dollar amount as an allowance toward the cost of completing what are essentially the real estate items within the leased premises. The tenant provides the decor and specialty finishing work peculiar to his occupancy at his own cost. In an enclosing project, the lease agreements with tenants in newly created space usually follow the familiar pattern and, as previously noted, kiosk construction is customarily wholly at occupant cost. In both cases, provision for tenant participation in maintenance of the common area, including its heating and cooling, is premised on the space being in an enclosed mall center.

Both capital costs and future income and operating expense of added building area and kiosks are predictable with reasonable accuracy in advance of even a tentative decision to proceed. However, when the financial planning gets to the heart of the matter, the enclosure itself and agreements with the existing tenants, things become much more complicated. The principal complication, as noted earlier, stems from the fact that the other parties to the negotiations are not prospects, to be accepted or rejected at the owner's discretion; they are tenants in possession with whatever rights are explicit in their remaining lease terms.

Two separate lines of negotiations are involved and in neither are the financial implications apparent until after negotiations are well started. One area of negotiation is the division between landlord and tenant of the capital costs to be incurred; the other concerns the tenant's ongoing financial obligations in the form of rent, tax participation, contribution to various common activities, and term of lease. Since capital and ongoing charges, when aggregated, become occupancy expense to the tenant, they are interrelated and involve a certain amount of trade-off as negotiation proceeds. In presenting them here there is an unavoidable tendency to discuss the details as though they existed independently of each other, and it is incumbent on the reader to keep in mind that in practice the two become merged.

Two kinds of capital costs are incurred in enclosure construction and concurrently or thereafter within it: those within or directly related to the individual tenant space, and those having to do with the common area. Illustrative of the former would be a new storefront, internal sprinklers, or the extension of interior finishes and mechanical systems if the space is enlarged. The latter category is exemplified by the roof and enclosing walls, new flooring, the mechanical installations to light and climate-condition the mall, and the overall exterior refurbishing of buildings and parking area that gives the whole center a bright new appearance. Some costs are not clear-cut, such as modification of the climate-control installation within a store to make it compatible with the mall system. But such items are usually minor enough to be split on an agreed basis without too much trouble.

The costs related directly to the individual leased areas are substantial even when there is no change in size, and only the addition of sprinklers is in any way self-liquidating. As noted in the chapter on insurance, the premium savings on content coverage will usually balance out the sprinkler investment over a period of time. The major cost to the tenant, however, will be a new storefront with its related peripheral improvements—and that is a must. An old, weatherbeaten, outdoor-type façade in a newly enclosed shopping center is a glaring anachronism; it is harmful to the tenant and his immediate neighbors, and to the image of the center as a whole. Its replacement with an indoor-type open front will automatically lead to a redecorating of the entire interior and at least partial refixturing. Taken with the necessary revisions of the lighting and HVAC systems it will represent a sizable investment, but in the eye of the shopper the store becomes an attractive new entity.

Generally, unless a large majority of the tenants are prepared to absorb all of the costs related to their own alteration and renovation, and agree to proceed with alterations in a timely manner, an enclosure will not be economically feasible. Marked reluctance to do this will signal the owner that there is rough weather ahead on two counts: (1) it will be difficult to improve the financial terms of the leases sufficiently to support the added investment, and (2) the owner has little chance of obtaining any significant capital contribution toward the costs related to the structural and other common areas.

Upgrading the leases is imperative, and if preliminary soundings indicate any serious difficulties are ahead the validity of the project becomes suspect. In the absence of a reasonably enthusiastic attitude on the part of the tenant group as a whole, an enclosure, other than of a quite simple form, is unlikely to be a prudent investment. The importance of the extent to which the present tenants can be persuaded to contribute to construction cost outside their leased areas tends to be directly related to the ratio of to-be-added GLA (previously referred to as Type Three space) to the existing amount. If the added space constitutes a major expansion, the costs of enclosing what is already there become less significant. When the Type Three space is minor, the extent of tenant contribution can become a controlling factor. In most such cases, the final go or no-go decision will largely depend on the extent to which the tenants are prepared to share that cost.

Tenant contribution to the enclosing cost may take various forms and is usually related to the area of the store, the volume of business, or a combination of the two. Most frequently, contributions are collected as a monthly surcharge, not recoverable via overage rent, assessed on a square-foot basis. The surcharge is sometimes a fixed rate charged for a uniform period of time. More often, however, it is weighted in accordance with a publicized formula that takes into account several variables. Among the factors commonly considered are: size of space, amount of mall frontage, proportion of mall level to upper or lower secondary space, and future length of lease term. Because the configuration of shopping centers and their internal pedestrian traffic patterns are so extremely varied, no simple, universal formula can be developed to determine tenant contributions. Each center constitutes a singular case to be thought out as such by the manager or someone else familiar with its workings and peculiarities. It is essential that the final assessment plan reflect as nearly as possible the relative benefits to be realized by the tenants, and if perceived as such by them will be accepted with no more than minor quibbling.

Exactly when to discontinue levying an enclosure assessment is a matter of individual judgment and, in most cases, does not take place until construction is well advanced. The timing is usually then determined on a pragmatic basis of what the market will bear. The most common practice appears to be to include the assessment in the leases of all tenants (new ones in both Type Two and Type Three spaces as well as the holdovers) expected to be in business at the time the enclosure is completed. In a strong center, such a procedure is usually accepted. As construction progresses, however, the enclosure becomes increasingly an accomplished fact in the eyes of prospective new tenants and their resistance to being asked to help pay for it stiffens. The likely result is that the requirement will have been quietly abandoned as completion becomes imminent.

A variation sometimes employed, alone or in combination with an area-based formula, calls for the tenant to pay increased percentage rent in the form of a temporary stepped-up rate on all sales volume in excess of that derived from the immediate past record, with a ceiling on the total amount thus collected. As a supplement the approach has some merit and is relatively easy to sell, but as the main provision it has serious deficiencies. It is inapplicable to tenants not subject to percentage rent, such as banks and travel agencies, or to newcomers signed up in anticipation of the enclosure. In addition, because of its contingent nature, this approach is of little help in the long-term financing.

For a relatively simple enclosure of a small center that has a limited number of tenants, it is sometimes possible to secure lump sum contributions. This plan has the obvious appeal of simplicity. Less obvious are some potential shortcomings in that approach if the owner is in anything less than a dominant position vis-a-vis the tenants. There is the universal circumstance that people tend to be more tight-fisted about cash on the barrelhead than when paying on an installment plan. There is a certain discipline inherent in amending a lease in accordance with a well-defined formula; without it there is danger that the procedure will deteriorate into a pass-the-hat situation with the fair-share concept dependent on voluntaryism. Naturally, whatever method of allocation is chosen, the degree of success realized will, in large measure, be governed by the relative bargaining position of landlord and tenant. In marginal situations the decisive factor will be the negotiating skill and ingenuity of the manager.

In practically every shopping center, particularly larger ones, there will be a number of tenants unable or unwilling to participate financially in a program of enclosing. In dealing with them it is important to differentiate between the two dispositions. Those unable to pay are typically small shops, the so-called "mom and pop" type, that do not have either accumulated capital or access to it. If they are desirable occupants, as rent-payers or contributors to the quality of the mix, a manager will ordinarily make an effort to assist them. For example, in renovating the store itself, help might take the form of a direct loan to be repaid out of a surcharge on future percentage rent, or it might consist of guaranteeing a bank loan. The same treatment could be accorded the tenant's share of the structural cost contribution, or that obligation might be waived altogether. The less said about the latter the better, but even if this arrangement becomes generally known few other tenants will be upset so long as the reason is apparent.

Replacing Tenants

Very often, those tenants that are unwilling, rather than unable, to contribute to the enclosure are the same ones it would be desirable to replace. In such cases, if the remaining term of the lease is relatively short it is advisable to have a frank talk with the tenant principals, as soon as a firm decision has been made to proceed with enclosure, in an effort to agree on a surrender of possession at the time of greatest mutual convenience. From the landlord's standpoint, the tenant should vacate early enough so that a replacement tenant can remodel, fixture, and be open for business in time to participate in the official reopening, but not so early in the construction period as to cause undue loss of rental income. The tenant's preference is more likely to be influenced by a combination of two factors: the seasonal characteristics peculiar to his operation and the extent to which he anticipates the construction activity will depress his volume. Frequently, a manager will find it expedient to offer some sort of special deal on the rent to either accelerate or delay the vacating.

A much more difficult situation is one akin to that described in the second illustrative example discussed in Chapter 8, in which the lease has several years to run but the space is relatively unproductive for the landlord and of marginal profitability to the tenant. In this case, the landlord is faced with years of money-losing eyesore and the tenant has no incentive to do other than sit comfortably still. If the tenant adamantly refuses to give up occupancy, and the space is large enough to be practicably subdivided, the answer to the problem may lie in the kind of deal explored in the referential example. Usually the best solution, and the only one involving areas too small for effective division, is to buy out the lease if it can be accomplished at a worthwhile cost/benefit price.

As in the example, determining the ceiling price calls for two parallel financial projections covering the remaining years of the lease—one setting forth the probable outcome of maintaining status quo, and the other depicting the possible results from obtaining possession of the space. The latter, of course, will need to take into account the availability and cost of capital. An intangible to be pondered by the manager is the possible negative impact on shoppers of an unmodernized store amid the general refurbishing, which may be important if the space is large and prominently situated. A partial amelioration of such a problem, all else having failed, can sometimes be achieved by encouraging other tenants to apply peer pressure toward

196

at least a minimum program of freshening the appearance of storefront, entrance, and display windows.

If the circumstances recommend an attempt to buy out the lease, it may be presumed that the tenant is already alert to such a possibility and has been giving it some thought. The finesse with which the initial approach is executed can influence the final result, and probably the surest way to get off on the wrong foot is to use the landlord's attorney as leadoff man. The lawyers will have their day when it is time to draw the termination papers, but the purely economic issues first must be resolved by the parties at interest and negotiations can be less friendly if the tenant gets a feeling that he is being subtly threatened with some sort of legal action. It is usually unproductive to simply ask the tenant how much money he wants to surrender possession. Such an approach tends to create the illusion that a blank check is being offered and the negotiation can quickly degenerate into a bluffing contest. Occasionally, of course, a tenant with several years remaining on his lease is doing so poorly that, given a face-saving excuse, he is fairly certain to move. In such a case, the proper tactic may be the direct offer of a relatively modest sum in an implied take-it-or-leave-it manner.

In the more typical case, however, the tenant is in a relaxed bargaining posture, and it is important to launch the discussion on a businesslike basis and try to keep it that way. It is usually desirable that the initial approach be made by either the center owner or a management representative who is empowered to make the agreement rather than serving simply as an intermediary. A good starting point is an unambiguous expression of intent to reimburse the tenant, within the limits of the landlord's ability to do so, for the losses he may incur in vacating within a specified period of time. Presenting the objective in a forthright manner implies that the owner knows what he wants, how much he is prepared to pay for it, and is ready to do business. Thus, getting off on the right foot can expedite the negotiations and, also important, reduce the possibility of mutual ill feeling if there is a negative outcome.

A useful technique for keeping the negotiations orderly is to proceed in two well-defined stages: (1) identify by mutual agreement the nature of all potential losses to be included and, (2) agree on how each is to be computed and the maximum reparation for each. The financial penalties will typically cover such matters as the unamortized portion of leasehold improvements; the unamortized costs of fixtures and equipment, less the recovery from resale; the loss on inventory resulting from forced liquidation or other removal; the expenses of physically moving out; and the expenses incidental to terminating employees and canceling service contracts such as advertising and insurance. The costs of all of the foregoing can be estimated in advance and a dollar amount determined after the fact. The same cannot be said for loss of anticipated profits, which is a topic sure to turn up during the first stage. Future profit in any type of retail or service business, other than in the very short term, is a highly nebulous thing and every effort should be made to avoid any consideration of it. Far better is it to assume a generous stance on the reasonably calculable loss than to get bogged down in an issue as subjective as anticipated profit.

Revising Leases

The other broad area of negotiations, having to do with revision of existing leases, will include most of the tenants in possession at the time enclosure is being considered. Since the center typically will be at least 10 years old, termination dates of the leases usually will be distributed in a random pattern over the succeeding 10 or more years. It is also typical to a center of that age that many, if not most, leases will contain provisions which are disadvantageous to the landlord under any conditions and intolerable as applied to the proposed circumstances. Some of the deficiencies needing correction will stem from weakness in the landlord's bargaining position at the earlier time, some from changes in accepted industry practice, and some from previously altered relationships within the center itself.

Every lease will have to be amended, supplemented, or otherwise altered to add the heating, ventilating, and air conditioning costs of the mall to common area maintenance expense, to establish the conditions governing storefront replacement, and to provide for participation in the structural construction cost. Further, the enclosing process will entail numerous minor changes in store size as well as the major ones undertaken to improve space productivity by reallocating it among tenants. Additionally, the remaining lease term of those tenants incurring substantial costs of their own must be adjusted to accommodate their need for a suitable amortization period. And, finally, the basic lease instrument used for the Type Three space will undoubtedly differ in both substance and form from the one previously used. In a large center, attempting to cope with all such changes, and correct existing deficiencies, by amending the present leases creates a jungle of paperwork, both in the doing and in future interpretation.

A fresh start with a redesigned basic lease form is a much more orderly procedure, one less prone to errors and omissions and easier to administer as the years go by. An important advantage of this approach is that the landlord can take the initiative in effecting changes designed to correct previous provisions, or the lack of them, detrimental to his interest. Negotiation incidental to revising the lease is essentially an adversary proceeding—gain for the landlord viewed, at least theoretically, as a loss for the tenant and vice versa. In such a situation, there is often a tactical advantage in making the other party assume the burden of presenting the arguments in support of either additions or deletions in the document under discussion.

The number, identity, and extent of the lease modifications will, of course, vary from center to center and from tenant to tenant. In preparing the revised basic form, it is helpful to pretend that the whole project is a completely new development and use language accordingly. The best current industry practice can be followed in such matters as common area maintenance, tax participation, store hours, and promotional activities, which form the background against which to establish individual rental terms. Needless to say, the basic instrument would make no reference to such things as offsets, ceilings, or tenant options and would contain nothing indicating such things ever existed. As in all such matters, the end result of such a broad-based renegotiation will be determined by two factors: the relative bargaining strength of the parties and the level of skill demonstrated by the center manager.

Establishing Priorities

As noted earlier, all discussions of financial matters with existing tenants have two objectives: (1) to obtain their greatest possible participation in the various capital expenditures required, and (2) to upgrade their lease obligations to the extent possible. Because these objectives are interrelated in all stages and finally merge in an overall lease agreement, they cannot be negotiated separately beyond the very early stages. Since it is unlikely, no matter how strong his position, that the manager will reach all of his goals, it is advisable to establish a system of priorities, as was discussed at some length in Chapter 8. Priorities for an enclosure might consist of two parts, the basic priority as between capital contribution and improved lease terms, and the specific priorities applied to the individual leases. Critical to the whole process is a continual realistic evaluation of the rate of progress with appropriate loosening or tightening of demands from time to time. If substantial physical rearrangement of tenants is required, a second system of priorities is indicated. The purpose this time would be to identify the sequence in which individual negotiations should be brought to a conclusion in order to clear the way for the ones dependent on their outcome. To a minor extent the workings of such a system would also have a bearing on the sequence of leasing Type Three space.

In dealing with tenants, it is essential that management have an adequate study of the market, a well-thought-out game plan, skilled personnel, and a constant monitoring of results. Lacking any one of the four components can at best bring some disappointments and at worst can result in disaster.

Planning Construction

Obviously management's first responsibility in the actual construction work is to select the architectural and engineering team, which may consist of a single entity or, within limits, various specialists. In a major enclosing project the interrelationships are so complex and pervading as to make a strong case against dispersion of responsibility in either professional services or construction. Unless the management has available a strong in-house capability of its own, the preferred course is to employ a single professional firm and, subsequently, a single general contractor. Specialists such as a traffic engineer can be associated with the architectural firm for administrative purposes and thus lessen the danger of the left hand not knowing what the right one is doing. Assuming availability and competence, there are advantages to rehiring the firms which handled the original construction. Even after as long as 20 years, frequently there are still people on the staff who participated in the earlier job and have useful memories of how things were done.

The architect must be involved from the very beginning. The usual practice is to enter into a two-stage contract with the architect that provides for a clear-cut termination on short notice by the owner at any time up to the final decision to proceed. The fee for that exploratory stage is commonly based on a cost-plus formula. The fee for the second stage, beginning with the start of working drawings, may be a fixed sum, cost plus, a percentage of construction cost, or whatever is customary in the community. In considering the financial arrangements, however, all concerned should remember that a typical enclosing construction program will differ from a new development of similar dollar size in several important ways. Preparation of plans and specifications will take appreciably longer, perhaps as much as 25 percent more time; the construction work will have a significantly longer time-span; and the precontracting estimates cannot be expected to be nearly as accurate because of the uncertainties in contractors' minds as they prepare their bids. Even after firm bids are in hand, experienced architects are inclined to cushion the final preconstruction estimate with at least 10 percent for unforeseen contingencies as compared to the 3 to 5 percent they would use for a new project.

Ordinarily the architectural work on the Type Three space presents no unusual problems. Once the schematics have established size and location, the detailed work proceeds as in any other addition, with care taken to isolate the construction from pedestrian traffic and minimize the interference with vehicular movement and parking. In Type Two space the architectural and engineering development of working drawings becomes complicated and close supervision by the center manager is called for. The working drawings are based on the game plan referred to earlier, which has put in sketch form the enlargement and rearrangement of the existing floor space in accordance with the occupancy pattern the manager hopes to achieve. The degree of accuracy attained in the game plan will significantly affect the final cost of the project. If the preparatory discussions with the then-present tenants have been both thorough and realistically evaluated, the game plan should prove to have at least 90 percent accuracy, with a 95 percent score possible under favorable circumstances.

It is extremely important that the general conditions usually included in the specifications detail the manner in which the contractors are to perform their work. Care must be taken to minimize interference with the business operations of tenants and also provide maximum protection against injury to the general public. Such objectives are accomplished by a statement of guidelines, such as: customer access to every store must be maintained during regular business hours; protected walkways must provide for adequate shopper circulation; temporary lighting must insure reasonable visibility. The difficult problem of dust control, both in the air and under foot, warrants special attention because this is likely to be the source of the single most recurrent tenant complaint and is a factor not normally of concern in construction work. The presence of a comprehensive description of such work rules in the contract documents is essential to an orderly construction program and to controlling the contract extras and tenant damage claims arising from unforeseen job conditions.

The seasonal aspects of shopping center activity being what they are, timing of the construction program has considerable significance. In the case of a relatively small center with a simple configuration it may be possible to start work in early January and have most stores, both old and new, in full, unobstructed operation by late November. In a major project, however, such a time span could be realized only by effectively closing down the center for a large part of the year. What it comes down to, therefore, is a choice between keeping the job going right through the Christmas season or closing it down and scheduling the work in two or more 10-month segments. For obvious reasons, the decision must be made before the work goes out for bids, and it is not an easy one. The extent to which the unsightly appearance and general confusion will deter shoppers and thereby depress sales volume during that critical period is impossible to estimate on any basis other than pure guesswork.

The costs of an intermediate shutdown, on the other hand, are largely calculable and can be substantial. The four factors to be taken into account are the direct costs of shutting down the work in progress and later reactivating it, the carrying charges on the capital already invested, the inflationary penalty attributable to rising prices during the idle period, and the indeterminate damage that may result from a loss of momentum. The direct cost of a shutdown will depend on the stage of progress at the time, but can be expected to run around 1 percent of total job cost. Financial carrying charges, of course, are determined by the cost of money at the time. The inflationary penalty will apply only on that portion of the work not yet in place. In a time of rapidly rising material and labor prices, such as was experienced during the early 1970s, this can amount to as much as 1 percent per month. The harm, if any, resulting from loss of momentum cannot be foretold and is rarely identifiable in retrospect. However, human experience indicates that progress in any endeavor that involves a number of people is always adversely affected by a temporary suspension of activity.

Although they will be affected by the decision, this is not the kind of problem that can be discussed with the tenants. Since they will share in the inconvenience and possible loss of income resulting from continued construction during the busy season but will not be required to participate in the added costs of a recess, their reaction is quite predictable. Human nature being what it is, if they have been consulted and the subsequent decision by the owner is to keep going, any resulting difficulties are likely to be somewhat magnified by the time they land in the manager's lap.

The Owner's Superintendent

When the contracts have been let and construction starts, the managerial responsibilities become such as to give the individual in charge a kindred feeling for the proverbial one-armed paperhanger with hives. Among the more insistent and time-consuming of those duties is the necessity of coordinating the day-by-day, and sometimes hour-by-hour, construction work with the normal business activity of a shopping center. When tenant work on storefronts and interiors begins, there may be dozens of independent contractors on the premises in addition to those working directly for the owner. The coordination duties become especially demanding.

In a relatively small center, a manager with a good working knowledge of construction practices may be able to handle that assignment personally without neglecting other equally important responsibilities, but in a project of any magnitude it becomes a full-time job. It is customary to employ an owner's superintendent on a duration-of-the-job basis, a position important enough to warrant both great care in making the selection and paying well to get the right person. In addition to a thorough grounding in the construction of commercial buildings, the individual chosen should know enough about business in general to have a sympathetic understanding of the operational characteristics of a shopping center and its tenants. And, very importantly, he must be an effective liaison between tenants and construction personnel; one who is perceived by both as a person who understands their concerns and an acceptable arbitrator of the countless little disputes endemic in such situations.

In order for an owner's superintendent to function efficiently, he must have reasonably broad authority, including power to make financial commitments within established limits without specific prior approval by management. If the work is such that frequent minor unforeseen contingencies arise calling for additional expense by a contractor, the project will move more smoothly and generally at lower final cost if a spot agreement can be made as to what to do and how much to pay for it. Matters involving substantial contract extras are better processed through the architect's office in the conventional manner and decisions made at the ownership level, particularly if they are to any extent optional. The small ones, which are bound to be numerous in alteration work, can seriously delay construction if allowed to accumulate.

Bulletins for center-wide distribution will serve to cover the general shape of things to come. Extremely important is the desirability, and in some cases the necessity, of alerting tenants to impending disruptions of their individual businesses. For instance, loss of refrigeration from afterhours electrical work requiring a temporary shutoff of power can be disastrous to a food store or restaurant unless there has been adequate time to take protective measures. Less damaging but equally annoying can be daytime work above the ceiling of an apparel store which causes precipitation of dust onto displayed garments without sufficient warning to permit their removal or covering. Such occurrences not only put a strain on the landlord-tenant relationship but, in aggravated cases, can result in expensive damage claims if there is no clear record of prior notice. In this phase of the operation alone a competent owner's superintendent, or construction coordinator as he also is called, will more than pay for himself.

An indispensible part of the superintendent's equipment is a camera that can take good color pictures under adverse lighting conditions. Photographs can be used to document any damage complaint by a tenant or shopper, no matter how trivial. It is sometimes useful to have on file a clear photograph of every storefront in the center, dated immediately prior to the start of construction.

The presence of an owner's superintendent should not be construed as a move to relieve the architect of any of the customary field responsibilities, such as inspecting the work for contract compliance, certifying progress payments, obtaining required governmental approvals, and similar administrative duties. The owner's superintendent should be viewed as a supplement rather than a substitute; he is part of the management team representing the owner and as such charged with making those decisions that are inherently a function of ownership. The superintendent plays a critical role in coordinating tenant work in both Type Two and Type Three space—particularly so in the former where the replacement and extension of storefronts is carried on in the midst of shopper traffic with numerous tenant contractors operating in close juxtaposition. Even if each work area is adequately fenced or bulkheaded, the movement of materials in and debris out can become a serious problem unless tightly controlled, and without a competent buffer the possible interference with neighboring tenants can make the center manager's life miserable.

204

Staging Tenant Work

There are two schools of thought on how to stage the tenant work in Type Two space. Some people advocate pushing vigorously to get it all done as promptly as possible after structural work is completed, accepting the fact that for a time shoppers will be greatly inconvenienced. Others favor trying to schedule the activity to avoid concentration in any one area of the public space. In weighing the two approaches it is possible to approximate the difference in rental income as it applies to minimum guarantees and other payments unrelated to volume. Assuming the upward revisions become effective on completion of the individual rearrangements, it is important to achieve that condition as early as possible. Since the major part of the landlord's investment has, at that point, been made, it is desirable to keep the lag between then and start of the enlarged income stream as brief as possible. The other side of the coin, however, is the difficulty of foretelling the extent of possible damage to sales volume, both short- and long-term, caused by prolonging the period of intensive construction activity.

With occasional exceptions, the unavoidable dust, noise, and general confusion will cause some temporary loss of business during the structural enclosing phase. As an offset, which will be discussed later, the usual practice is a relatively low-key public relations program which culminates in a highly publicized grand reopening as soon as the new mall has been cleaned up enough to be presentable. Experience is conclusive that individual store remodeling, if well contained and not in overwhelming quantity, can then go on indefinitely and be fully acceptable to the public if it does not interfere with general circulation. In considering the relative merits of a crash program of tenant improvements versus spacing them out, one more subtle factor must be taken into account—the potential erosion of the center's constituency of regular shoppers.

It is self-evident that a shopping center being converted from open to enclosed is in a competitive environment—every consumer in its trade area has ready access to other marketplaces—and it is a well-documented finding of retail market research that store loyalty has little to do with buying decisions. Research has also demonstrated that convenience has much to do with a shopper's choice of destination, and that convenience as perceived by the shopper is not synonymous with proximity. Still further, there is evidence that most people, being creatures of habit, develop patterns of repetitive visits to certain shop-

205

ping facilities although many are available to them. What this all adds up to is that the longer the center's physical condition serves to inconvenience the shopper, the greater the danger that individuals will change their shopping patterns. This can only result in a long-term loss of sales volume.

Financing

Management decisions on the rate at which to schedule the individual tenant improvements, on whether to shut down construction during the Christmas season, and on other matters affecting the overall pace of the project from start to finish will, to some extent, be governed by financing requirements. If the additional hard income—such as minimum rent guarantees, tenant contributions to capital cost, standby fees, tax participation, and common area maintenance charges—to be derived from all three space types is immediately needed to support the financing, speed will be the order of the day. That this may be costly in future soft income as represented by overage rent, and even in the staying power of some small tenants, is another illustration of a manager's responsibility for constantly analyzing financial decisions in terms of the time value of money, as discussed in Chapter 3.

The method employed to finance a shopping center enclosing, with or without addition, depends on the state of existing indebtedness, on the general financial condition of the owner, and, of course, on what is available. In a typical case, the original mortgage indebtedness will have been partially, and usually considerably, reduced and the equity will have been additionally enlarged by the combined influences of trade area growth and inflation. When there is thus created a substantial borrowing margin, the financing will commonly take one of the three forms identified in the refinancing section of Chapter 12—a new first mortgage, a second, or a wraparound. Where the owner has an independently strong financial position, coupled with a comfortably large margin of borrowing power in the center itself, it is frequently desirable to see the project through to completion with a short-term bank loan and hold off on arranging the long-term financing until there is a finished package. That procedure, when possible, permits flexibility in working out deals with tenants, with necessary changes in the plans being made as things go along.

It is more common, however, to identify the source and amount of the long-term financing at the earliest possible date, at least before becoming firmly committed to tenants, present or future. The first step is commonly taken when schematic drawings are available and preliminary cost and income estimates are sufficiently developed to establish in a tentative way the economics of the proposal. A conference with the present mortgagee or a selected alternate will be held to establish acceptability in principle of the project and a general idea of the amount and terms of a loan. As the planning proceeds a series of meetings and negotiations are held, culminating in a firm agreement contingent on the borrower having fulfilled certain stipulated conditions. Sometimes the agreement provides that the lender make partial advances as work progresses; more typically it will be in the form of a take-out commitment used to support interim borrowing, usually from a commercial bank on a monthly or quarterly basis until the project is completed. The complexity of the negotiations and the final agreement is related to the ratio of size of loan sought to lender's appraisal of market value of the center in its completed form, and the amount of the loan is not necessarily limited to the cost of the enclosure and addition.

Frequently, the financial condition of a shopping center at the point where it has become timely to undertake an enclosing is similar to that described in the refinancing section referred to above. That being the case, an owner will give thought to undertaking a withdrawal of equity capital in excess of the amount necessary to pay for the improvement. This usually means that in a propitious money market he will go after the maximum loan obtainable, which will tend to put pressure on the manager to meticulously detail both construction costs and anticipated income in the pro forma financial statements used in the borrowing negotiations. The same is true if there is little leeway between the cash requirement of the construction program and the borrowing margin of the property. In the former situation it will help convince a lender that the proposal has been thoroughly studied and the presentation contains a minimum of guesswork; in the latter instance the detailed presentation will be a matter of self-preservation since either a major cost overrun or a substantial income shortfall can have dire results.

Promotion and Publicity

To coordinate the construction work while also maintaining as much of the current flow of income as possible, a manager must accept the fact that the center is in for a protracted period of an inherently obtrusive and noisy operation. The construction specifications can go only so far in placing restrictions on the contractor's freedom of action without imposing a prohibitive penalty in both cost and time, and there is no way of muffling the sounds of the jackhammer, the riveting gun, and the power saw. That being the case, groundwork for dealing with the inconveniences is best laid during the exploratory phase by freely acknowledging to tenants that there are going to be some problems which can be minimized by the concerted efforts of all concerned when the time comes. There is little likelihood that an otherwise favorably inclined tenant will be deterred by the prospect of some temporary hardships in the future, and if he has been conditioned to expect them they will have less impact when they do occur.

An important consideration in getting the tenants involved well before construction begins is the lead time required in rearranging the ongoing promotion and publicity program. In the typical open shopping center preparing to be enclosed, the joint promotional effort will be funded largely by the tenants and controlled by them through a merchants' association or similar organization. In a center that has been in operation for several years, the promotional program usually follows an established annual pattern, with all on-premise events geared to the outdoor condition. During the construction period, presentation of special events other than in the parking area will be severely restricted if not impossible. On completion of the enclosure the opportunity for special events will be enlarged, but different kinds of events will have to be planned. The promotional program, therefore, will go through two drastic alterations—preparing for a year or more with no special events and adjusting to the new environment of the enclosed mall that, in all probability, will demand a program significantly greater in scope.

Providing the necessary leadership to engineer such a change in direction calls for a certain amount of specialized knowledge as well as quite a lot of time and patience. The manager of a community-size center might be able to handle it personally in addition to his other duties, but for a regional center such a program is a full-time job. It is very advantageous that the promotion director be an employee of the center rather than of the merchants' association during an enclosing program. During the construction period the inevitable disruptions and aggravations, coupled with a loss of volume, can severely strain the manager-tenant relationship and place a promotion director employed by the merchants' association in an uncomfortable and, at times, impossible position. If the director is a part of management, and this is

208

understood by the tenants, he can do his job much more effectively while also making life easier for the manager. Where the existing condition has the promotion director employed by the merchants, it will be prudent to establish the alternative arrangement early in the exploratory stage. Doing so may result in the owner having to pick up a slightly larger share of the tab, but all experience indicates the benefits will outweigh the costs.

For convenience of presentation, the promotion and publicity program as an integral part of the total project can be divided into five parts:

1. Informing the tenants of the overall plan, what is currently going on, what is going to happen next, and how well the schedule is being maintained.

2. Communicating to the general public the nature of the overall plan and what progress is being made.

3. Advertising and other promotional activity directly aimed at attracting people to visit the center for a specific purpose.

4. Interior signing and similar measures designed to facilitate shopper's movements and diminish their feeling of confusion and inconvenience.

5. The grand reopening.

As was suggested previously, it is a good idea to conduct the early explorations of financial feasibility in as discreet a manner as possible. If the anchors or other key tenants display a lack of enthusiasm, or other reasons appear to cast doubt on the economic soundness of enclosing, the less said the better. Once the program has become a probability, however, tenants should be informed about every detail that affects them in any way, including the disagreeable as well as the beneficial aspects of enclosure. By that is meant avoiding overselling by glossing over the fact that there will be a certain amount of business disruption accompanied by some substantial costs to be shared by all concerned. It has already been noted that early conditioning to expect some difficult operating conditions tends to soften the blow when it arrives, and that is also true to some degree with the costs. Experience demonstrates that getting money matters on the table in at least approximate terms early in the proceedings lessens the chance of later disappointments in establishing the game plan.

As soon as any specifics on which to structure a program are available, it is a good idea to set up a general meeting of all tenants, with special effort to secure attendance by principals as well as store managers. The presentation should include architectural renderings of finished appearance, an outline floor plan of added buildings with identification of principal prospective tenants by name or type, and revised site plan depicting proposed parking and traffic changes. An effective method of presentation is a well-rehearsed two-man team comprised of the center manager and the architect; the former to set forth the reasons for the project and what it is expected to accomplish, the latter to explain the physical aspects. Such a meeting should have no time limit but continue until audience questions have been exhausted. In a large center it is sometimes expedient to stage two such meetings a few days apart in order to achieve maximum coverage. If the meeting is carefully planned and well executed, it can do much to get the venture off on the right foot. Announcing that a meeting will be held just as soon as there is anything concrete to talk about will help control the rumors that will inevitably begin to circulate soon after the exploratory phase is started.

A second such meeting may be in order before construction begins but at the point where working drawings are substantially complete and the timing of the major construction stages has been established. Since the tenants could then start planning and scheduling their own individual renovation programs, this meeting could be enlarged to include tenant architects and construction managers. If that is the case, center management should then be represented by personnel competent to discuss all phases of the construction procedure and particularly the conditions governing tenant work. Whether or not there is a second general meeting, it is essential that the initial one be followed by a series of tenant bulletins at fairly frequent intervals to keep them informed of how things are going and what to expect next. Such communications, in reasonable detail, right up to completion of construction will do much to maintain internal harmony while facilitating the work. Since most of the surprises during the construction period will be unpleasant, it helps to have as few of them as possible.

Informing the Public

Making an effort to inform the general public in the trade area of what is going on derives its value from the workings of what industrial psychologists call the Hawthorne effect. Expressed in simplest terms, the Hawthorne effect states that when people feel you are interested in their aspirations they will reciprocate by taking an interest in yours. If shoppers, both present and potential, understand and sympathize with what you are trying to accomplish, they will tend to accept temporary inconvenience as a means to an end. A way to get started on such a campaign is to hold a press conference when the scope and timing of the program has been firmly established. There should be suitable printed and pictorial matter for distribution. Attendance at the conference can be bolstered by including representatives of the anchor stores and other tenants who happen to be strong advertisers. Subsequently, many people can be reached by having speakers available to tell the story and show visual material to audiences such as service clubs and similar neighborhood groups. If the center has perimeter pylons with integral message panels, they can carry occasional short notices of progress. If there is an adjacent high-traffic road a temporary billboard may be effective.

A limited amount of purely institutional-type advertising may sometimes be helpful, but the main effort should be directed toward inspiring publicity pictures and stories dramatizing the construction work. In most cases, the advertising dollars are better spent on straight merchandising efforts designed to create an immediate response, and this frequently calls for special attention to the problems of the smaller tenants. As has been repeatedly stressed in this book, it is difficult to generalize about shopping centers. However, experience indicates that with few exceptions the burden of lost sales during an enclosing falls much heavier on the satellite tenants than on the anchors. In addition to traffic generated through continual advertising, the anchor stores almost always have important entrances directly from the parking area that are unaffected by the obstructions of the enclosing work. The normal spillover of that traffic tends to be inhibited during the period of structural work, which has particularly severe impact on those stores largely dependent on the passing flow of pedestrian traffic.

Often, those least able to absorb the interim loss of income from impaired volume are desirable tenants for whom the forthcoming renovation of their own stores is going to be a financial problem. The expectation that this is almost certainly going to happen needs to be taken into account when the promotional program is being revised during the construction period. That portion of the budget previously allocated to special events could be redirected into tabloid or similar cooperative efforts that would provide small tenants the opportunity for item advertising designed to stimulate shoppers to seek them out.

211

Center management might find it worthwhile to make some additional contribution to the cost of such efforts. With such a program it is desirable to get an early start on the planning so that participating tenants would have time to select and procure the specific items. The willingness of the public to move about in a construction area often can be encouraged if the temporary bulkheads and fencing contain wire mesh at eye level that obstructs visibility as little as possible. This approach helps shoppers locate particular stores and can minimize tenant feelings that they have been "fenced out of business."

Temporary Signs

While major construction activity is being carried on in the midst of a busy retail area it is all but impossible to post too many temporary signs, provided they are smartly executed, convey an accurately useful message, and are posted and removed in a timely manner. Conversely, nothing creates a poorer public impression than a handwritten sign, penciled on a piece of old carton, warning of a break in the pavement after a dozen people have already fallen in, and then left in place long after the hazard has been eliminated. The signs can be of two general types—those intended to warn of possible danger or inconvenience, and those that direct people to various objectives. The necessity for both kinds, particularly the former, changes often and frequently with little advance notice. Coping with the problem, therefore, calls for prompt perception of the need and quick response. Responsibility for warning signs properly rests with the contractors, and the insurance company inspectors can generally be relied on to keep after them about it. However, the inspector is only intermittently on hand and a hazard can be created inadvertently. Therefore, charging the owner's superintendent with policing the installation and maintaining the signs can be a worthwhile precaution.

Signs that direct both pedestrian and vehicular traffic constitute a less pressing problem from a timing standpoint but are much more difficult to plan. When a parking lot entrance must be temporarily closed or a main footway is obstructed, the signs required to reroute traffic are relatively simple, but can be made confusing if not properly planned for that specific use. Outdoor signs must be sized and located for adequate visibility and convey a message readily understandable by a stranger to the center. The problem of temporary signing within what will become the enclosed area, however, is much more perplexing and because of its direct effect on tenant sales warrants constant, thoughtful attention. The objectives are, first, to reassure the shopper that the center is not a trackless jungle but has well-posted trails and, second, assist the shopper in reaching any desired destination. The task is frequently complicated by a drumfire of tenant complaints, ranging in tone from plaintive to bellicose, to the effect that they have been isolated beyond any hope of being found by a customer. All of this must be dealt with tactfully but within the framework of an orderly program.

For obvious reasons, the placement and content of interior signs will be governed by the configuration and store pattern of the individual shopping center and will change frequently as construction proceeds. A good practice, however, is to maintain well-marked routes connecting the larger stores by name. Doing so will inevitably provoke some howls from the smaller tenants but experience demonstrates that this approach functions reasonably well. Habitual shoppers tend to associate the location of small shops with the more prominent stores in the immediate vicinity, and if shoppers can be induced to move around within the confines of the center all stores get visual exposure.

The preferred type of sign for use in weather-protected locations is a standard 22 x 28-inch posterboard with black lettering on a white or pastel ground. It is easily attached to any surface or mounted in movable standards and is adequately sized for nearly all uses. It is usually worthwhile to invest in a sign machine as a permanent part of the center's equipment because of the continual need for such postings in connection with various events in an enclosed center. The machine will be of special value during the enclosing period when there is a premium on prompt response to a perceived need. Such a machine is usually simple to operate and the job typically can be handled by a high school or college student working part time. Some of the cost can be covered by supplying the needs of tenants at a price competitive with an outside source. If not feasible for the center to acquire its own machine, it is sometimes possible to work out a sharing arrangement with an anchor tenant who does have such equipment. However it is done, the effectiveness of the interior signing will depend on how quickly the sign can be posted after the need is perceived.

Grand Reopening

Although the expression "grand reopening" is something of a misnomer as applied to an event where there has been no actual closing, it is as good a term as any to describe the burst of publicity celebrating completion of an enclosure. The format of the reopening is generally similar to the initial opening of a new shopping center with suitable modifications to fit the changed circumstances. The funds for institutional advertising and special events planned for the celebration come from the merchants' association's regular budget for that year or from a special fund made up of contributions from both landlord and tenants as stipulated in the new lease agreements.

In establishing the date for officially opening a new center, particularly one strong in the apparel field, the usual practice is to point for a month to six weeks before Easter, the beginning of August, or the end of October. But a "Grand Reopening" may be controlled by other considerations. If there is a major addition including a lot of new stores, then certainly the fashion dates of Easter and August are important. If it is largely the same family of tenants, particularly if there has been a serious loss of business, the reopening celebration is better staged just as soon as the overall appearance is bright and fresh. As mentioned earlier, the presence of a limited amount of individual store remodeling is not apt to mar the occasion, but every effort should be made to have the parking area and mall entrances in spic-and-span condition.

In addition to the specific activities identified in this chapter, management must plan and implement those corollary details having to do with the ongoing operation of the center in its altered form. New procedures and schedules for housekeeping and maintenance must be thought out and established; security routines will need revision; insurance coverage will have to be reevaluated; the new real estate assessed value will require time at the city hall, as will new police and fire department procedures; overhauling the annual promotion program will involve protracted discussions with the merchants' association directors. In general, every facet of the center's operation will need to be thoroughly reviewed to ensure that it is consistent with the new reality.

QUESTIONS FOR DISCUSSION

1. *What role does additional leasable area play in the enclosure of the open shopping center?*

2. *Explain circumstances under which tenant participation and long-term financing for enclosure would not be available.*

3. *Discuss the economics of the three types of new lease space available resulting from a center's enclosure and expansion.*

4. *What are the problems inherent to any tenant rearrangement resulting from expansion?*

5. *Discuss the owner and tenant financial implications resulting from enclosure and expansion.*

6. *What is the role of the owner's superintendent during the construction?*

7. *Compare the merits of the two divergent approaches in scheduling tenant construction.*

8. *Discuss the promotion program transition from an open to an enclosed center.*

9. *Why is it important to keep tenants apprised of construction plans and progress?*

10. *Discuss the Hawthorne approach of keeping the general public in the trade area informed of the construction progress.*

RECOMMENDED READING LIST

Applebaum, William and S. O. Kaylin. **Case Studies in Shopping Center Development and Operation.** New York: International Council of Shopping Centers, 1974. 280 pp.

Casto, Don M. III and Richard W. Trott. **Renovating a Small Center.** New York: International Council of Shopping Centers, 1977. 16 pp.

CHAPTER **12**

Some Special Considerations

Market Research

In the shopping center industry, market research is a valuable tool for two different but closely related purposes. As noted in the opening chapter, it is essential in the course of planning all but the simplest of centers. After a center has passed through its opening flurry and has stabilized, which may take from one month to one year, periodic research projects can be useful in directing attention to possible improvements in the effectiveness of its appeal to potential customers. In the latter applications, however, it is probable that considerable energy and money are wasted in the belief that market research will supply the answer to all performance problems.

To begin with, true research involves more than the simple survey; it is a specialized and highly technical business. A survey can discover the facts of a given situation; research can then find the reasons underlying those facts and can allow an extrapolation of future courses of action from them.

On this more sophisticated level, research is a job for professionals. It is expensive and should not be undertaken without first clearly defining the nature of the information sought and having a definite plan for the uses to which it will be put. All too often, shop-

216

ping center managements or merchants' associations go to the trouble and expense of gathering an ill-assorted collection of facts and/or opinions that, after some discussion of their possible significance, are filed away and forgotten.

Whether survey or research, there is a distinction between field work carried on within the center and that performed in the trade area at large. In evaluating the results, it must be recognized that data gathered internally are representative only of that segment of the market already using the center; the data will not necessarily be accurate or reliable if extrapolated to cover the entire community.

The professional market research firm will structure its questionnaires to eliminate bias and subjectivity in either the answers or in the interpretations they can elicit. This must be kept in mind if a center undertakes a do-it-yourself survey. As a general rule, it is nearly impossible to secure true objectivity in an amateur project for any survey above the most elementary level.

The question of who is to bear the expense of a research project —the owner or the tenants—calls for an early and explicit understanding. Theoretically, the costs should be spread pro rata to the anticipated benefits, but it is usually futile to seek an agreement to this method. The immediate and largest benefit will usually accrue to the tenants, who can gain guidance on merchandising their stores and properly aiming their advertising, with the owner consequently benefitting from increased rental income. The only practical way to allocate costs is by negotiated agreement between landlord and the merchants' association, with the tenants' share taken from the association's treasury.

A survey, or any part of one, that is directed at sampling customers' opinions on the operating characteristics of the center itself— as distinguished from the tenants' stores—rarely produces new and useful information. A manager who needs an outside survey to tell him that there are potholes in the parking lot and noisy children in the mall should seriously think of going into some other line of work.

In weighing market research as a management tool, a sensible guideline would be to observe two precepts. First, avoid research simply for its own sake—the shotgun approach that, if enough information is gathered, some of it may turn out to have value. Limit, instead, the activity to projects for which it is possible to prepare exact definitions of the data sought and the reasons they will be of use.

Second, test all proposals—for both their validity and their methodology—by exposing them to disinterested expert advice. Within reach of every shopping center there are colleges of business administration whose faculty members are qualified to offer guidance for a reasonable fee.

Long-Range Projections

In discussing preparation of the annual budget in Chapter 3, reference was made to the desirability of maintaining an outline of a tentative budget for the following two or three years. The purpose of such a forward look is to facilitate decision-making, particularly as regards capital expenditures, during the immediately coming year. To the extent that probable future activities justify the effort, it is worthwhile to enlarge that concept by creating and maintaining an annual income and expense projection extending well into the future—say 15 or 20 years.

Such a projection becomes, in effect, a model on which to test the probable results of actions such as additions, major alterations, or refinancing, which will affect the capital structure of the center. It is of particular value when there is a choice between two or more alternatives—a good example is the second illustrative case of replacement leasing in Chapter 8.

In that situation, the manager was confronted with a succession of alternatives. The first was the basic choice between leaving the matter in status quo or proceeding with a division of the space. To make that decision, however, he must first develop a financial plan for the use of the 10,000 square feet that will thus become available, and in doing so he is faced with a new level of multiple alternatives. The space can be rented as a unit or it can be subdivided into two, four, six, or eight individual shops, each plan having different costs and income potential with concomitant changes in the financing requirement and future depreciation charges. Thus, in order to arrive at the final decision on what to do, each one of the secondary alternatives must be projected out for at least ten years ahead. If a basic model is in existence, and particularly if it has already been put into a computer, a thorough exploration of the alternatives is greatly encouraged, with a resulting improvement in the quality of management decisions.

To test profitability and explore various alternatives in financing and methods of depreciation, experienced developers commonly extend over several years the pro forma operating statement prepared in the planning stage. Such a projection is usually not done in complete detail, however, and since it is based entirely on assumptions it tends to become increasingly invalid after the center goes into operation. There is no set rule, but probably a three-to five-year history of substantially full operation is necessary to provide the background for a reasonably solid long-range projection. And once established, it needs careful scrutiny each year to determine if the accumulating history continues to substantiate the patterns on which forward assumptions have been predicated.

The format of a long-range projection can vary in length and extent of detail, both of which may be related to the size and complexity of the shopping center. A ten-year projection is about the minimum that is of any real value, and anything for more than 25 years is almost certainly wasted effort. In the absence of a specific reason for doing otherwise, the standard practice is to use the same categories of income and expense as are present in the annual operating statement, i.e., including depreciation but excluding payments on debt principal and any costs that have been capitalized. Future-year cash flow can be readily ascertained by reversing the treatment of depreciation and principal payments, as demonstrated in Chapter 3.

The actual preparation of a projection calls for neither a crystal ball nor any particularly esoteric financial skill. It does require a reasonable familiarity with the center's past workings and a good understanding of its accounting system. The former characteristic is necessary in order to correctly identify extraordinary, or nonrecurrent, items of income or expense that may distort the pattern. In regard to the accounting system, it is important to have a thorough grasp of the depreciation practices in use, since accelerated and/or component methods result in significant annual changes as the center edges up on middle age.

The procedure is to produce a spread-sheet with the income and expense items arranged vertically (in the same manner as in the annual report) and the years spread out horizontally, starting with the first year considered sufficiently stabilized to be meaningful for the purpose in hand. For past years the pertinent items of both income and expense are adjusted by the deletion of amounts considered to be extraordinary by usual accounting standards, and the adjustments are carried right down to the bottom lines. The current year is inserted in accordance with the operating budget with no adjustments.

The past years are then analyzed for patterns, which are expressed in terms of percentage rates for use in projecting the individual budget items into the future. For instance, if overage rent shows an increase at an average compounded rate of 3 percent annually, that rate will be projected into the future, using the current year as the base. The same procedure is applied to other income categories and to repairs, salaries, utility charges, insurance, taxes, and other variable expense items. Excepted, of course, are mortgage payments, depreciation, and any other budget item that can be computed exactly. The necessity for yearly adjustment of the percentage factors will largely depend on the length of the background, since a three-year history, for instance, is not likely to have the stability of one embodying seven years of operating experience.

Such a projection is not, of course, an infallible guide to the future since it is subject to derailment by any number of unforeseen events. Yet it does offer a preview of the probable results in terms of reportable income and cash flow if the property is operated in exact status quo, and thereby provides the base against which to test proposed changes. Superimposing the assumed results of a change on all of the affected items in the model, if done manually, can be such an onerous task as to discourage doing it very often, but a manager who has access to a computer will find that such a projection takes some of the guesswork out of his decisions.

Tenant Mix

In the description of the development process of a shopping center in Chapter 1, there was reference to the occupancy pattern, in terms of retail classifications, to be sought in the initial leasing program—commonly referred to as the "tenant mix." In Chapter 8, the term was used again in the two illustrative examples involving a manager's efforts to correct initial leasing decisions that had subsequently proven undesirable.

To a manager of an established, successful center, some of those early decisions may seem inexplicable. An understanding of the background is often helpful in approaching present problems; for that reason this section is devoted to a description of the typical evolutionary process that the originally planned tenant mix might undergo. As employed here, the qualifying adjective "typical" excludes small strips and major regionals, both of which are leased under conditions peculiar to their size. Some of the considerations referred to are present in varying degrees of intensity regardless of size, but the focus here is

220

on centers in the 100,000- to 500,000-square-foot range.

As in most other human endeavors, the validity of a planned tenant mix can vary from pretty bad to very good, with the quality depending on competence and thoroughness. When the mix is done by qualified market research people, it presents a theoretical occupancy plan, by store types, that will have maximum attractiveness to the population of that specific trade area. In most cases, the study is performed within the framework of an assumption of the identity, by name or type, of the anchor tenants, and when prepared by independent professionals it is free of the subjectivity that tends to taint plans formulated entirely within the developing organization. However, the plan ordinarily presents a theoretically ideal composition of the tenant group; the transition from desirable to obtainable is up to the developer to engineer.

An expedient has been defined as an ideal that has had to go to work for a living, and that pretty well describes what happens from there on. The developer, or his leasing agent, is limited by four factors that vary in flexibility and in potential for trade-offs among them. Not necessarily in order of importance, the factors are:

1. *The availability of equity capital.* The tighter the budget the less room there is to move around in some of the other matters.

2. *The strictures imposed by the prospective mortgagee.* Typically, a lender will demand that a specified minimum amount of the GLA be leased to prime credit tenants, that the leases must run for a stated minimum number of years, and that the aggregate guaranteed minimum rents must total a certain figure. Such requirements are sometimes absolute, but more often there is an understanding that if the exact amounts are not met there will be a proportionate reduction in the amount of the loan.

3. *The aversions of the anchors or other major tenants.* In the light of recent Federal Trade Commission activities, the status of objections from that source was up in the air at the time these pages were written, but as a practical matter developers have normally taken into consideration the wishes, or the presumed wishes, of their anchors when deciding upon the tenant mix of their centers.

4. *The marketability of the product itself,* which determines the respective negotiating strengths of lessor and lessee. Obviously, a center that, in the collective judgment of many retailers, will be a good place to do business is going to enjoy a smoother leasing path than one not so favored. The weaker his bargaining position, the more a developer will be forced to compromise the initial plan in order to achieve occupancy within the limitations of the other constraints.

In some cases, deviation from plan is caused simply by a total lack of qualified prospects in the desired category, in others because the cost of staying with it is deemed prohibitive. The latter situation sometimes requires difficult decisions, as is illustrated by the following example.

The tenant mix analysis points strongly to the desirability of a good-sized better women's wear store to serve as the nucleus for a cluster of small shops offering similar merchandise, and there are three such retailers now established in the entire community. One is presently positioned elsewhere in the trade area on a long-term lease, and another is so weak financially as to be an unacceptable credit risk; this leaves one real prospect, who is well aware of his bargaining position. As the negotiation proceeds, it becomes evident that a deal can be made, provided the developer will accept a very low guaranteed rent and finish the store interior well beyond his contemplated standard. The combination of the two concessions will simultaneously shrink the mortgage while enlarging the construction budget and, thus, assuming the developer has the cash to bridge the gap, will automatically act to depress the rate of return on his investment, at least for the near term.

Some fairly simple calculation establishes that, for the developer to recoup via overage rent the financial disadvantages of the early years, the tenant's sales volume will have to reach the outer limit of the probability range almost immediately after opening. This is not, however, the crux of the matter, since the extent of risk in the direct financial outcome of that specific lease can, at least approximately, be mathematically quantified in terms of dollars on a time-value basis.

The true dilemma involves the far more subtle question of the extent of damage, if any, that will be done to the long-range, overall performance of the center if the planned tenant mix is altered by elimination of the entire better women's wear grouping, the satellite units of which are dependent on the presence of a bellwether. The probable difference in rental income, either better or worse, from an alternative use of the space can be estimated, but not the effect of the intangible change in the image of the center on that segment of the trade area's population that would have been attracted to it by that original group of stores. The decision made cannot be reversed for many years, if ever, and it is situations like this that give developers grey hair early in life, and a few years later do the same for shopping center managers.

Problems along this line tend to be less acute in small centers because of their relatively simple tenant mix requirement, and in major regionals because these centers usually have the money and the muscle to attain their objectives with relatively little adulteration.

Defensive Expansion

Not infrequently, a shopping center owner is faced with a dilemma—the choice between making a major additional investment of dubious profitability or suffering an economic blow of uncertain severity to his present investment. It becomes a choice between two evils, with neither possible of more than approximate quantification.

As an example, assume the case of a 12-year-old medium-sized community center, showing a good rate of return on the invested capital, and anchored by a junior department store on a 15-year lease. The center has no surplus land, but adjacent acreage can be purchased.

The department store tenant informs the center management that it needs more space and, unless the center will substantially enlarge its facility, will relocate at the end of the lease. If the owner will undertake the required expansion, the tenant proposes an additional 15-year lease on rental terms that will provide effectively no net profit on the new investment, and might very well result in a loss if projections of future sales volume prove to be overly optimistic.

Without attempting to identify every last nuance of the center owner's dilemma, he must certainly ponder the following questions:

- Is this a bluff? If I sit tight will the store either renew for a few more years or raise the ante enough to give me a decent profit?

- If the department store does vacate, what are my chances of obtaining a satisfactory replacement?

- Is the tenant likely to relocate under conditions that will do minimum damage to my center, or is it apt to become the anchor in a new center close enough to be ruinous?

- If I go along with the proposal, is this a propitious time to buy enough additional land to concurrently expand the satellite store groups in the hope of averaging out with a fair return on the total added investment? If I elect this course, how close can

223

I come to mortgaging out on the total cost?

A variation of the problem, but presenting essentially the same alternatives, would be the situation in which the center has surplus land and is approached by a major newcomer to the local retailing scene, seeking to either buy land at a below-market price or have a store built for lease on unprofitable rental terms. In this case, the choice is between adding drawing power to the center at the expense of a poor investment, or having the new arrival locate down the street with an unpredictable impact on the center's future.

In most situations of that kind, preparing long-term income/expense projections of alternatives for comparative purposes is largely futile. The assumptions on which to project results are necessarily so highly speculative as to reduce the whole exercise to a guessing game. In the final analysis, the shopping center management makes what is essentially a gut decision.

Refinancing

After about ten years of operation, shopping center management must give thought to the desirability of refinancing. The typical center, regardless of size, has the following characteristics:

- As a business form, it is capital-intensive.
- It is capable of sustaining a high debt–equity ratio.
- The debt is subject to constant and accelerating amortization.
- True capital value, as expressed in terms of the available sale price, tends to show a net increase over depreciation for a fairly long period of time after completion.

Given such conditions, consider the following example, which has been somewhat simplified for the purpose of illustration. All amounts are stated in constant dollars.

A developer assembled a parcel of land at a cost of $50,000 and thereon built a shopping center at an additional cost of $800,000, for a total of $850,000. His input of entrepreneurial skill and effort resulted in a market-value appraisal of the finished product at $1,000,000, enabling him to secure a long-term mortgage in the amount of $750,000. In the first full year of operation, the center's net cash flow was $20,000.

At that point, the developer is in a position to choose between selling for an immediate profit of $150,000 or accepting an initial rate of return of 20 percent on his actual cash investment of $100,000.

Both options, to be sure, are cited here without considering applicable capital gains or income taxes.

Now, assume that ten years have passed and the following changes have taken place:

- The working of the percentage leases has tripled the annual cash flow to $60,000.

- Influenced by the increased productivity of the leases and the rise in construction costs, the center's market value has increased at an average straight-line rate of 3 percent per year to $1,-300,000.

- Amortization has reduced the principal amount of the mortgage to $500,000, leaving the owner with an equity of $800,000.

At this time, the income looks pretty good as related to the original investment, but not at all as good as a return on the present investment, which consists of the equity less the capital gains tax incurred if the property were to be sold. Looking ahead from this point, and assuming the center to be healthy and having a good long-range outlook, the management is faced with one probability and two certainties. The former is that the gross income will continue to rise; the latter are that both interest and depreciation will progressively decline. The likely net affect will be a growing erosion of cash flow by income taxes, resulting in a still further decline in the rate of return on the increasing amount of capital employed.

At that stage of the center's life cycle, the owner is effectively put into the position of having to make another choice—sell or refinance.

If he sells at the indicated market value of $1,300,000, he will receive $800,000, representing a gain of $700,000 as against the cost basis of the original $100,000 investment. In the absence of an offsetting loss, and depending on his general tax situation, he might expect to walk away with a net on the order of $550,000 to $600,000.

Should the owner elect to refinance, and the state of the money market is propitious, a new 75 percent mortgage of $950,000 might be negotiated. The $450,000 of capital thus withdrawn from the investment, as borrowed money, would have no tax consequence, thus would all be spendable income. Further, there would remain as continuing income whatever portion of the cash flow was not required to service the enlarged debt, together with ownership of the equity and thus the future benefit of potential further appreciation in value.

225

It should be clearly understood that the foregoing analysis is a great simplification of what might be termed a broadly typical condition. It should not, however, be treated in any way as a guide in dealing with a specific situation. The figures and ratios used are in the context of ownership by an individual, and both the considerations and the arithmetic would be significantly different for a corporation.

In most cases, refinancing takes one of three forms: (1) a replacing first mortgage with the previous balance discharged out of the proceeds; (2) a second mortgage constituting a lien junior to the remaining balance of the first; (3) what is commonly referred to as a wraparound, which technically is a second mortgage with the holder assuming the servicing of the first mortgage out of a single monthly, or quarterly, payment received from the borrower. The choice is a matter of shopping around to see what is available to suit best the needs of that particular situation.

In analyzing the various alternatives, particular attention should be given to the penalty clause in the existing mortgage. With rare exceptions, long-term mortgages contain a provision calling for payment by the borrower of a stipulated percentage penalty on any prepayments of principal. Ordinarily, the severity of the penalty diminishes with time and the absolute amount concurrently lessens as the principal balance becomes progressively smaller. If the prepayment penalty is quite stiff, it may be an important factor in determining the optimum time for refinancing and the selection of method. A new first mortgage would involve payment of the penalty while a second or wraparound avoids it, and that could tip the balance if it is a tight choice.

From the standpoint of the shopping center manager, the important thing is to recognize the necessity of refinancing and to determine the probable timing well in advance. For that purpose, a long-range projection of the kind discussed elsewhere in this chapter is an essential tool serving three purposes:

1. It identifies the approximate point in the future at which the diminishing expenses of interest and depreciation and the increasing tax bite become critical in their combined effect on spendable income.

2. It permits an informed guess as to market value from time to time—and from that an approximation of borrowing power at various future dates.

3. It provides the basis for analyzing the probable financial results of various courses of action in advance and for evaluating the alternatives actually available when they are known.

In the absence of an extraneous influence, such as an addition, a major alteration, or a poor general economic climate, it is generally practical to pick the optimum time for refinancing at least two or three years in advance. The manager doing this is provided with adequate lead time to set the stage. He moves chiefly in two directions:

- First, he gears his re-leasing program to present the fewest possible uncertainties by the time he reaches his target date. If, for example, the tenth year is selected, he is sure that all renewals of ten-year leases have been fully negotiated during the ninth year. Uncertainties on the tenants' stability of occupancy are negative factors in the eyes of both prospective purchasers and lenders.

- Second, he makes sure that maintenance—particularly that of a cosmetic nature—is up to snuff. The basic determinant of value will be the financial record of the past and the outlook for the future, but physical appearance always carries some weight.

The actual negotiations for refinancing will be conducted by the owner, in most cases, but the manager will usually be charged with preparing the exhibits. It is important that they be complete, readily understandable, and organized for convenient reference. Typically, they will consist of such physical data as the site plan, leasing plan, basic specifications, and photographs; the financial data accompanying them will include annual operating reports, lease summaries, and tenants' sales-volume records.

The factual and historical material are customarily augmented with a forecast of the estimated future operating results, based on anticipated growth of sales volume and improvements in the lease structure. That document represents another use of the long-range projection—but it seems plausible to perk it up with whatever optimistic embellishments are available in the circumstances.

Options

An option is defined as follows:

The privilege, granted by contract, of demanding a specified fulfillment during a specified future time.

As incorporated into shopping center leases, options can be favorable to either landlord or tenant, and their presence in the center's early years is usually indicative of the relative bargaining position of the two parties in the development stage. A subsequent manager can change them only in the course of a renegotiation at renewal time, or as incidental to some other event that opens the lease agreement for mutual consideration of changes.

It ·an be useful for a manager to go beyond simply becoming aware of an option's existence and to try to ascertain the motives of the parties at the time the agreement was made. It is not at all unusual to find that reasons of compelling force during the initial leasing period are no longer important or even applicable, and the option can therefore be eliminated or modified with a minimum of effort.

Options can take many forms, ranging from the utmost simplicity to a complexity bordering on the esoteric, and no attempt will be made here to catalogue them. However, some brief comment on the more common types found in shopping center leases may be of interest.

Probably one of the most common, and certainly one of the least desirable from an owner's standpoint, is a tenant's option to renew for a specified period on identical terms. The worst type of such options is one in which the renewal right takes the form of a string of short periods—for example, as an initial lease term of ten years to be followed by ten successive options for one year each. Somewhat less horrendous from a management view is the renewal option containing an element of increased rent, expressed either as a stipulated amount or as a formula related to certain conditions existing when the lease was drawn.

In older centers particularly, strong tenants frequently obtained the right to terminate without penalty in the event of certain specified physical changes in the center that might be damaging to them. For instance, the taking of land by a public authority, which diminished the parking ratio, or a casualty resulting in a stipulated amount of the center's GLA being untenantable beyond a certain length of time, were such changes.

Another burdensome type of tenant option, again most often found in older leases, is one requiring the owner, on stipulated conditions, to provide additional space for tenant use. Typically such an option, if exercised, results in a thoroughly uneconomic use of the owner's funds because of the relative inadequacy of the specified additional rent to the cost of making the space ready when the time arrives.

228

A listing of such tenant options could go on ad infinitum. Every one is disadvantageous to the owner and is present only because, under the exigencies of the situation at the time, the developer was unable to reject them. It becomes a manager's responsibility systematically to attempt their elimination, or mitigation, in the same manner as he works to overcome limitations on contributions to common area maintenance or other provisions contrary to the owner's interest.

To the extent that circumstances may require the granting of tenant options as part of a re-leasing program, management should make every effort to steer clear of four characteristics.

1. Avoid what might be called "free" options, i.e., the kind calling for no quid pro quo if exercised by the tenant. For example, a lease extension with no improvement in the rental terms, or a right of cancellation without penalty, are completely one-sided arrangements that can sometimes be improved with a little persistence despite a relatively weak bargaining position.

2. Regardless of how attractive the concomitant rental terms may seem at the time, be especially wary of options calling for the expenditure of unspecified sums of money at any indeterminate future date to be established by the tenant. It is surprising how often what appeared to be a first-rate deal in the light of that day's circumstances can look like a disaster five years later.

3. Make every effort to keep an option's life short. It does not necessarily have to run for the full term of the lease if it has to do with something other than a renewal. Obviously, the shorter the period of exposure the less the chance of an unpleasant outcome.

4. Insist on adequate notice of the tenant's lease extension so that there will be sufficient lead time for planning purposes. In the case of a renewal option on a ten-year lease, for instance, a year's notice is none too long and it works no real hardship on the tenant to be so obligated.

Options in favor of the owner may be broadly categorized as being of two types, the first of which are those uniformly applicable to all, or a large number of, tenants. These options are ordinarily made a part of all agreements during the development process, are thereafter perpetuated in renewals and replacements, and lose effectiveness if exceptions are made. Typical of such an option would be the one referred to in Chapter 10: the right of an owner to demolish a building if a major portion was destroyed by fire. Incidentally, an option of that nature invariably includes a requirement for tenant indemnification by the owner for unamortized fixture and leasehold improvement costs not covered by tenants' insurance. If not included in the original leases, any universal option program takes a long time to implement, but to the extent that it is reasonable it can be accomplished with persistence.

The second type of owner options, those peculiar to individual leases, are typical of, and largely limited to, situations in which the landlord's bargaining power is overwhelmingly strong. They are designed in most cases to give the lessor a right to take some form of action that will almost certainly be unwelcome by the lessee at the time. An example would be a provision giving an owner the right to relocate a tenant in another, and possibly smaller, space at any time following the third lease year, in the event of the tenant not reaching and sustaining a specified sales volume.

The essential point concerning lease options granted to tenants by a shopping center manager is that they represent a future price to be paid for a present benefit, and they must be so evaluated. Unfortunately, the tradeoff cannot be quantitatively measured because there is no way at the time of decision to determine accurately the future price. When that day comes, the lost freedom of choice may be inconsequential or it could be quite onerous, depending on circumstances at the time.

As in so many other aspects of management, no rule or formula covers the granting of options in lease renewals or replacements. In each case, a manager must balance the strength of his bargaining position, the desirability of that particular tenant, and the potential harm of the proposed concession. The extent to which he can keep the agreements free of tenant options is one of those subtle things that make the difference between adequate and good management.

Community Rooms

Since the early days of the industry, shopping centers have sometimes included meeting rooms for public use apart from the space provided for occupancy of rent-paying tenants. The areas have ranged from bare halls, equipped with folding chairs capable of seating perhaps fifty persons, to quite elaborate facilities accommodating several hundred and providing kitchens, tables, stages, special lighting, and sound equipment. The objective has been to help establish an identity with the community and to build shopper traffic as a by-product of the meeting facility's use.

There is no hard evidence indicating the extent to which results have justified the investment, and there is no practical way of developing such evidence. The community room is essentially an amenity and as such cannot be part of a financial analysis. Opinion within the industry is mixed and tends to be rather subjective. Not all installations have achieved the intended results and some have turned out to be more trouble than they were worth. Again there is no hard evidence, but observation leads to the opinion that the unsatisfactory experiences proceed from poor planning or inept management, or a combination of the two.

Not surprisingly, the degree of enthusiasm with which community rooms are viewed by various segments within the industry is also colored by both proximity and financial considerations. Promotion directors, to whom the rooms can be very useful, are unanimously in favor; managers generally like their availability; but owners tend to be more skeptical and their doubts are likely to become more pronounced as a center grows older. According to one school of thought, such a facility has a time value—its importance diminishes as a center becomes firmly established and a maturing community around it provides alternative accommodations. It is significant that the conversion of community rooms to income-producing uses is not unusual in mature centers, whereas additions where they did not previously exist are extremely rare.

It is probable that the underlying cause of eliminating community rooms in most cases is the increasing financial burden of subsidizing the operation in older centers. During earlier years, the general industry practice was for the owner to assume all expense of operating the community room and pocket as income the revenue from rental charges. This income rarely, if ever, covered expenses, and the deficit thus became a charge to general overhead, a charge that grew steadily as time passed. The practice more recently has been to structure the leases so that the operating expense, less the income, is included in the common area maintenance charge passed on to the tenants, thus relieving the landlord of the deficit, except when a share of that charge is not passed on by reason of limitations in individual lease agreements.

Another practice of the early years that has been largely abandoned is that of making the facility available free of charge on an indiscriminate basis. Doing so invariably invites overuse by small groups of little standing in the community, which limits gatherings of the kind

231

contributing to the center's business purpose. Current practice generally calls for free use only when there is a direct tie-in with one of the center's own promotions, or for a few carefully selected community gatherings of wide appeal; for example, the kick-off meeting for the annual United Fund campaign. Exceptions to the general policy can always be made for special situations sufficiently unusual as to minimize the risk of being precedent-setting. For instance, if a nearby church shou'd suffer a fire it might be good community relations to offer the congregation complimentary use of the center's hall on Sunday mornings during the repair period.

In establishing a schedule of charges, the usual objective is a level that will permit recovery of the direct expenses for lighting, heating, cooling, and cleaning plus, where possible, some contribution to maintenance such as painting and equipment repair. Except in unusual and usually short-lived circumstances, it is rarely possible to recover depreciation or any return on the investment if the rates are to be kept at a level that will attract users. Other than in the newest of communities, there are alternative facilities available in churches, schools, libraries, and other public buildings with use charges geared to custodial expense. The economic justification for the unrewarded capital investment in community rooms is that, as noted before, the installation is an amenity increasing the overall attractiveness of the center to shoppers in its trade area. The extent of the intangible payoff thus derived from the investment is undoubtedly directly related to the management skill applied to utilizing the asset to the best advantage.

Statistics bearing on number, size, and distribution of community rooms on an industry-wide basis are not available, but observation indicates that their incidence tends to follow the same general pattern as for on-site managers—uncommon in centers of less than 400,000 square feet of GLA and quite common in those of more than 600,000 square feet. Based entirely on relatively limited observation, there does not appear to be any correlation between size of center and size of community room, but the facilities do appear to be better planned and equipped and more attractively decorated in centers of recent construction. The scarcity of installations in centers with less than 400,000 square feet undoubtedly reflects the severe operational difficulties inherent in servicing such a facility for intermittent uses during the day and evening other than with salaried personnel who are on the premises for different purposes.

Successful operation of a community room on a really active

basis calls for the exercise of managerial competence along several lines. One is the planning and attention to detail required to schedule, without embarrassing conflicts, both the center's promotional events and the meetings of community groups. Another is the ability to maintain at reasonable expense a housekeeping staff capable of fast, efficient service when one use is quickly followed by another.

Still another management requirement is to promulgate a comprehensive set of rules covering rental and use of the facility, expressed in terms readily understandable by both employees and patrons. Finally, and sometimes most difficult, is to exercise the combination of tact and backbone necessary to make the rules stick, especially the unwritten one about free uses. In this respect, a manager soon finds out that the world is full of worthy but impoverished causes, all represented by sincere and persuasive spokesmen. He also becomes quickly aware, if he was not already, that there is no such thing as a confidential arrangement—a special deal today is all over town tomorrow.

The manager must be aware of uses that one or more tenants may think of as inimical to their interest and of rentals to groups that, by their nature, have a high potential for disorder or abuse of the property. An example of the former might be a cooking demonstration featuring a kitchen range bearing the house-brand name of a department store not among the center's anchor tenants. Among possible users to be leery of are high school-age groups unless there is positive assurance that there will be strict adult supervision.

Where any form of kitchen equipment is provided, the general practice is to restrict the service of food in the facility to that brought in by a caterer or in fully prepared form by the group members themselves, the only exception being the making of coffee. In most communities, a kitchen used for food warming or cooling purposes only, as distinguished from restaurant-type cooking, is relatively free from the rigid licensing and inspection procedures otherwise applicable.

In the matter of general conduct, the successful operations invariably have certain rules requiring strict compliance—such matters as no gambling, no alcoholic beverages, or no loud music, and an exact observance of closing hours. Probably most of the unhappy experiences with community rooms are attributable to a combination of poor housekeeping and the failure to maintain discipline.

Educational Programs of ICSC

Shopping center managers, regardless of their original education and training, occasionally feel the need to improve old skills and acquire new ones. Some managers, indeed, ambitiously seek advanced instruction on a regular basis—usually because they know that the greater their ability, the higher their potential income. Such training is available through specialized classes in real estate or merchandising at many colleges and universities or at other institutions, and numbers of good books are useful to those capable of self-instruction. But organized upgrading and advancement programs are also valuable, and the most systematic of these are offered by the International Council of Shopping Centers.

From its earliest days, ICSC has engaged in vigorous and expanding educational activities for its members. The objectives have been, for the most part, to encourage the development of personal skills and the improvement of business methods. A secondary aim has been to familiarize the industry with new circumstances affecting it—such as the national movement to protect the environment and ecology.

The Council's chief teaching technique has been the organized exchange of experience among the members; relatively little reliance has been put on professional educators and formal classroom situations. These programs have taken several forms, which may be summarized as follows:

Publications. ICSC publishes books, technical reports, legal and other specialized bulletins of a topical nature, and checklists designed for quick use in the field. Manuscripts are solicited from experienced members of the Council or outside specialists, and often contain distillations of materials prepared by several individuals or groups.

The book-length works usually deal with broad-ranging subjects (as does this volume), but the shorter publications concentrate on particular aspects of shopping center development or operation. Distribution of the Council's publications is widespread throughout the organization's membership and to individuals in allied fields, and efforts are made to sell some of the materials to interested outsiders, libraries, and selected educational institutions.

Institutes. Using the facilities of well-known universities, ICSC offers several highly concentrated education programs throughout the year. Among them are Management Institutes I and II—the first for basic instruction and the other for more advanced training—and a Promotion Institute which focuses on that special aspect of shopping center operation. Each Institute is taught by teams of senior professionals, who through intensive lectures, workshops, and seminars provide basic instruction as well as practical application of the principles of shopping center operations. Class size is small to allow for maximum interchange between faculty and students.

University. As its major educational activity, ICSC conducts an annual, week-long University of Shopping Centers, which offers a large number of courses in development, finance, leasing, management, design/construction, and promotion. Again, the faculty is drawn from the ranks of highly qualified professionals, and the University attracts large numbers of students. As a result of this appeal to all comers, the University has won recognition as the outstanding self-advancement activity for both beginners and experienced personnel at all levels.

Conferences and seminars. From time to time, the Council holds two- or three-day meetings for the exchange of experience and opinions on various specialized topics. Typical subjects include multicenter development, construction techniques, management methods, antitrust legislation, promotional activities, and leasing problems. Attendance at these conferences varies from a few dozen to several hundred.

Idea Exchanges. Some thirty or forty regional meetings are held by the Council every year, devoted to intensive discussion of topical problems that arouse general interest. These one-day meetings are usually attended by members of ICSC from the area in which the Exchange is held, and serve as an excellent way to keep abreast of current industry thinking.

Convention. ICSC's annual convention is attended by a major portion of the entire membership. The four-day program usually features speakers of national stature, who address themselves to broad issues of public policy, economic development, and industry growth. By tradition, a limited number of topical meetings during the convention draw large audiences. An important aspect of the annual event is the trade show and exhibition, at which a great variety of products and services are displayed to the participants.

CSM and ASPD programs. To encourage a spirit of professionalism in the industry, the Council established in 1964 a program to designate Certified Shopping Center Managers (CSMs)—individuals who have met certain high standards of experience, education, and conduct, as determined by rigorous examination and personal evaluation. A similar program was begun in 1970 to cite Accredited Shopping Center Promotion Directors (ASPDs) for comparable professional achievements in the field of promotion. More than 700 men and women have been honored in the two programs as this book was written.

As a group, CSMs and ASPDs constitute a cadre around which the Council has worked to improve the standards and quality of shopping center management to the benefit of the industry.

Where Do We Go from Here?

During the thirty years following the end of World War II, the shopping center industry experienced a period of explosive growth and, on the whole, great prosperity. Among the thousands of centers built, the failure rate, as measured by involuntary change of ownership because of inability to meet financial commitments, was negligible —a small fraction of one percent. Population increase in the metropolitan-area fringes, where the industry concentrated, was universally so rapid that it was all but impossible to make a disastrous mistake. The suburban shopping center represented an idea whose time had come, and it flourished accordingly.

The size of the industry thus created within a relatively short time is impressive. The estimated 15,000 centers now in business in the United States serve as vehicles for the distribution of a major share of goods sold at retail, and they provide employment for hundreds of thousands of people. It is typical of a young industry, however, that a scarcity exists of statistical data on its financial nature. But, by applying some admittedly rough averages to the tabulation of centers by size, included in the first chapter, it seems probable that the total capital value of land and buildings at this time is in the range of $45 to $50 billion.

Toward the end of the 1960s, symptoms of maturity became apparent within the industry. Some of the symptoms take the form of trends that will probably continue for some time and, as they intensify, increasingly affect the management process. Four trends, in particular, will be briefly examined in this section: concentration of ownership, market saturation, influence of government, and specialization of centers.

1. *Concentration of ownership.* In the early years, development and the consequent ownership of shopping centers was extremely fragmented, with the ratio of the number of owners to the number of centers being practically one for one. A natural outcome was that direct owner-operation was the almost universal rule. By the mid-1950s, a limited number of multicenter developers had emerged, nearly all of whom, however, confined their activities to relatively small centers in compact geographic areas. These owners were thereby in a position to continue what was effectively direct management. It was largely men from that group, incidentally, who founded the International Council of Shopping Centers in 1956.

About 1960, there began to appear on the scene a growing number of developers whose scale of operations, geographic dispersion, or both, necessitated the use of managerial assistance. At the same time, original owners, who were running out of permissible depreciation deductions on their properties, began to sell centers. Many such sales were made to investors who were not in a position to conduct their own management. In combination, these two developments fostered a growing dependence on the use of professional managers, either as employees or as fee agents.

Both phases of the trend accelerated in recent years and show no present sign of slowing. The creation of new shopping centers has, to a considerable extent, become dominated by a relatively few developers, some of whom finish a dozen or more each year. Concurrently, there has been a sharp increase in the purchase of centers by institutional investors, notably insurance companies and real estate investment trusts. As the size of the total investment continues to grow, ownership devolves into proportionately fewer hands.

2. *Market saturation.* As was discussed briefly in Chapter 6, for at least 15 years following the end of World War II there was relatively little business competition among shopping centers. With few exceptions, each center offered its consumers only an alternative to much less convenient retail facilities—not to other centers. Now that condition has changed in all except a few of the major metropolitan areas—those that are still experiencing rapid population growth —and it is also ceasing to be a governing factor in most of the minor metropolitan trade areas.

Thus, by the early 1970s there was little difference in terms of overall shopper satisfaction between what a new shopping center was able to offer its customers and the available facilities in other organized retail areas. The obvious result has been a steady growth of intercenter competition, particularly among those in the over- 200,000-square-foot GLA class, whose tributary trade areas are extensive enough for significant overlapping.

It was pointed out in Chapters 2 and 4 that a modern shopping center is a hybrid type of entrepreneurial activity—partly a real estate investment and partly a going business. The owner's customers are the tenants to whom he sells the use of his floor space, but the real centerpole of the tent is the consumer, without whose steady support the whole enterprise collapses.

Thoughtful developers and owners realized by the late 1960s that the industry was running out of virgin territory. There began a shift of emphasis from what had been a dominant concentration on real estate economics of centers to a greater understanding of the necessity for ongoing marketing programs. Owners' interest in the quality of both esthetic appeal and of tenant mix took a sharp upturn, and sustained efforts were launched to strengthen the funding of centerwide promotional programs. As of this writing, there is every indication that the trend will continue and will be increasingly important from a management standpoint.

3. *Influence of government.* For many years, the hand of government rested lightly on the shopping center industry. The nation's real estate tax assessors—always notably quick on their feet in such matters—had demonstrated by the mid-1950s that they knew a good thing when they saw it. There were also occasional problems with planning commissions and zoning boards, but in general local governments were cooperative and exercised relatively little regulatory authority. And contacts with the state and federal governments were almost nonexistent, other than in matters relating to employment practices and working conditions.

Starting toward the end of the 1960s, the general public's increasing interest in environmental conditions began to be expressed in a stiffening of administrative procedures and in the enactment of new legislation bearing on the development and operation of shopping centers. At the local government level this was principally manifested in two forms: planning bodies put more emphasis on the inclusion of such neighborhood amenities as building setbacks, peripheral landscaping, and access sidewalks, and zoning boards displayed greater reluctance to grant variances, even those of a minor nature.

It was at the state and fede-al levels, however, that the major legislative activity took place. In rapid succession, new laws were aimed at reducing water and air pollution and at establishing greater governmental control over all aspects of land planning and use. The initial impact of these far-reaching regulatory powers is being felt at the development stage, but as the powers predictably take root and expand, they will become an increasing factor in operations as well.

It will probably be necessary to take government into account, for example, in planning any but the most minor additions and alterations as well as in many operating practices.

4. *Specialization.* During the early postwar period of rapid growth, a basic appeal of shopping centers was the concept of one-stop shopping. Neighborhood centers—built around a supermarket, drug store, and variety store—emphasized the convenience to the suburban housewife of being able to meet most of her day-to-day retail and service needs. Then the first regionals made a big impact with their broad range of retail classifications, competing head-to-head with what was generally available downtown. These centers sought to make available all the convenience goods and services plus an assortment of the kinds of merchandise associated with comparison shopping.

Starting in the early 1960s, the concept of the regional center began to change. As noted in Chapter 1, the department stores changed their isolationist thinking and sought each other's company. This had two direct results: the size of the typical regional increased, and the costs to the developer of producing and operating satellite-store space went up sharply, since the department stores were almost invariably subsidized by the developer in one way or another. Concurrently, and independent of that cause-and-effect relationship, there was throughout the entire 1960s and into the 1970s an extraordinarily rapid rise in construction costs.

Taken together, the effect of the two trends was progressively to price out of the rental market certain types of stores. Retailers whose sales per square foot and/or gross margins were relatively low could not sustain the occupancy costs necessary to justify economically creating space for them in regional shopping centers. Increasingly, the tenant rosters of new regional centers no longer included furniture, variety, hardware, paint and wallpaper, floor covering, and appliance stores, or supermarkets. The emphasis was heavily on apparel and allied soft goods; sales of merchandise such as home furnishings was confined to department stores.

The thus-dispossessed merchants, to some extent, tended to flow into the older regional and community-type centers. There they often replaced apparel stores that had found the locations no longer profitable. Accordingly, there has been gradually emerging a pattern of specialization in which some shopping centers, other than the strictly neighborhood type, tend to be strong on apparel and weak on hard goods, or vice versa. That trend has been further refined with the development of smaller centers specifically designed to be specialized, as noted early in Chapter 1.

Future directions. Any attempt at projecting into the future the effect of current trends must be mindful of Benjamin Disraeli's admonition that, "What we anticipate seldom occurs; what we least expected generally happens." With that qualification, there are offered some thoughts on the direction in which shopping center management seems to be heading.

Management will become more professionalized as centers increasingly are placed in the hands of people to whom such activity is a full-time business. That will, in turn, act to stimulate the general level of competence among managers. Owners will become more demanding in terms of forward planning, reports, and analytical studies on which to base operating and investment decisions. To satisfy such demands, managers will need constantly to improve their skill in the understanding and use of electronic data processing and in the science of decision-making.

There will be an increase in the amount of managerial attention and money devoted to promotion, and that phase of the business will also become more professionalized. As the pressure of intercenter competition becomes more acute, there will be a further rise in demand for the services of people capable of planning and executing sustained marketing programs. It will no longer suffice to develop such programs on a year-by-year basis; rather they will need to be integrated into the overall forward planning for the center.

The increasing presence of government above the municipal level in the affairs of shopping centers establishes a new requirement for managers. They will need to become familiar with a growing body of regulations and keep up to date with what are bound to be frequent changes and interpretations. Additionally, they will find it useful to learn the procedures and techniques for dealing with governmental agencies more remote than the city hall.

The trend toward specialization, taken in combination with increasing competition and the ceaseless flow of demographic change, emphasizes the requirement for managerial effectiveness above the custodial level. The world outside is in a constant state of flux and a manager must be alert to any changes necessary to keep in step with the times. As noted in the foreword of this book, a shopping center is in the nature of a wasting asset and its span of useful life is greatly influenced by the skill with which it is managed.

240

Finally, and probably most difficult, is the need for developing the understanding and the methods required to cope with problems of lessening economic virility. It was noted at the beginning of this section that the financial failure rate of shopping centers had been minute, and it is also true that of all those built in the last 35 years, extremely few have been demolished or otherwise ceased operations. Yet with each passing year an increasing number of centers move that much closer to the end of their economically useful lives and, as was mentioned in Chapter 8, the most severe test of a manager's skill may be in how well he is able to prolong the economic viability of a center that has seen its best days. With the arrival of full maturity, here lies the real future challenge to the management sector of the shopping center industry.

QUESTIONS FOR DISCUSSION

1. *Give an example of market research that would be of importance to a shopping center in the growth stage of its life cycle.*

2. *What effect does a long-range projection have on the management of shopping centers?*

3. *Discuss the factors that cause developers to deviate from a planned tenant mix.*

4. *What are the financial hazards of defensive expansion of shopping centers?*

5. *Why would a shopping center owner consider refinancing his center?*

6. *What role should the center manager play in the refinancing of a shopping center?*

7. *What role should the center manager play in the re-leasing of a shopping center?*

8. *Explain the pitfalls of tenant options as a part of a re-leasing program.*

9. *Develop a plan for the effective use of a center's community room.*

10. *Discuss changes in shopping center management practices that are likely over the next ten years.*

RECOMMENDED READING LIST

Baker, Martin S., Joseph S. Kaming and Richard E. Morrison. **Environmental Impact Statements: A Guide to Preparation and Review.** New York: Practising Law Institute, 1977. 334 pp.

Godschalk, David R., David J. Brower, Larry D. McBennett and Barbara A. Vestal. **Constitutional Issues of Growth Management.** Chicago: The ASPO Press-American Society of Planning Officials, 1977. 295 pp.

How Shopping Centers Are Meeting the Energy Crisis. New York: International Council of Shopping Centers, 1974. 8 pp.

McAndrews, James P. **Air . . . For Sale or Lease.** New York: International Council of Shopping Centers, 1972. 8 pp.

Merritt, Robert E., Jr. **Local and Regional Regulation of Land Development.** New York: Practising Law Institute, 1977. 416 pp.

Shopping Centers: The Next 15 Years. New York: International Council of Shopping Centers, 1975. 96 pp.

Appendix

a dditional information, or other viewpoints, on the topics discussed in this book may be found in the publications that are part of the recommended reading lists offered at the end of each chapter.

Some of these titles may be found in local libraries or bookshops, or they may be ordered directly from their publishers.

Of particular note, ICSC issues a number of technical bulletins and topical reports on specialized subjects of interest to shopping center managers. These are in addition to a monthly newsletter devoted to news of the industry. Many of these publications are available only to members. A complete list of publications may be obtained from ICSC, 665 Fifth Avenue, New York, N.Y. 10022.

For the convenience of readers, following are the names and addresses of the publishers of the various books and reports cited elsewhere in this book.

American Institute of Real
Estate Appraisers
430 N. Michigan Avenue
Chicago, Illinois 60611

American Management
Associations
135 West 50th Street
New York, N.Y. 10019

The ASPO *Press*
1313 East 60th Street
Chicago, Illinois 60637

California Continuing Education
of the Bar
2150 Shattuck Avenue,
6th Floor
Berkeley, California 94704

Chain Store Age Books
425 Park Avenue
New York, N.Y. 10022

Crain Books
740 N. Rush Street
Chicago, Illinois 60611

243

Downtown Research and
Development Center
270 Madison Avenue
New York, N.Y. 10016

Executive Enterprises
Publications Co., Inc.
33 West 60th Street
New York, N.Y. 10020

Fairchild Publications, Inc.
7 East 12th Street
New York, N.Y. 10003

Richard D. Irwin, Inc.
1818 Ridge Road
Hanewood, Illinois 60430

Institute of Real Estate
Management
430 N. Michigan Avenue
Chicago, Illinois 60611

International Association of
Assessing Officers
430 N. Michigan Avenue
Chicago, Illinois 60611

International Council of
Shopping Centers
665 Fifth Avenue
New York, N.Y. 10022

McGraw-Hill Book Co.
1221 Avenue of the Americas
New York, N.Y. 10020

National Institute of Real
Estate Brokers
430 N. Michigan Avenue
Chicago, Illinois 60611

National Parking Association
1101 17th St., N.W., Ste. 906
Washington, D.C. 20036

National Retail Merchants
Association
100 W. 31st Street
New York, N.Y. 10001

Practising Law Institute
810 7th Avenue
New York, N.Y. 10019

Prentice-Hall Publishing Co.
Route 9W
Englewood Cliffs, N.J. 07632

Reston Publishing Co., Inc.
Box 547
Reston, Virginia 22090

Shopping Center World Books
6285 Barfield Road
Atlanta, Georgia 30328

Howard W. Sams & Co.
(ITT Publ.)
4300 W. 62nd Street
Indianapolis, Ind. 46268

The Urban Land Institute
1200 18th Street, N.W.
Washington, D.C. 20036

Van Nostrand Reinhold Co.
450 West 33 Street
New York, N.Y. 10001

Warren, Gorham &
Lamont, Inc.
210 South Street
Boston, Mass. 02111

Periodicals

The following monthly periodicals, some of which are available regularly in libraries, publish current news, informative articles, and product advertising of general interest to shopping center managers. Subscription rates may be obtained from the publishers.

Buildings. 427 Sixth Avenue, S.E., Cedar Rapids, Iowa 52406.

Chain Store Age—Shopping Center Executives Edition. 425 Park Avenue, New York, N.Y. 10022.

Journal of Property Management. 430 North Michigan Avenue, Chicago, Ill. 60611.

National Mall Monitor. (bi-monthly). Suite 104, Arbor Office Center, 1321 U. S. 19 So., Clearwater, Fla. 33516.

National Real Estate Investor. 6285 Barfield Road, Atlanta, Georgia 30328.

Real Estate Review. (quarterly). 210 South Street, Boston, Mass. 02111.

Security World. P.O. Box 272, Culver City, Calif. 90230.

Shopping Center Digest. (twice monthly). Box 2, Suffern, N.Y. 10901.

Shopping Center World. 6285 Barfield Road, Atlanta, Ga. 30328.

Stores Magazine. 100 West 31st Street, New York, N.Y. 10001.

Index

Accredited Shopping Center Promotion Directors (ASPDs), 235-236
Advertising, 64-65
Advertising agencies, for promotion, 106-108
Anchor stores, 5-6, 7, 9, 11, 13-15, 74, 108, 122-123, 137-138, 139, 211, 221, 223
Appraisal, real estate, 159, 160; market value, approaches to estimating, 160-161
Assessing, real estate, 157-159, 163; estimating market value for, 160-161; relations with assessors, 160
Audits, 67

Budget billing, 54-55
Budgets, annual, 43-47, 48-52, 58, 218; for capital expenditures, 45, 48-52; expense overruns, avoiding, 46-47; for operations, 45, 48
Bureau of Statistics, Dominion (Canada), 18

Capitalization rate, 19-20
Cash flow, 22, 39, 40, 49, 50-55, 57, 121, 169, 219, 220, 224, 225; discounted (DCF), 52-54, 121; monthly forecasts, 53, 55, 56; summary, 58
Census of Population and Housing, U.S., 18
Census tracts, 18
Certified Shopping Center Managers (CSMs), 235-236
Charitable solicitations, handling, 89
Collection problems, manager's, 66-70
Common area expense, 20, 49-50, 54, 68, 69, 70, 120, 125-126, 129, 135, 141, 161, 163, 164, 172, 173, 181, 192, 198, 199, 229, 231
Community relations, of shopping centers, 80-81, 91-92, 231-232; handling unwelcome elements, 86-91; and security measures, 81-86
Community rooms, 230-233

Construction, Operating, and Reciprocal Easement Agreement (COREA). *See* Reciprocal Easement Agreement (REA)

Construction coordinators. *See* Owner's superintendents

Cost-benefit analyses, 56, 132, 134, 170

Country Club Plaza, 5

Defensive expansion, 223-224

Demographic changes, 139, 144, 181

Department stores: in centers, 6-7, 9, 108, 137, 169, 239; and internal security, 85-86; land ownership by, 23, 117, 169

Discounted cash flow (DCF), 52-54, 121; projections, 52-54

Dollars and Cents of Shopping Centers, The, 58

Federal Trade Commission (FTC), investigation of shopping centers by, 72, 221

Funds, no commingling of, 55, 69

Gross leasable area, 7, 8, 9, 11, 42, 58, 140, 183, 221; increasing, in enclosings, 182-183, 186-188

Handbills, problem of, 89

Hawthorne effect, 210-211

Housekeeping, 119, 125; divergent interests in, 126; and fire risks, 175

Income, 19; evaluating future, before undertaking maintenance, 122-123; immediate vs. future, 40-41, 183-184; net, 19-20, 161; reportable, 22, 39-40, 220

Income taxes, 157, 164-165, 225; information for, 58

Insurance, 167-168; actual cash value vs. replacement value, 171; basic policy, conditions affecting cost of, 174-177; broad categories of, 167; casualty, 172, 173-174, 178; consequential loss, 170, 171-172; coverage, responsibility and planning for, 168-170; deductibles, 170-171, 176, 178; distinction between agent and broker, 168; financial considerations of coverage, 169-170; fine points of coverage, 171-173; Fire and Extended Coverage policies, 170, 172; personal injury claims, 177; public liability costs and security force, 85; sprinkler system, cost savings in, 174-175, 176-177; subrogation, right of, 172; tying in tenants' own, to center's, 173, 174, 177

International Council of Shopping Centers, 9, 119, 124, 237; advanced managerial instruction from, 234-236

Juveniles, disorderly, problem of, 90-91; and community assistance, 91

247

Kiosks, 186, 187, 188, 192

Landlord-tenant relations, 62-65, 99-100, 101, 105, 172, 176-177, 186, 192-199, 204, 208, 209-210, 211-212, 213

Leases: buying out, 196-198; fixed-rent, 67; limiting obligation to rebuild after major loss, 172-173, 229-230; options in, 227-230; percentage, 28-29, 42, 63, 67, 96, 225; restrictive clauses in, enforcing, 75; revising, in case of enclosing, 198-199; tenants' own insurance, requiring appropriate, 173, 177; terms of, 137-138, 142; upgrading of, 30, 98-102, 108, 193; violation of, 72-73

Leases, renewing of, 137-143, 162; as affecting refinancing, 227; factors affecting, 139-142; lead time important in, 152; proposed physical changes and, 142-143

Leasing plans, developer's, 20, 154; for enclosings, 189

Letters of intent, 189

Maintenance, 40-41, 43, 47, 48-49; basic methods of, 127-129; complete plans needed, 125; diverse interests involved in, 120-121; factors affecting, 117-118; independent contractors, using, 127-128, 129-131; informational facilities available, 118-119,

124-125; preservative vs. restorative, 123; quality of, and fire risk, 175; record-keeping needed, 124, 126-127, 129-130; and refinancing, 227; snow-removal program, planning a, 131-133; structural and mechanical, 123; terms involved in, 119-120; three divisions of program, 126

Management, shopping center, future directions of, 240-241

Management records, 42-43, 141; insurance, 168, 173, 174; for maintenance program, 124, 126-127, 129-130

Managers, shopping center: compensation of, 34-36; counseling of tenants by, 76-78; decisiveness, need for, 65-66; enforcing lease provisions, 75; fee-contractual, 32-36; growth in industry use of, 237; importance of, 27, 29-31; instruction for, advanced, 233-236; maintenance, skill needed to supervise, 117-119, 120-135; owner-controlled, 32-34; owners' objectives, understanding, 38-41; 199-200; professionalization of, increasing, 240; promotion, problems of, 108-115; promotion director, relations with, 105-106; roles of, 30-31, 65; services for tenants, providing, 69-70; and tenant

mix, 220-223; tenants, relations with, 42-43, 65-78; unwelcome elements, handling,
86-91
Market research, 17-18, 216-218
Merchants' association, 20, 31,
32, 65, 68, 69, 74, 76, 86,
99, 100, 101, 102, 104, 105,
106-107, 108-112, 114, 142,
173, 174, 176, 208, 214, 217
Money: surpluses, investment of,
59, 169; time-value of, 50,
52-53, 121, 183-184, 206
Mortgages, penalty clauses in,
226

Nichols, J. C., 5
Northgate, 6
Northland Center, 6

Obsolescence, 27-28, 181
Operating statement, 47-48, 219
Options, lease, 227-230; owner-
favoring, 229-230; types of,
228, 229-230; types to avoid,
229
Owners, shopping center: objectives of, 20-21, 38-39, 40-
41, 165; payout to, 55; two
or more, 169
Owner's superintendents, 203-
204, 212

"Pad," 23
Parking, employee, problems of,
72-73
Percentage leases, 28-29, 42, 63,
67, 96, 225
Picketing: in labor disputes, 86;
social or political, 87-88

Political candidates, problem of,
88
Population data, 18
Preservation of center property,
70-72
Presumptive value, 19-20
Pro formas, 18-19, 20, 47, 185-
186, 191-192, 207, 218-219
Projections, long-range, 191, 196,
218-220, 224, 226, 227
Promotion, 94, 95, 108-115, 240;
enclosing, in case of, 208-
212, 214; impact of, on return on investment, 96-98;
selling, to tenants, 99-104,
199. *See also* Advertising
agencies; Promotion directors
Promotion directors, 65, 89, 94-
95, 101-102, 103, 104, 231;
Accredited Shopping Center
PromotionDirector(ASPDs),
235-236; enclosings, in cases
of, 208-209; optimally center employees, 104-106
Prospective tenants, locating, 153-
154
Public relations program, 205
Publicity, 94, 95-96; enclosing, in
case of, 208, 209, 211

REA. *See* Reciprocal Easement
Agreement
Real estate taxes: ad valorem,
157; appealing assessment
change, 159-160, 164; tenant participation in, 68-69,
97, 142, 161-164, 199

249

Reciprocal Easement Agreement (REA), 23, 117
Records, management, 42-43, 141; insurance, 168, 173, 174; for maintenance program, 124, 126-127, 129-130
Refinancing, 206, 207, 224-227; decision for, 225; possible forms of, 226; or sale, 225; timing of, 226-227
Re-leasing, 138-143
Renewal leasing. See Leases, renewing of
Rent, 19, 20; ancillary agreements affecting, 67-68; factors affecting terms, 155; franchise, 155; guaranteed, 20, 66, 97, 141, 155, 181; overage, 42, 67, 97, 109, 141, 142, 148, 162, 163, 194, 206, 220; percentage, 20, 53-54, 66-67, 97, 141, 155, 161, 162, 164, 195
Repairs, 43, 47
Replacement leasing, 143-152, 162, 188; hypothetical examples of, 144-148, 149-152, 218; reasons for, 143-144
Reportable gain (income), 22, 39-40; equation for, 40
Reports to owners, 41-60; annual budget, 43-47, 58; annual report, 43-44, 58, 219; interim operating, 55-57, 59; of unusual events, 59-60
Restaurants, fire hazards of, 175

Satellite stores, 6, 7, 23, 137-138, 211, 222, 223, 239
Sears, Roebuck & Co., 5
Security, of shopping centers, 80, 81-91; arming of guards, 82; and community relations, 80, 81, 84-85; contract guards vs. center's forces, 82-83, 84; electronic devices available, 84; full-time patrol, 81-82; and insurance costs, 85; shoplifting, education to prevent, 86; and tenants' measures, 85-86
Service contracts, 129-131
Services for tenants, providing, 69-70
Shoppers, dual role of, 65
Shoppers World, 6, 7
Shopping Center World, 7, 8
Shopping centers: as business investments, 27, 28, 31, 36, 238; creation of, 17-20; customer appeal, changing the, 144; definitions of, 4-5; financing of, 23-24; historical development of, 5-7, 161-162, 236; life-cycles of, 121-122, 138; maturing, making changes in, 142-143; net income of, 19-20; number of, 4, 7-8; "owner" and "developer" distinguished, 21-22; owners' objectives, 20-21, 38-39, 40-41, 165; ownership arrangements, 21-24; sales volume of, 8; size distribution of, 8; types of, 5-6, 9-16